5O Years and
5O,OOO Miles
of Sailing

by

DALE PARSHALL

Make a Wish !
Go Sailing !
— Dale

50 Years and 50,000 Miles of Sailing

by

Dale Parshall

Published by Dale L. Parshall, 13501 Ranch Road 12 #103-324, Wimberley, Texas 78676

Cover Art by Jim Dewitt

Cover Design by Katherine McGee

Editor: Marcia Baker

Readers: Bill Danly, Zaneta Matkowska, Cheryl Rankin, Valerie Schwartz

Printed in the United States of America

ISBN 978-0-615-36845-0

Cover Art by Jim DeWitt

About the Cover:

In 1997, Giggles was the first boat to finish the Long Pac Race, a 400-mile, offshore, singlehanded race. At the end of that race, Dale, alone on the boat, carried the spinnaker under the Golden Gate Bridge and across the finish line. The Race Committee took pictures. The following year, Dale and Giggles won the Singlehanded Transpac from San Francisco to Hawaii.

The Singlehanded Sailing Society commissioned Jim DeWitt to provide the artwork for a poster advertising the next Singlehanded Transpac. Working from the photos taken in 1997, Jim DeWitt created this fabulous rendering of Dale and Giggles under spinnaker.

About the Artist:

Jim DeWitt is a native Californian and always excelled in art. He trained at the California College of Arts and Crafts and the Los Angeles Art Center.

Jim is best known for his paintings of racing sailboats. A number of these paintings hang in yacht clubs and private collections throughout the world.

In addition to painting sailboats, Jim has designed and raced them. He has raced from San Francisco to Hawaii, in Europe, on both coasts of the United States, and in Nassau, Mexico, and the Caribbean.

In 1963 he was the first West Coast skipper to win the North American Men's Sailing Championship and brought home the Mallory Cup. Later, in 1982, Jim won the International Masters Sailing Championship in J-24s. For 33 years, he owned a sail loft in the San Francisco Bay Area, specializing in racing sails.

For more information about Jim, to view his online gallery, or to contact him, please visit www.dewittgalleryandframing.com and www.jimdewitt.com.

Table of Contents

Disclaimer

In writing a memoir today, a serious conflict exists between telling it all exactly as the author remembers it and protecting oneself from a law suit. Even where facts can be verified, the events from which they flow may place someone in an unfavorable light, causing that person to consider retribution. Worse, when memories of the author cannot be verified, someone may take exception to what was written and start a struggle that is difficult to conclude.

On the other hand, a biography of any kind carries the responsibility to be true to the life it represents. The truth in a situation is what has a special appeal to the reader. Truth is a fundamental in the contract between author and reader.

However, in telling a story, many deviations from complete and strict truth are both necessary and commonly taken. If a story is to be fully faithful to the truth, it needs to include all the details. But, then, it would no longer be a story. In fact, it would be unreadable, and the essence of the story would be lost. That very essence is what the story tries to capture and bring to the reader in a succinct delivery.

The conflict between truth and safe position, I believe, remains unresolved. In facing this conflict, I tried to represent my sailing situations in a way that was true to my memory, enjoyable and poignant to the reader, and yet not directly offensive to anyone.

To protect myself from controversies, I have, at times, taken the following liberties with truth: I left out people who were actually there. I used a title or descriptor rather than a personal name, e.g., watch captain. I changed living people's names and boat names except when I had written permission to use them. I created literal quotes out of what I remember being said. And I left out many, many details.

In the Epilogue, Changing of the Watch is a dream I've had about my own death. It is not truthful in that I'm still alive today. Other than that, I have been a part of, and witnessed, every event in the story—except, of course, my own death.

While I took some liberties with absolute truth, I worked steadfastly to remain true to the essence of life that prompted the telling of the event. My hope is, while attempting to be nonoffensive to everyone, that I've still been able to write each chapter in a joyful, instructive, and memorable way for the reader. This is my contract with you.

This is also my contract with myself.

Acknowledgement

I am fortunate. I have lived great sailing experiences, and I've been mentored by wonderful people who already knew how to sail. While the best of my memories are told in this book, my mentors should not go unmentioned.

The people who came into my life taught me most of everything I know—from how to tie a knot to how to live life. Some of the people who had an impact on my life I never knew by name. Some I only knew by their first name or their boat's name. Others I have forgotten completely.

I owe a huge debt to all those who helped me find my way.

To everyone who showed me how, thank you for helping make my adventures both possible and rewarding. To those whose names are absent, I apologize.

Gary Albright	Bob Klein
Nick Barnhill	Bob Lieopld
Peter Barrett	Rob Macfarlane
Charlie Brochard	Bruce Nesbit
Dick Carlton	Harry Nye
Tom Carr	Gregg Potter
Gary Comer	Dennis Robbins
Bill Danly	Ken Roper
Alan Ely	Rick Van Mell
Harry Forni	Skipper Van Mell
David Hunter	John Vetromile

Foreword

Growing up in Kansas isn't the most likely place to acquire the skills you need to master the world's oceans. When Dale went to college in Chicago, The Fates must have been in control. Dale excelled at swimming in Kansas and had begun training life guards. But Lake Michigan was far bigger than the biggest swimming hole in all of Kansas. Swimming was no longer the best relationship to water.

I first met Dale when he graduated from the Star fleet at Belmont Harbor into the cruising class boats in Monroe Street Harbor. Everyone had heard about that Star fleet—they had some of the top-ranked sailors in the world. Anyone who could begin racing by sailing against those guys every weekend must be either really good or really willing to learn. Dale's mind was like a sponge looking for a bucket of water.

Dale and I both had a bad case of Adventure Sailing Fever. When I was still in high school, my brother and I delivered a 29-foot sailboat from Chicago to San Diego. We powered down the Mississippi and sailed from New Orleans to San Diego, transiting the Panama Canal. Dale's sense of adventure was just as strong and he followed it all his life.

When Dale's employer relocated him from Chicago to San Jose, The Fates were back in control. San Francisco Bay is one of the world's true meccas of sailing. High summer winds, tricky currents, and fog banks make the Bay one of the most challenging places to sail.

First, in a Santana 22, and then in a Cal 2-27, Dale added knowledge of currents and sailing in 25 knots of wind to his already considerable experience. Putting it all together, he began to win races.

Along with racing on the Bay and cruising in the Delta, Dale gave back his knowledge by teaching in the junior sailing program at the Richmond Yacht Club, one of the most active sailing programs for kids on the Bay. The program is so successful that graduates of the program have gone on to compete in the Olympics and the America's Cup.

Then, The Fates intervened twice more. The first time was to give Dale a berth on a race to Hawaii, giving him a taste of long distance sailing.

While sailing to Hawaii would certainly meet most people's need for adventure, for Dale, it was only one-third the way across the world's largest ocean.

The next intervention by The Fates was to make it possible for Dale to take time off from work to follow his dream. His adventures would take him half-way around the world. And, after that trip, he could come back to his day job.

Dale made the long ocean voyage to New Zealand while visiting the archipelagos of the Marquesas, the Society Islands, the Kingdom of Tonga, and other fascinating places in between.

When he returned from 18 months at sea, Dale had a different perspective on career needs and life goals. With his professional career winding down, Dale looked forward to retirement. And, most of all, he looked forward to more sailing.

Always one to challenge himself and his sailing skills, Dale dreamed of racing across the Pacific Ocean—alone. The chapter titled "Singlehanded Transpac" is the ultimate story for any sailor or person who strives to reach their highest accomplishment.

After the 1998 Singlehanded Transpac and delivery home, Dale settled down to more leisurely, fully crewed fun races, and cruising along the southern California and northern Baja California coasts. He also created a new kind of sailing contest: an on-the-water contest in Dead Reckoning.

Some of Dale's misadventures didn't make his book, though. I remember him steering the boat one day after too much cheap wine the night before. Dale said it hurt to turn his head, and he asked me to keep him posted on our competition and any traffic. He sat perfectly still, hunched over the tiller, and stared fixedly at the leading edge of the jib. By the end of the first leg, Dale had no idea where the competition was. I just kept saying they were "over there." In fact, Dale opened a huge lead by concentrating better than ever before. For the next several months, Dale claimed it was a learning experience and tried to make the crew do all the work, while he sat perfectly still. Even when he wasn't steering.

I am lucky to have sailed with Dale on several of his adventures—from winning races in the San Francisco Bay to ocean passages across the Pacific. And I am grateful to have experienced them first-hand. I know all Dale's experiences are real and he does a terrific job at re-creating the sailing atmosphere.

You, the reader, can live Dale's adventures with him. By the end of the book, some of you will be glad to have shared Dale's experiences. And some of you will want to experience the real thing for yourselves.

—Bill Danly

Web Site Pictures

Far too many pictures from Dale's adventures are available to print in this book, but you can see all the pictures on Dale's web site:

www.CaptainDale.com.

As you read each chapter, you may want to look at the pictures from that time in Dale's adventures.

A Special Thank You

I was especially fortunate to have had Zaneta's vision and support. When I rambled on about my sailing memories, it was she who saw it would make a book. She insisted I write it, and encouraged me continuously during the process.

The good stuff was truly wonderful.

50 Years and
50,000 Miles
of Sailing

Sailing in the ocean always filled me
with a sense of high adventure.
Whether flying a spinnaker all alone,
fighting the fatigue that comes after two weeks of no rest,
or sailing in a storm . . .
every time I thrilled at exceeding my previous limits.

Part I

Fresh Water

Chapter 1

Cartwheel

About the time young boys turn into young men, they begin to test the world around them. Sometimes it may be to understand how things work; sometimes there just doesn't seem to be any good reason.

Before I ever owned a sailboat, my friend, David, and I had summer jobs at a music camp in northern Michigan. The tall green pines and crystal blue lakes were a welcome relief from college classrooms. David worked the hotel desk. I worked on the waterfront as a lifeguard and water craft instructor. Once a week, we both had the same afternoon off and we went sailing on David's Super Sailfish.

Normally, the winds in northern Michigan were fairly calm and the sailing was quite gentle. But, one afternoon, a storm was brewing. The wind preceding it was much stronger than either of us had sailed in before. We looked at the swaying branches overhead and the white caps on the lake with innocent teenage excitement.

This was going to be a great sail!

We raised the sail as it jerked from side-to-side in the wind, pushed the boat out into waist-deep water, and climbed aboard as fast as we could. David sheeted in and the boat immediately heeled over hard, lunging forward. Scrambling to climb out on the high side, we barely kept the sail out of the water as the boat jerked to a new heel with each blast of wind. Together, we were barely heavy enough on the weather rail to keep the boat upright.

The first beat was awesome. In the lulls, we could just keep the boat on its feet, driving hard. In the puffs, however, only by luffing hard could we keep the boat upright. We only had a slim margin between sailing and going for a swim! We lived on the thrill.

The first tack was almost a disaster. The boat would not come head to wind. When it did cross the eye of the wind, it spun down on the new tack as the wind filled the sail.

Instinctively, David pushed the helm down and eased the sheet to keep from capsizing. Before David could get control, the boat turned down onto a broad reach and, at full power, shot up onto its bow wave and began planing. We flew over the water, spraying a bow wake out on both sides.

I still don't know why, but I turned back to David and said, "Permission to go forward! Sir!" As I turned forward and jumped up, I heard David say something like "Huh?"

On my feet, I started forward as fast as I could go. My second footfall was forward of the mast, and my weight was enough to submerge the bow of the Super Sailfish into the next wave as we flew along. The boat was on a full plane when the bow dug into the water and stopped. The sail above the boat, still driven by the wind, continued on.

The sail pulled on the mainsheet, the mainsheet pulled on the traveler, and the traveler pulled the back of the boat up and out of the water. David was catapulted high in the air and clear of the boat. The transom continued up, and then directly over the bow of the boat. When the sail hit the water in front of the boat, we were halfway through a cartwheel.

Spectacular!

When we came back up to the surface of the water, we were both laughing so hard, we could hardly right the boat and climb on again. When we got back to shore, we were still hyped from our airborne adventure. We told everyone we could find about the crazy thing we had done. "Kids," the people replied and went on about their business.

When I look back at it now, I realize that adventure was the beginning of my living through perils and recounting them as sea stories.

Chapter 2

Magic

When I was first introduced to sailboat racing, I didn't know it would become a life-long passion. I only knew I was fascinated by high-performance sailing and I wanted to become good at it.

I started reading sailing magazines and sailing books. I talked to anyone who seemed to have sailing knowledge. I began crewing on a Tripp 30 out of Monroe Street Harbor in Chicago. At the same time, I tried one small boat after another.

After a couple of summers, I bought a Star and began skippering my own boat. That's when my desire to become good met reality.

Sitting on my back porch, I tried to figure out what had happened. Clearly, everyone had sailed away from me. But what was not clear was why. At least it wasn't clear to me.

A couple months earlier, I started a "post-race diary," where I wrote down my experiences. I wanted either to cement what I was doing right or understand what I was doing wrong and try to change. Theoretically, my idea was to look honestly at my mistakes. I was ready to be brutally honest with myself, at least in a book no one else ever saw.

All I had to do was figure out what I'd done wrong. The problem was I simply didn't understand why everyone else sailed faster than I did, so I had no idea what to write.

I looked back over the notes I'd written in previous weeks. At one time, I'd been reading an article about sail trim by a big name sail maker. My notes contained a lot of uncertainty about whether I was doing it right. On the race course that day, I wasn't sure if the shape of my sail was the same as what I'd seen in the article.

In another place, I compared the start I'd made to the perfectly timed start described in the latest book I was reading on sailboat racing[1]. I'd timed my sailing away from the starting line and back to the starting line, just as the book said. When the gun went off, I was a long way from the starting line. My start should have worked, but it didn't.

When I went back to the book to make sure I remembered the write up correctly, I found 13 pages of variations described by the author. Light air, heavy air, starting line canted this way or that, fast or slow boat, starting at this end or that end of the line, and late changes to the starting line. As I read through it again, I couldn't remember the variations I'd just read, let alone the author's recommendation for each. How was I supposed to remember all that under pressure in the middle of a real start with lots of boats around me?

Today, I'd just followed the pack across the line and started sailing for the first mark. Not knowing where to go, I decided to play it safe. I went up the middle of the course.

Well, that was a mistake! All the fleet leaders went way off to the right and got a nice wind shift. By the time I got to the first mark, I wasn't even in the race any more.

Now, looking down at my diary, I realized the last five minutes had been more fussing and fuming than writing. Today's page was still blank. I just didn't know what to write. I was getting tired of sitting on my back porch every Sunday evening, unable to answer the same question.

After the race today, I asked one of the guys in the fleet about the wind shift. I had just set my Star, Busybox, on the trailer when Gary walked past me. Gary had finished so far in front of me, he had already put his boat away and was on his way to the club house. "Gary, in the last race, I went up the middle. You and all the boats in

---

[1] *Scientific Sailboat Racing,* by Ted Wells. New York: Dodd, Mead & Company, 1958, p. 80.

the lead went all the way to the lay line on the right side of the course," I started slowly.

Gary's eyes twinkled. "Yeah . . . ?"

"Well, because *all* the leaders did it, I gotta believe they *knew* there'd be a wind shift over there. I couldn't see any wind shift. How did you know to go over there for it?" I was struggling.

Gary just smiled and said "Oh . . . uh . . . Just lucky, I guess." Gary was very soft-spoken.

"No, Gary. How did they *KNOW*?" I really needed an answer I could put to use in the future.

"Well . . ." Gary drawled by way of clear explanation, "Did you ever notice how the same guys are always lucky?"

Sitting on the back porch, I wondered if I should write down Gary's advice.

Eventually, I came to know the sailing history of the guys in the local fleet at Belmont. Gary was an Olympic Bronze medalist in the same Star boat he was now racing at the local club. Another guy was the latest American to win a Gold medal, and he did it in Star class. The middle of the fleet included a North American champion, a regional champion, and so on, all in Star class. In the next fleet north of Belmont, the top guy was tuning up for the next Olympics, where he went on to win a Silver medal.

When Gary first said they were just lucky, that seemed like the most reasonable answer. After I understood how good these guys really were, I continued watching them from the back of the fleet. But, now, it seemed more like magic.

I never did write anything in my diary.

Chapter 3

Wait a Minute

Sailing against people who have much greater skills can be bluntly humbling. However, when the people are nice, as well as good, the message is easier to take.

The sailors at Belmont Harbor call Chicago "The Windy City," not because of the politicians, but because the weather is just plain fickle. Today was one of those abnormal, unusual, fickle wind days.

Before the start, I sailed around in the starting area, tuning the sails and getting ready mentally. When I passed a competitor I knew, I'd nod or say "hello," or maybe "good luck." I don't know why I ever said good luck. I was the novice. These guys had traveled all over the world racing the best, sometimes bringing back the silver that sat in the yacht club until the following year. They didn't need good luck. I did. They were being nice to me. I was trying to be sociable with them.

The start was, from my perspective, typical. The good boats timed it just right and sparred with each other for the best start right next to the Race Committee boat. I started just behind a clump of boats on the committee boat end and congratulated myself on getting better.

After I crossed the starting line and cleared the committee boat, I tacked off to the starboard side of the course, thinking I would get my air clear. Maybe just to take fewer tacks or something, I beat most of the way to the lay line before I tacked again.

This time, the fickle winds of Chicago played to my advantage. Just as I tacked to starboard, the wind shifted to the right and lifted me up to the mark. In fact, I was able to crack off and foot a little faster. All the other boats were way off to the left and had to sail the knock on a hard beat all the way to the first mark.

13

For the first time in my life, I was the lead boat at the weather mark—and against world-class sailors, too! I knew it was luck, but I was still pumped.

At the mark, I rounded all alone. No one was even close. What a thrill!

When I rounded the mark, I turned down and eased the sails for the reach to the jibe mark. I looked out in front and, to my horror, there weren't any boats to follow. I couldn't see the next mark. I had no idea where to go.

As I sailed away from the first mark, the next boat to approach the weather mark was still in front of me. That next boat was my friend Gary on a hard beat, not even close to the mark yet. He was going to pass just below me on a port beat. And we were closing fast.

I had such a comfortable lead and I was on such a high! I wanted to say something, but I had no idea where the second mark was. When I opened my mouth, the only thing to come out was, "Gary, where do I go?"

Gary, who'd seen hundreds of rookies before and loved understatement, drolly replied, "Wait a minute; I'll show you."

And darned if he didn't.

That night, I wrote in my post-race diary, "It takes more than luck to beat the good guys."

Chapter 4

The Broken Mast

*Learning comes from many sources: books, articles,
trying new things and making mistakes, as well as advice
from a friend. When the friend is a past National Champion,
his advice is difficult to ignore.*

Crack! BANG!

The whole boat jerked, and then shuddered as the rebar
sticking out from the breakwater caught the starboard upper shroud
and let go.

I was returning into Belmont Harbor after a day of racing my
Star. I knew I was close to the breakwater, but I thought I could
squeeze by. Then I saw the rebar sticking out from the breakwater.

The mast stayed up, but I was sick. My first accident. I had just
"crashed" my boat.

I sailed over to the hoist and pulled the boat out of the water.
As soon as the boat was back in its dry storage space, I unstepped the
mast and laid it on a couple of sawhorses in the boat yard.

The mast was made of perfectly clear straight-grain Sitka
spruce, varnished to a clear, bright finish that showed off the beautiful
wood and craftsmanship. It also showed a break about six feet above
the deck a third of the way through the mast. Up and down from the
break was a classic green-tree split, extending about a foot or two
above and below the break.

I couldn't believe I had done such a thing. Half in denial, I
hoped the damage wasn't all that bad. Maybe it could be repaired. I
had no idea.

After several minutes of dithering, I decided to get advice. In
the yacht club, I ran into Harry, an old-time Star sailor and a really

nice guy. I think I needed the nice-guy part more than the advice, but I didn't realize it at the time.

I told Harry I needed his help. "My mast is broken . . . uh . . . just a little, and . . . I . . . uh . . . wonder if it can be repaired." After only a few words, Harry wanted to see the mast. So, back we went to the yard.

Harry looked at the mast and the ugly crack, and then rolled it over to get a better look. I desperately wanted him to tell me the mast could be repaired. It would make the damage, and my mistake, a lot less painful.

Without looking at me at all, Harry put both hands on the mast right next to the break and lunged at the mast.

CRACK!

The green-tree split now extended another three or four feet in both directions.

I was sick.

Harry calmly announced, "Your mast is broken too badly to be repaired. I think you should call your insurance agent and get a new mast. And, uh, by the way . . . I think your boat will be faster with a little lighter mast."

Chapter 5

The 1970 Mackinac Race

The Chicago to Mackinac Island Race runs 333 miles up the length of Lake Michigan, through the Mackinaw Straights, and on to Mackinac Island. In 1970, a severe Midwestern line squall drove force seven winds across the sailboats for over 16 hours.

During the storm, the course to the finish line was a beat.

Spirits ran high as the crews of Avanté and all the other boats gathered at the yacht club for the annual prerace festivities. This race—Chicago to Mackinac—was the biggest and most-anticipated race of the year. The noise level at cocktail hour attested to the emotional involvement of all those people who would cross the starting line the next day. Old friends and competitors met, swapped stories, and occasionally, made bets on the outcome of tomorrow's race. Both the noise and the bets were more ego-satisfying than monetary.

This was my first season on Avanté, a Vanguard 32. So far, we were pleased with our standings and we had high hopes of doing well in tomorrow's Mac Race. Being honorable and sober seamen, we had not made any bets with any of our competitors. We had, however, shared a few modest remarks about our unsurpassed sailing skills and astounding performance.

Both dining rooms were packed full of tables and chairs. More were set up in the meeting rooms, in the open space near the entrance, and even outside. In due time, the milling crowd began to find their boat names on the tables, and to settle down for dinner and speeches. The head table began to fill as the NOAA (National Oceanic and

17

Atmospheric Administration) weatherman, city government representatives, and the dignitaries from the yacht club found their seats.

The six seating cards for the crew of Avanté had been set on a table fairly close to the head table. Dick, the owner of Avanté, was pleased our table was in the main dining room where we could hear and see the NOAA weatherman. We knew a storm was coming, so we wanted the best information we could get for our race strategy.

Not long after we sat down, the yacht club maitre d' came to our table with a long and pained face. We all knew him . . . in the past, he had cheerfully seated us many times for lunch or dinner. One of our crew was a woman. "I'm sorry," he said to our female crew, "but you can't be seated for dinner." To Dick, the owner, he said, "This is a stag dinner. She can't eat here." Then, more quietly, he confided to Dick, "You are right in front of the head table."

Our female crew got up, saying, "That's OK. I'm a member of the yacht club next door. I'll eat there."

No sooner was she on her feet than the rest of the Avanté crew also rose. Dick said it first, but we were all of one mind: "If she can't eat here, then we'll *all* leave." Together, we left the main dining room and the yacht club, leaving six empty seats in front of the head table.

We chose one of Chicago's best barbeque restaurants and a personal favorite of many of us, Twin Anchors, for our dinner of pork ribs. While we all enjoyed our meals, we never heard the weatherman tell about the strength of the approaching storm.

Two days later, we were flying the spinnaker in the middle of Lake Michigan when the wind began to blow harder. Avanté picked up speed until the bow wake and the stern wake were as close together as they could get. After that, the boat simply plowed a deeper trough between the two wakes and went no faster. Trying to go faster than max hull speed, the boat began doing mini-death rolls as the spinnaker oscillated from side-to-side.

We opted to keep the spinnaker up as long as possible. But it didn't take long, Mother Nature made the decision for us. As the spinnaker oscillated back and forth, the tack tore out. The luff tapes held, but the body of the sail tore away from the luff tapes all along the starboard luff and the foot. The sail flagged out from the one good side. Only the luff tapes remained attached to the pole, outlining where the spinnaker had been.

When the power came off the boat, it was suddenly easier to steer. Even so, it took all hands to douse the spinnaker with the two loose luff tapes. Our plan was to go back up with a heavier and smaller spinnaker, but the storm rolled in over us first.

The wind shifted and began to blow much, much harder. We instantly went from a heavy spinnaker run to being overpowered with only the main up. We reefed the main, set the storm jib, and reefed the main again. Still overpowered, we took the main down completely and tied it to the boom.

The seas built in response to the wind. They became steep, short, and powerful. And, it wasn't long before we were in the heart of the storm, the area where the waves were as big as the wind could create.

Just before dark, I realized I was looking at something I'd never seen before. The wind was blowing the tops of the waves off and scattering them downwind as gray spume. The surface of the water looked as though it had a loosely knit gray blanket over it that was sliding sideways.

The gray spume drenched the boat. The remaining solid water part of each wave crashed against the forward part of the hull and kept the entire boat, and anyone on deck, drenched under running water. Being on deck was awful. Absolutely awful.

The solid-water part of each wave tossed the boat around like a cork. In the violence of the storm, and especially after dark, I couldn't tell which way the boat was being turned by each crashing wave. The movement of the boat was simply too random and disorienting. The only way to tell which way the boat was headed was to see the numbers on the compass.

Seeing the compass had to be done between walls of flying water. After each wave sprayed across the boat, I wiped my face, wiped the compass, read the compass, and decided which way to turn the boat to get back on course. I usually had time to move the tiller one way or the other. About the time the boat began to respond to the tiller, the bow hit the next wave and sent the next wall of water across the cockpit. Wipe my face. Wipe the compass. Read it. Change the helm. Hit the next wave. Wipe my face. Wipe the compass.

The storm jib was hanked onto the forestay. With the sail area all the way forward, the boat was badly balanced. As long as the boat stayed 45 degrees to the wind, it sailed OK. Every time a wave knocked the boat off course, the sail on the bow stalled and acted as a wind block on the forward end of the boat. This spun the bow downwind until we were headed away from Mackinac Island. Every time the boat turned broadside to the waves, it rolled violently. Immediately, we eased the jib sheet until the sail filled and started pulling the boat forward again. When the boat began to sail, we turned back upwind and cranked the jib back in against the blasting wind.

The first few times we came off watch, we never removed our foul-weather gear; it was too wet and cold below. After a few watches, the clothes inside our foul-weather gear were too wet to provide any insulation. When we came off watch, we looked for something dry in our sea bags, stripped off our foul-weather gear and soppy wet clothes, and put on the dry ones. We put our wet foul-weather gear back on, right over the dry clothes, sacrificing the dryness.

Because we had no place to put the soppy wet clothes we removed, we dropped them on the cabin sole. With our wet clothes on the cabin sole, we could walk on them, squeezing the water out and into the bilge, where we could then pump it overboard. During the fatigue caused by the storm, our minds considered this a good idea.

Everything in the boat got wet. The bunk was wet from water in the air and from our foul-weather gear. The cabin sole slowly filled up with wet clothes. The bulkheads and the counter top got wet every time we brushed against anything. The mast was mounted through the deck and supported by a stainless steel U-beam across the cabin top. The mast boot leaked and dripped water from the overhead onto everything.

Each time the boat turned down and rolled, everyone below was thrown from one side of the boat to the other. Life below was just as bad as on deck. In fact, being on deck and pumping in the jib sheet was probably better. At least the jib trimmer had his back to the wind and spray, and he stayed warm from cranking the winch.

It went on for hours.

Below, rest was nearly impossible. With three people on a watch, the other three went below and tried to sleep. The Vanguard had a settee in the main cabin that made up into a double bunk. The boat was heeled at such an angle that sleeping in the fore and aft position beside each other was impossible. Whoever slept on the low side would be crushed by the two people above falling onto him as the boat bounced and rolled.

We tried sleeping athwart ship, face up, braced in place by our feet on the low side of the double bunk. It didn't work. Whenever someone did fall asleep, their knees would automatically buckle just after they drifted off. A few waves later, the sleeping person would bounce and slide downhill over their bending knees, to be rudely awakened by their body weight crushing their bent legs. The only way to sleep, we found, was to lie face down on the bunk, feet on the low side, knees pressed into the mattress. Then when our knees buckled, it didn't matter. Our legs couldn't bend.

Before the race, we packed the ice box using dry ice to supplement the regular ice. The dry ice would keep the regular ice frozen for the first day or so. Then, after the dry ice was gone, the regular ice would keep the food cold for the rest of the race.

During the storm, we had more water inside the boat than ever before. The water from the mast step ran down the walls and across the countertop. It seeped into the crack around the ice box lid, where the dry ice froze it solid. The frozen water in the crack around the lid welded the lid to the countertop. We simply couldn't open the ice box.

We lived on cookies and carrots, the only edible things left outside the ice box. Of course, we had to eat the cookies quickly to save them from the flying water. The carrots lasted longer, though. Much longer. Eventually, someone in the cockpit placed the bag of uneaten carrots on the seat beside him, but it wasn't long before they fell to the cockpit sole. No problem, we seemed to have an inexhaustible supply of carrots.

21

No one could use the head below because the boat was bouncing around much too violently. On deck, walking up the low side to the shrouds simply wasn't safe—you'd be washed off your feet and thrown overboard by the rolling of the boat and the water rushing along the leeward rail. When necessary, the guys would aim at the scupper in the cockpit sole. Every wave washed the whole boat, including the cockpit sole. It was all washed away in minutes by the flying water, so that was the safest place to go. At every change of people on deck, the on-deck crew cautioned the new people, "Not *those* carrots!"

We started the race with two watches carefully balanced in skills. During the storm, the watch schedule became subject to who could take how much punishment of wet, cold, and being thrown around in the boat. Those who could keep going sailed the boat as best as they could. When they became exhausted, they traded with someone fresher. We had no rules about who went on watch or when. We did what we had to and tried to give others a chance to rest.

By the time the wind dropped below 40 for the first time, the watches had reorganized themselves. Our careful division of skills across the two watches broke down in favor of friendships. During the storm, the people who knew and trusted each other naturally wanted to be together.

By the time the storm began to ease up, we were wet, cold, tired, and hungry. Saying we were grateful when the wind eased off is the understatement of the century. I remember a kind of euphoria at seeing daylight through the clouds and knowing we were through the worst of it. Then, I could finally sleep.

The shortest course to Mackinac Island lies between the Manitou Islands and the eastern shore of Lake Michigan. As boats sail the length of Lake Michigan, they first tend to separate, and then to converge at the South Manitou Passage. As boats come back into sight of each other, the crews try to identify the boats they see. If the nearby boats are bigger and faster, then it's reasonable to assume you're doing well. But, if some of the boats are smaller and slower, then prospects for silver at the finish line grow dim.

As we entered the Manitou passage, we never saw another boat. We sailed the rest of the course and across the finish line, as alone as we had been in the storm.

After we crossed the finish line, we motored to the coal dock to find a place to tie up. Normally, larger boats would finish first and be tied to the dock long before the smaller boats finished. But the coal dock was nearly empty! How strange to be the smallest boat and tie up to the wall, instead of being rafted outside several other boats.

When we tied up to the dock we discovered it was much higher than the deck of our boat. We had to pull ourselves up by the shrouds to step onto the dock, and we noticed the shrouds were all terribly loose. We figured it must have been some storm because all the shrouds had stretched.

Walking along the dock, we began to hear the scuttlebutt about the race and the storm. The Race Committee was carefully trying to identify the location of every boat in the race. Many of the boats had taken refuge in the harbors along the eastern shore of Lake Michigan. As the dwindling numbers of boats arrived in each harbor, the Race Committee received telephone updates and posted the whereabouts.

Boats still out on the race course weren't listed. The Race Committee had no idea where they were.

The escort boat for the race was a Coast Guard ice breaker named The Mackinaw, which served as the emergency communications boat for all the sailboats within VHF range. The Mackinaw carried a chopper, which would be used if an evacuation was necessary. It also carried a few select, grey-haired, blue-blazered dignitaries.

During the storm, the Mackinaw tried to anchor while waiting for the sailboats to beat upwind against the storm. The storm blew the Mackinaw back against her anchor so hard that she dragged. To hold her place over the bottom, she turned on her screws and steamed into the storm over her anchor.

The bridge kept a steady watch on the anemometer. For 16 hours, they reported the lulls never dipped below 40. The highs went over 60.

23

Beating upwind in a sailboat against 40 to 60 miles of wind is on the edge of impossible. The pounding while going to weather took a toll on every part of every boat, as well as on all the people onboard.

Probably the most impressive story on the dock was the failure of a winch. The bolts holding the winch to the deck were sheared off by the force of the wind and the winch was catapulted out into the night.

On a more humorous note, a holding tank that was fiberglassed to the hull of the boat cracked loose, spilling its contents into the boat. The crew claimed they preferred to sit on the rail in the driving rain rather than go below, even off watch. Eventually, when they got seasick, they grimly told each other "Save Our Lake!" and pulled back the hatch cover to throw up into the boat rather than over the side into the lake. After the race, they took the boat out into the lake, opened a sea cock, filled the boat to the cushions, washed it out, and pumped it dry again. Three times.

At the awards ceremony, Avanté was awarded First in Class. She was also given Honorable Mention for being the smallest boat in the fleet to make it to the finish line.

Before we left Mackinac Island for the sail back to Chicago, we tightened the shrouds and retuned the mast. On the way back, even though the weather was quite nice, the shrouds stretched again. This time we got serious about finding the cause.

The real culprit was the U-beam across the cabin top that supported the mast. In the center of the U-beam, directly underneath the mast, the weld between the side walls and the bottom plate of the U-beam had cracked and parted. Without the support of the side walls, the bottom plate couldn't hold the load of the mast. The mast had deformed the bottom plate, bending it down into the cabin just above where we learned about sleeping with our knees against the mattress. Fortunately, the bottom plate never parted and the mast never joined us in the bunk.

After the race was over and the boats returned home, the yacht club surveyed the boat owners to find out what happened. Of the 167 sailboats in the race, 88 reported boat damage and seasick crew, and took refuge in the small harbors along the eastern shore of Lake Michigan.

Nearly all the boats reported some equipment failure. The lists of broken parts included many blown-out sails, snapped lines, exploded blocks, broken masts, goosenecks, and sheaves. Just about anything that had a purpose and carried a load had broken on one boat or another.

Even though considerable damage had occurred, most of the boats could still be jury rigged and sailed. The dominant reason for boats retiring from the race wasn't physical damage, it was crew fatigue. The boats, it seemed, could take more punishment than the people.

Chapter 6

Birth of a Spinnaker

Each summer, the city of Chicago sponsors a yacht race as part of the downtown festival. The race is designed as a beautiful backdrop for the city dwellers who flock to the parks along the lake front. Each boat's starting time is based on the boat's handicap, making the first boat to finish the winner. The picnickers along the shore can watch the boats sail by and tell who is winning . . . at least at the finish.

"Fifty seconds to our start" came the quiet call from the cockpit. On the foredeck, I was getting the spinnaker ready for the downwind start, and trying to watch my wristwatch at the same time. Tom was at the mast ready for the hoist. The pole was up and back. The spinnaker bag was open. I had one hand on the head and clew to keep the sail from pulling out of the bag. My other hand was on the headstay. We were ready.

Now, all we had to do was time it right.

Before the race, on the way out to the starting line, we talked about the start. Because our start was delayed until our handicap ran out, and because we were the only boat with our handicap, we knew we would be all alone at the start—something none of us had ever experienced before. So, we planned an all-alone-start. The idea was simple: get the spinnaker up well before the gun, and have the boat moving at full speed and close to the line when the starting gun went off.

"Forty-five seconds."

Dick was at the helm. He would have to judge boat speed, distance, and the time remaining, and then decide when to raise the chute.

"Forty."

Quiet tension.

"Thirty-five."

Absolute quiet on the boat.

"Thirty."

A few seconds later, Dick called out: "Hoist." The entire crew went to work as one. Tom became all elbows as he hauled on the halyard as fast as possible. The head of the spinnaker shot out of the bag past my hand toward the top of the mast. The sheet snaked back along the leeward rail pulling the clew out of the bag.

"Twenty-five."

"Two blocked!" called Tom to the cockpit. The sheet ran faster down the side of the boat, and then snapped tight as the spinnaker filled and began to draw.

Clean set, I thought.

"Twenty."

The spinnaker began to pull; the boat heeled and began to accelerate.

"Trim a little. You're pretty close. Pole is right on."

"Coming up a little," called Dick

"Pole forward a little. Trim on the sheet."

"Fifteen."

"Course."

"Pole's good. Nice curl in the chute. Lookin' good!"

The boat heeled a little more and gained more speed.

We stood by with focused attention and a little anxiety. I looked for the starting line. We were close, but I thought we'd be OK. Then, I took a better look at the distance and our increasing speed. Well, maybe.

"Ten."

The boat was moving well now.

Everyone was quiet, waiting to see if we'd be over early.

"Five."

28

Quiet on board.

The boat was at full power and closing with the line. Going to be close! I watched the bow pulpit and the line flag on the committee boat.

"Gun."

Bang!

I thought we were OK and looked down course. I looked up at the spinnaker to check the trim.

Bang! The second gun. Someone was over early.

A second gun? I thought. Then, it hit me. The spinnaker was five feet in front of the bow pulpit.

Our spinnaker was over early.

Now we had to go back and restart. How could we do that with the spinnaker up? "Get that thing down!" came the cry from the cockpit.

"Pole forward." I jumped into the pulpit to release the tack from the pole. My mind was leaping ahead, reviewing the steps.

A takedown is normally preceded by putting the genny up, but we needed to get the spinnaker down fast, so Dick could turn back upwind to the starting line, now receding behind us. No time to put up a jib, not now. We'd just sail farther away from the start line. Maybe we could set it after the spinnaker takedown. We needed to get the chute down now.

We'd have to get the pole down, remove the topping lift, repack the chute, and re-lead the spinnaker sheet. After we sailed back to the right side of the starting line, we would have to put it all back together, and then hoist again.

We were going to be in all-out panic mode for the next few minutes.

Then, my mind took a leap. We didn't have time to put up the genny before the spinnaker takedown. What if we never put the genny up and we didn't take any lines off the spinnaker? It would go back up clean! "Dick Can you sail back to the line on the main only?"

"Pole coming forward."

"This is going to be a normal takedown." The cockpit was shifting gears, from post-start to restarting. "Everyone stay calm, we've done this a million times. Let's not mess it up. This is just like normal. We'll dump it down the main hatch."

The spinnaker collapsed and the boat began to coast.

"Ease the sheet!" I hollered.

No response from the cockpit. People were moving into position for the takedown.

"Ease the sheet!" I called again.

"Well, I guess I could sail back on the main. Why not use the jib?" Dick asked.

Another voice from the cockpit, "Ease the sheet? We need it to take down the chute!"

"Tom, are you ready on the halyard?" I knew Tom was ready. This was more coordination than question. And then to the cockpit, "Yes, ease the sheet! To me! Give me ALL you got!"

"Ready on the halyard." Tom's voice was the only calm one.

"Easing. Tell me how much. . . . What are you doing?"

"I don't want to disconnect all this stuff and repack the chute." I started gathering the whole foot into my hands. "Ease some more."

I had the whole foot in my hands. "Tom, start the halyard down. Work with me." I started to pull the lower part of the spinnaker down into my lap, making a pile. Then, I realized just how much cloth I would have to hold in my lap.

"Ease the halyard some more."

"Easing the sheet," came a confused voice from the cockpit.

"Easing the halyard." Tom was on board with my plan.

The guys who were getting ready for the takedown at the side of the boat were trying to figure out what was going on.

Now I had more cloth in my lap than I knew what to do with. And a lot more was to come.

"Right!" Dick understood my plan, even though I hadn't been able to explain it. "We're getting farther from the line. Can I head back to the line? Will you be OK?"

"Ease some more," I told Tom. I gathered cloth as fast as I could into the pile. The pile was getting more uncontrollable. Then, to Dick, "Sure. Head back to the line."

The sweatshirt I was wearing had a zipper down the front and was half unzipped. I was desperate. I started shoving the spinnaker down into my sweatshirt.

The guys at the main hatch realized they weren't going to do a normal takedown. "Dale, what are you doing?" came the question from the cockpit. "You going to hold the whole spinnaker in your lap? You'll never make it. It'll blow overboard."

"Easing," Tom said. "Dale, I can see you, I'll ease as fast as you can take it."

"Coming up," Dick said.

The guys at the main hatch jumped to get back into normal position for a beat. There was no jib, so they had fewer jobs to do. The boat started to turn up.

I was stuffing cloth as fast as I could into my sweatshirt. The top of the spinnaker filled with wind as we turned up and the apparent wind increased. This was a tug of war and the top of the spinnaker was winning. It was pulling me off the boat.

Tom saw my problem and gave the halyard a ten-foot ease. The top of the spinnaker dropped and floated off to leeward. Both of us were too busy to talk. The wind spilled out the top of the sail and I dropped back down on the bow pulpit.

I pulled and stuffed like mad. Soon my sweatshirt had stretched to the limit and was absolutely full. It wouldn't take another wrinkle. Back to making a pile in my lap. The last four feet of the spinnaker were wet. Silently, I thanked Tom I was still on the boat.

I held the last of the spinnaker in my lap. I couldn't move or I'd lose some of it. If it went over the side and into the water, it would surely fill with water as the boat sailed along. It would drag the rest of the sail into the water and me with it. I held on tight to keep it in my lap.

Finally I caught my breath and began to explain: "We're going to put the spinnaker right back up. We don't have to repack or reload

31

anything. We'll just put it back up when we're on the prestart side of the line."

The boat was now headed back upwind. Halfway back to the line, Dick tacked the boat and headed directly for the line to restart. With the wind now on the other side of the boat, the pole was on the leeward side. With the spinnaker in my lap, I couldn't move to reset the pole. "Dick, we can't set the spinnaker on this side. The pole and everything are on the wrong side." This wasn't going to work after all.

"I'll jibe when we get across the line. Then we'll set the chute on the original side." Dick saved my bacon. "So this will be a jibe-set."

"Settle down everybody. Get ready for the jibe."

"OK. A jibe-set. But without a jib to jibe or take down. This'll be easy." The cockpit was on board with the plan.

"Set the pole back about where it was when we started," I shouted back to the cockpit.

As the pole moved back, it pulled cloth out of my sweatshirt. The tack of the spinnaker was the first to go into my sweatshirt. It was on the bottom, and it started to pull the whole wad out of my sweatshirt. I panicked. "Hold the pole!"

Then, more calmly, "That's as much as you can have right now." I didn't have time or wits to explain what was wrong. Just, please don't do that.

"Holding."

The boat crossed the starting line in the wrong direction and the Race Committee gave us a little courtesy nod. Dick turned the boat down and crossed the starting line, restarting, but on the wrong tack. He kept turning down and spun right into the jibe.

"Main's over," came the call.

"Pole back. Hoist!" I called, and then "Trim the sheet!"

Mostly the halyard, but also the sheet and the guy all pulled sail cloth out of my sweatshirt at the same time. In an instant, I went from fat to empty. Bang! The spinnaker was up, full and drawing. Feeling my stretched and empty sweatshirt, I couldn't help wondering if we'd restarted in a delivery room.

Chapter 7

Beer and Chicken Sailing

The port-to-port racing from Chicago created friendships among competitors like nowhere else I've ever sailed. Racing to St. Joe, Michigan City, Racine, or Milwaukee on Saturday, and then back on Sunday created the opportunity for a giant Saturday night party at the destination yacht club.

The mingling of crews from the 50 to 100 boats, plus all the wives, sweethearts, and wannabes allowed competitors to get to know each other. Sometimes, good friendships developed.

One day at work, I received a phone call from Rick, the bowman on his father's C & C 39. It was a sultry summer day in Chicago—a lot hotter than normal. "Would you like to go sailing after work?" Rick asked. "Some of the people coming are good sailors and some aren't. We aren't going to do anything fancy, no spinnakers or anything, just cruise around off Belmont Harbor while it gets dark."

I jumped at the chance to go sailing during the week. It sure would beat going home to a hot, stuffy apartment. "Sure," I said. "What can I do to help?"

"Well, why don't you stop by that chicken place and bring a bucket of chicken?" he said. "Paul is going to bring some beer. I think that's about all we'll need. So don't stop for dinner. Just get down to Belmont as fast as you can."

"I'll be there!" I answered.

The chicken and I arrived at the harbor as fast as I could manage it. But, Rick was way ahead of me. After work, when I went home to change, Rick went directly to the boat and changed on board.

By the time I arrived at the yacht club, he'd brought the boat into the guest dock and was waiting for the rest of us.

I'd never done much social sailing, so I had a whole new protocol to learn or, rather, the absence of a protocol. Some things were the same, like leaving the dock and getting under way. Some things were a lot more relaxed.

"Someone go below and get the Number Two out of the forepeak," Rick asked. "We'll be underpowered tonight, but who cares. It's such a pretty night."

So we hung a jib that was too small . . . too small by my racing training. I had to learn going fast wasn't the goal in social sailing.

We sailed out of the harbor on a gentle evening breeze, just enjoying the feel of the boat as it quietly slid over the small waves. We ate chicken and drank beer. We declared life was, indeed, good. We talked as the Sun went down behind the city and dark descended on a lake without lights. We sat in the dark cockpit and talked about the good things in our lives. And we talked about the things that didn't make any sense.

In the dark, by the glow of the instrument lights, we could barely see each other's faces. In a night full of stars and thoughts about sailing and life, each person's presence was far stronger than the dim outline I could make out with my eyes.

In a way, each person seemed like a navigation light in the night. Each was signaling to the others with what knowledge he had. We were all free to use that knowledge and, yet, we were free to sail wherever we chose.

When the time came to return, the hour was well past normal bedtime. Reluctantly, we turned the boat in the light breeze toward the distant city lights. The location of the harbor entrance was long lost to our awareness, so we looked at Chicago's skyline from the lake and guessed where Belmont must be. We looked and looked for the navigation light at the harbor entrance. Eventually, someone found the red light. Then, after a moment, it turned green, and we imagined the traffic starting through the intersection on shore.

We continued looking for the harbor light, all the time gently sailing toward the apartment buildings. Eventually, the harbor light separated from the city lights behind it and we were nearly home.

The hour was late and the good-byes were quiet. We each carried the wonderful inner feeling of the evening home with us.

Going fast wasn't the goal. Good friends were.

Chapter 8

A Higher Vision of Sailing

In 1975, for the hundredth anniversary of the Chicago Yacht Club, the race organizers wanted to attract as many entrants as possible to the Chicago to Mackinac Race. The yachting fleet in Detroit was sizable and boasted some excellent sailors, but only a few ever came to Chicago. Detroit's fleet had their own sailing regattas, including their own race to Mackinac, the Port Huron to Mackinac Race. To encourage the boats from Detroit to come to Chicago for the Chicago race, a new race was conceived: the Port Huron to Chicago Race. At 631 miles, it was the longest fresh-water race ever staged.

"I'll go down and get the RDF[2]," Rick concluded as he stared out at the wall of fog obscuring everything more than a hundred feet away. I'd just come on watch and Rick's explanation of our situation left me as cold as the water in the air. Basically, we had to find Cove Island Light, a buoy some fifteen miles ahead of us, somewhere out there in the fog, and round the buoy.

The last time we knew where we were for sure was at the start, 150 miles ago. Since then, every five miles or so, each helmsman had estimated the average direction and speed he thought the boat had gone during his time on the helm, and logged it. These log entries were carefully plotted on the chart. Each advancement of our position

---

[2] In 1975, Radio Direction Finding was the only electronic navigation tool available. LORAN, Sat Nav, and GPS were still in the future.

was based on the results of the previous estimates, compounding error onto error.

Now we had to steer directly toward, and find, Cove Island Light buoy. In truth, we didn't know exactly where we were. If the fog held like this, we would need to pass within two or three boat lengths of the mark for it to be visible in the fog.

Now that my watch was all on deck, Rick's watch was officially off. They began to stretch and go below for a well-deserved rest. With only fifteen miles to go, we would either find Cove Island Light buoy or pass it . . . on my watch.

When I looked up, I realized Rick was looking right at me. "I'll get the RDF," he repeated quietly as he got up to go below. "Maybe it will confirm our DR or, if not, it'll give us new data to work with."

When Rick came back on deck, he was holding a small device trailing a long wire that ran back below. "The way this model works is I have the antenna and compass here, and it's connected by these wires to the radio receiver down below. These ear phones let me hear what the radio receives. I'm supposed to get the antenna part outside of the cone of the shrouds and stays. Less distortion that way. Supposed to be the most accurate RDF available."

Rick went to the side of the boat and back as far as the wire trailing below would allow. As he aimed the antenna/compass out into the fog and began mumbling to himself, I wondered if the RDF could possibly be accurate enough. RDFs typically had a five or ten-degree error in measuring the direction to a broadcasting tower. Cove Island Light buoy was only fifteen miles ahead of us. But, the broadcasting stations would be on land near the populations they served, much farther away. If Rick's stations were 30 or 40 miles away, a ten-degree error could lead us to believe we were five miles or more away from where we actually were. And we had to pass within a few boat lengths of the mark to see it. I didn't relish the idea of getting there on my watch.

Rick went below for a moment. When he came back on deck he moved to the other side of the boat. I tried to concentrate on sailing as straight as I could in the fog. There wasn't anything to look at but the binnacle compass. The wind was light and the water flat. On a close reach under spinnaker, the boat sailed quite nicely. The only sounds were from our own gentle bow wake . . . and Rick's muttering.

A little later, Rick took the same bearings again. And then he took them a third time. Eventually, he went below, gathering up the wire lead as he left. He plotted all the bearings, advancing them for the distance the boat had traveled between readings. In a few minutes, Rick stuck his head and shoulders out of the main hatch, and he announced, "Cove Island Light lies at 46 degrees magnetic and 8.2 miles away."

I had checked the dead reckoning just before coming on watch. "Rick, our DR says 35 degrees and fourteen miles. Which do you think is right?"

"Probably neither," said the Skipper from below. Rick and I were the watch captains. The Skipper was the seventh person. He had not assigned himself to either watch. He floated between them as the situation dictated, and he was always there when a decision had to be made. In truth, the Skipper probably got less sleep than either watch.

"Well, nothing's certain," Rick replied. "When I took the bearings, I felt I had good signals. I know the stations are a little far away, but it felt good when I did it."

"If we are where the RDF says, and not where the DR says," the Skipper reasoned, "then we would have been going a little higher than we realized. On a close reach, rounding up a little and averaging a little high seems pretty much believable. Let's take a chance on the RDF."

"I'm okay with that," Rick muttered. "I'm exhausted. I'm going to get some sleep. Wake me when we get there."

"Yeah. Right." But I was thinking *if* we get there.

So, I came down to 46 degrees magnetic and held the course as steady as I could. In my mind, I kept multiplying our boat speed by the minutes as they passed, counting down the tenths of miles to Cove Island Light buoy. If we were off by a little, we would sail right past the buoy in the fog and never know it. Then which way would we turn to try to find it?

Maybe the fog would lift.

Rick stuck his head back up, "Hey, I just heard the Race Committee call the stake boat that's supposed to be at Cove Island Light. If you want, I'll turn the VHF on in the cockpit, so you can listen."

"Sure. Maybe we'll learn something."

". . . approaching Cove Island Light, but we're not on station yet. Over," blurted the VHF.

"Well, OK. But the lead boats must be there already. Over."

"I don't see how they could be. It's as thick as I've ever seen it. We've got to be close, but we haven't actually seen it yet. Nobody around here can see anything. Over."

"It'll be dawn soon. Maybe that'll help. Call us when you're on station. Over."

"Roger. Race Committee One standing by."

"Race Committee Base standing by."

We laughed. The Race Committee couldn't find the mark.

Then we realized we, and every boat in the fleet, had the same problem they had. The visible circle within the fog was only about 100 feet. We had to pass close enough to the buoy to make it come within our visible circle or we'd never see it as we passed by. For the hundredth time, I wondered where it was and where we were.

Time ticked down slowly. The steady light breeze and our boat speed held. Time, speed, and distance. Time, speed, and distance. How many times could I run the same calculation in my head?

We sailed on in fog, gliding quietly under spinnaker. Occasionally, we could hear a fog horn. Once, we heard a bow wake right behind us and a little to starboard. With no time for the fog horn, we hollered "Hello!"

For a reply, all we heard was the terse conversation on the boat just off our transom. "Look out! There's a boat there."

"Where?"

"Over there."

"Coming down a little."

"Easing."

"They still there?"

"Not sure."

40

At the closest point, we saw an outline of a dark spinnaker in the fog. Immediately, it turned to grey, and then disappeared again. We hollered back into the now empty fog, "I think we're OK." Our one glimpse of the dark shadow hadn't been enough for us to identify the boat.

Then we heard someone joke, "See you at Mackinac." Like the shadow of their spinnaker, they were gone.

After the close call, everyone on deck was wide awake. We sailed on, carefully following the compass, but the spinnaker needed little adjustment in the steady, damp, gray breeze.

We were staring out in every direction into the blank fog when our bowman began recounting a conversation he had the night before the start with some guys from a local boat. They told him the original course of the Port Huron to Mackinac Race was simply the shortest course to Mackinac, which followed the gently curving western shore of Lake Huron. Unfortunately, this course created a follow-the-leader parade along the shore line.

In 1939, to make the race more interesting, the Race Committee made the Cove Island Light buoy, on the eastern side of Lake Huron, a mark of the course. All the boats had to sail out of sight of land for half the length of Lake Huron, and then approach the buoy from the middle of the lake, adding a navigational challenge to the race.

As chance would have it, a thick fog settled down on Lake Huron that year, and the boats had a terrible time finding the Cove Island Light buoy. Crews who missed the buoy in the fog, eventually figured out they were sailing at racing speeds with no visibility ahead straight toward the shore beyond the buoy.

The Race Committee considered that too dangerous so, after only one race, Cove Island Light buoy was removed from the course. It wasn't until 1972 when Cove Island Light buoy was brought back as a mark of the course, again to make the race more interesting.

The VHF broke into our conversation: "Race Committee One. Race Committee One. Race Committee One. This is the yacht Flyer."

"Race Committee One here. Over."

"Are you guys on station? Over."

"Negative. Over."

"The race circular says you'll take our sail numbers as we round. If you aren't on station, how are you going to know who rounded? Over."

Silence.

The radio operator on the stake boat must have asked the Race Officer what to say. The silence was long enough that they probably had a conference trying to decide exactly how to say it.

"This is Race Committee One. Every boat should round the mark as proscribed in the Race Circular. We'll begin recording sail numbers when we arrive on station. Over."

Another long silence. This time there must have been a conference on Flyer.

Then, "Thank you Race Committee. Flyer standing by."

"Race Committee One standing by."

Like every other boat in the fleet listening to their VHF, we dug out the Race Circular to see what it said about rounding. When we found it, it was a simple "Leave Cove Island Light to port. A stake boat will take sail numbers of the boats rounding."

It had been nearly an hour-and-a-half since the RDF fix. I kept thinking we've got to be there. What do we do if we pass by it? Ten more minutes at this speed and we'll have to start asking hard questions. There was no sound in the fog except our own quiet bow wake.

The fog seemed to be lighter now. No, I realized it was the dawn beginning to brighten the fog. The circle of visibility wasn't any bigger, just brighter.

I looked at my watch and calculated the distance again. Where are we? The bow wake continued to ripple as we sailed blindly ahead.

ding

I almost missed it. Cove Island Light buoy. Way off to the port. Barely audible.

I forgot we had a spinnaker up and turned the boat toward the ding in the fog.

"Hey, where're you going? The spinnaker collapsed," came the immediate complaint.

"I heard the buoy. I'm going to head toward the sound before I lose it," I explained. "Get the spinnaker down and the big jib up, as fast as you can!"

"Give us a chance." They were already running to the foredeck.

It was a scramble, but we got the spinnaker down and the big jib up. We tacked and turned the boat upwind in the fog toward the area where I thought the sound had come from.

We listened intently for the next ding. Nothing.

A boat under spinnaker going the direction we were when we had our spinnaker up popped out of the fog, slid past us, and disappeared. Apparently, they hadn't heard the buoy. They sailed on past it without knowing.

Under jib and main, we coasted back upwind over a flat sea, listening as hard as we could for another ding. The tack roused the off-watch crew and they came on deck, with the obvious questions: "Are we there? Where is it?"

The buoy popped out of the fog.

The very light breeze we were sailing in wasn't enough to create any wave action. Without waves, there wasn't enough movement to swing the clapper away from the bell on the buoy. So, the buoy remained as silent as the fog. The only sound from the buoy resulted from our wake just after we passed close aboard. When our wake rolled past the buoy, it rocked the buoy a little and the clapper scraped on the side of the bell.

Almost immediately after we sailed away from the buoy, it disappeared back into the fog. Another boat passed just ahead of us under spinnaker.

Without wave action to actuate the clapper, none of the boats could hear the buoy. They had to sail close enough to see it. We had been lucky to hear the one rare ding.

As we set a course for Mackinac Island, the boats back at the mark continued to sail back and forth, searching and searching. The more times they tacked and sailed back and forth, the more error they introduced into their dead reckoning. After a while, random chance became more important than good navigation.

43

"Race Committee One. Race Committee One. Race Committee One. This is Frantic Caper. Over."

"Race Committee One. Go ahead. Over."

"Race Committee One, we have plotted our course and we know we are well past the mark. We have not actually seen the mark, so we are rounding it navigationally. Over."

Silence.

More silence.

Eventually, it became clear the Race Committee did not intend to respond.

"This is Frantic Caper, standing by."

"Race Committee One standing by."

"Rounding 'NAVIGATIONALLY!?'" burst out one of our crew. "How can they do that? How do they know they ever rounded it?"

Once the dam was broken, several more frustrated boats called the Race Committee, claiming Navigational Rounding.

Frustration in the heavy fog brought out lots of creativity. Decision, one of the best boats in the fleet, wondered if a man at the top of the mast could see the buoy from farther away. If he did see it, they sure didn't want to tell the rest of the boats how they found it. Very quietly, they hoisted a man up the mast. When they got him to the top, he started laughing.

"What do you see?" they demanded, as quietly as they could. "Well? What do you see?"

"I see the tops of about 20 masts, all sticking up out of the fog, and all going in different directions!"

Chapter 9

Frostbiting

The kids in the junior program at our yacht club in Chicago were taught how to sail in Lehman dinghies. The club owned a couple dozen of these modest sailing, round-bottomed, unstable, and unforgiving charters. The kids sailed them all summer. In the winter, when no kid would get in a sailing dinghy and go out on the water, the adults exhibited their superiority.

In the winter, no one talks about the weather in Chicago. We just call it "unpredictable." All winter long, it just keeps getting more and more unpredictable. The water temperature was the only predictable thing. And that would, undoubtedly, keep going down until spring.

Back when Rick convinced me to race in the Frostbite Series, the weather was a little brisk, but not terribly cold. "Great fun!" Rick continued excitedly. "It'll give you a chance to hone your tactics and apply the rules in close quarters. Dinghy racing is the only place where the action is so close and fast. You'll learn a lot."

Now that the series had begun, the thermometer had been in the teens for weeks. My desire for dinghy racing was closely following the mercury down.

Despite my aversion to cold, here I was, beating to weather on the first race of the day.

It was bitter cold. Way below freezing.

Last week, I put on enough layers of clothes to keep warm, but I couldn't move around in the dinghy. I almost capsized when I got hit by a puff. I couldn't get out of the bottom of the dinghy and up on the rail. I think capsizing would have been like jumping naked into a glass of water between the ice cubes.

This morning, I put on fewer layers. Now I could move better, if I didn't freeze first.

Darn, Paul just tacked on my wind. Got to tack! My legs were so cold and stiff, it hurt to move to the other side of the dinghy. It's impossible to roll tack when you're too cold to move.

I should have stayed home this morning, but, somehow, I couldn't do that. It would have given bragging rights to Rick and I'd never hear the end of it.

Oops. A big puff. Hike out! Keep the dinghy upright.

This morning when I stepped onto the dinghy dock to rig the boat, I started sliding down the incline toward the water. Sheet ice! The wind last night must have splashed enough water up on the dock to cover it with water and, this morning, it was frozen. I grabbed the dinghy to stop my slide. When I did, I heard the ice crack between the bottom of the dinghy and the dock.

"You'll learn a lot," Rick had said.

Still a long way to the weather mark.

When I went to bail out the dinghy, I tried to pick up the sponge from the bottom of the dingy. Not only was the sponge frozen into a brick, but it was also frozen solid to the bottom of the dinghy. But, as it turned out, that was OK. The water I wanted to bail out was also frozen.

Another blast of wind hit the sail and the dinghy did a jerk roll to port. I hiked as fast as I could move. I was almost fast enough. I only shipped a little water.

The water was cold on my feet.

I wished it would snow, then it wouldn't be so cold. No! I take that back. It did snow a couple of weeks ago. I couldn't see the next mark. I rounded the weather mark and sailed off into the falling snow, just like into a thick fog. It was a new experience to have "fog" and no way to dead reckon.

By gentleman's agreement, if someone found the next mark in the falling snow and rounded it, they were supposed to shout out for

46

everyone to hear. I never figured it out; some misinformation was always going on.

Thanks for the experience, Rick.

I remembered the whole harbor had frozen over last year. I wondered how cold it had to be for that to happen. Maybe then we could all stand at the bar and declare how disappointed we were. Secretly, we'd be terrified it would thaw before Frostbite Season was over.

A violent wind shift! The dinghy stood up and rolled to weather. I leaned in and steered down as fast as the dinghy would turn. Now the seat of my pants was sopping wet.

When I had the dinghy under control again, I looked upwind to see which gods were trying to send me swimming on this cold, blustery day. Oh! There they are! The tall apartment buildings that overlooked the harbor. The wind had to pass between the buildings before it came to me. The slots between the buildings created the world's largest wind burble. And I had to beat in it to get to the upwind mark.

Not too much farther to the weather mark. Seems like I've been beating for hours. I'm cold.

Then I saw a big mess just past the mark.

Someone had capsized and the crash boat was there getting the person out of the water. All the other dinghies were steering around the crash boat and the overturned dinghy.

One more tack and I'd lay the mark. I held on a little longer to make sure. I couldn't think about adding two more tacks.

In a few boat lengths I decided I had over-stood enough to be safe. It was time to tack.

The water in the harbor had warmed the bottom of the boat. The sponge and ice frozen to the bottom were still frozen together, but they had come loose from the bottom. This thin, one-foot ice cube floated in the water I had shipped. I tried not to step on the slippery sheet while going through the tack.

After the tack, I found I was plenty high, and I'd lay the mark easily. I remembered the tall buildings and the wind shifts. I worried some more. I didn't want to go swimming.

Wait a minute. Why was that guy turning back upwind? That made no sense at all. He just rounded the weather mark. He should be going downwind on the free leg. I didn't get it.

Now I was at the mark.

I turned down and eased the sheet, but the sail didn't go out! The main sheet wouldn't run through the block! The sheet was frozen in a straight line. It wouldn't bend over the pulley, and it wouldn't run out.

The dinghy was already headed down toward the leeward mark. The sail stayed trimmed in flat for a beat.

The apartment building gods struck again. WHAM! The wind drove the dinghy over on beam's end. The open dinghy began to fill with water.

I was still standing in the sinking, open dinghy as the icy water found my feet, climbed up my legs to my waist, and then covered my chest and neck.

Thanks, Rick.

The last thing I heard before my head descended under the icy surface was the two-blast whistle from the Race Committee signaling the abandonment of the race.

Completely submerged in ice cold water, I resolved to learn about the weather in California.

48

Part II

Salt Water

Chapter 10

Welcome to San Francisco Bay

In 1975, my employer transferred me to San José, making San Francisco Bay the place to sail. Having sailed in everything from light air to winds over 60 miles an hour, I expected to hold my own on the race course.

My first boat in California was a Santana 22, which I chose for its popularity on the Bay. The people in the Santana fleet were kind and helpful. They offered advice and showed me what to do.

"Don't forget to check your backstay tension," Charlie hollered at me from his boat. We had been about a boat length apart on a hard beat since clearing Peninsula Point. My backstay adjuster was just behind me on the transom. I knew I had adjusted it when we started on the beat. I looked at the jib luff. *Not too much sag,* I thought. Why would he tell me to check the backstay when the jib luff looked OK?

I was still checking the leading edge of the jib when Charlie suddenly turned down.

So! This was to be a game of chase! If I had turned around to look at the backstay, I'd have missed his turn. Instantly, I turned down right on his track and eased the main. Both our boats surged up to hull speed and we reached across the Bay, barely a boat length apart.

Back at the yacht club, when we were putting Fetish and Tacky Lady in the water, Charlie had been all friendly. He had offered to be a trial horse for me and to show me the Bay.

Once on the water, it seemed more like sparring than sightseeing. Maybe he just wanted to check out the new guy.

Thanks for the reminder about the backstay, Charlie. I smiled. *I know you now. Lead on! I had worked to weather of you on the beat, at least a little. Then you pulled that backstay trick. I'll catch you again before we get back.*

As we crossed the Bay, we trimmed sails, pumped the main, and worked our boats over the waves to maximize boat speed and gain inches on each other. When we roared into Harding Rock, I was still back about a boat length. Clearly no overlap at the two boat-length circle.

Charlie jibed and headed down for the west face of Angel Island. I came into Harding a little higher, cleared the buoy by inches just as the main went over, and exited the jibe on a higher course. As a result, I gained on him relative to the wind and ended up with the edge of my wind shadow across his boat.

I sat on his air as best as I could. Very slowly, my half wind-shadow made a difference, and I gained on him. Slowly, I pulled up into a better coverage position.

Gottcha! I pulled up to where I had control of his air, and then came down on him to present a bigger, closer wind block. I was careful not to get close enough for him to spin up and tag me, but I camped on his air as long as I dared. He looked like he was thinking about spinning up once, but he didn't try it.

By now, I had a boat-speed advantage on him and sailed clear ahead. Then, Charlie got his wind clear again and stopped falling back. I expected him to head up and try to pass me to weather. I was all set to go up with him, but it never happened.

Charlie continued to sail toward the shore of Angel Island, seemingly content to sail behind me. I didn't trust this for a moment, and I divided my attention between watching where I was going and Charlie behind me. There wasn't much he could do that far astern and to leeward. I had him where I wanted him.

As we sailed closer to Angel Island, the breeze began to ease off. Both of us slowed down with the lower wind and adjusted our sail trim.

Still, Charlie didn't head up and try to go to weather of me. He continued to drift below me, until he was quite close to the shore.

Thinking he would have to go up at some point, I stayed a little to weather of him. If he tried to go up, I'd be well ahead.

Then, somehow, Charlie began going faster. He started gaining on me. Confused, I checked my sail trim. He continued to gain. I checked again.

"Check your sail trim!" Charlie hollered. I had already done that and stared in disbelief at how fast he was gaining on me.

When he sailed into my wind shadow, he slowed a little, but only a little. Then, he sailed right on through my lee and kept going.

Now he was clear ahead of me. And still to leeward.

What had I done? I was confused. No way should he have broken through my lee. I checked the sail trim again. Perfect!

"Come down here behind me!" Charlie hollered back.

What an insult, I thought. He wanted me to sail behind him.

"Come down here behind me!" he yelled again. "Sail in my track." Charlie was still pulling away from me.

OK. I'll come down, I thought reluctantly. I sailed down to well back on his quarter.

"No, not there. Down more. Get right in my track. Not above it. Right *behind* me."

I sailed down and did as Charlie directed. He stopped pulling away from me.

"Tide," Charlie hollered back at me. I was now so far back, I could just hear his words. "Countercurrent, close along the face of Angel, in a strong ebb." I could barely hear him. "You'll have to learn about tides."

Chapter 11

There's the Photo Boat!

The winds and tides in the San Francisco Bay make it one of the most difficult places in the world to sail. Those same conditions make it one of the most exciting places in the world to sail. This draws both the sailors who challenge the conditions and the photographers who take incredible action photos of people and sailboats.

"We have a lot more wind now than we had out in the ocean," George said from the helm. He was an experienced racer from the East Coast, but new to San Francisco Bay.

"Just hold the boat steady. We're not quite to the Gate yet," Frank replied. Frank had gotten the racing crew together for George and asked me if I wanted to go, too. I was new to the San Francisco Bay and jumped at my first chance to sail out beneath the Golden Gate Bridge on a day race.

"No, I mean it's really building," insisted George. He had just taken delivery of the boat. This was his first race in the San Francisco Bay, and his first spinnaker run back in under the Gate

"Nah, this is pretty much normal. You see, back between Point Bonita and Mile Rock, the entrance to the Gate is quite wide. By the time you get to the Gate, it's a lot narrower. As the sides come in, it acts like a funnel. As you sail down the funnel, the wind gets stronger," Frank explained. "Watch your course!"

The boat heeled sharply as the apparent wind came forward a little.

"Got it. On course," mumbled George as he steered back down.

The boat settled down as George concentrated on steering a straight line and keeping the wind well aft. After a few minutes of concentration, George said, "It wasn't blowing this hard when we left this morning."

"Blows harder in the afternoon as the inland valley heats up," Frank said. He was more tense now. "Hot air rises. Sucks in the cool air from the ocean."

A wave picked up the stern of the boat and pushed it a little. The boat started to turn up. George steered back down and controlled the boat just fine.

"Almost under the bridge," announced George.

"Careful. You need to concentrate here," Frank reminded him.

The bow wake roared and spray sheeted off to both sides. We had to be at max hull speed.

"There's the bridge," George pointed out, as he looked up at the bridge 220 feet above. "Sailing in under the Golden Gate! I love it. We're back inside. What a great day!" George was obviously enjoying his new boat and sailing in San Francisco Bay.

"We've got a good ways to go yet. Stay with it," Frank cautioned. "Watch for wind shifts. We're almost to the tricky spot."

After passing beneath the bridge, we began to look for the finish line over on the city front. Someone pointed out the yacht club on the shore.

"The swells are calming down. I guess that's because we're inside now," George tried to make his point. "It sure is easier to steer."

"Just concentrate on steering," Frank said. "The bridge creates a big burble in the wind. It starts way high up where the bridge is. As we sail downwind from the bridge, the burble spreads out . . . sideways, and up and down, too. Some of it may come down to the water. You gotta be alert when it does." Frank focused George's attention back on steering.

We were on port tack, and the yacht club and finish line were way to starboard. We would have to do two jibes before the finish— one pretty soon and one as we approach the line.

Two jibes in this wind! I was glad I was in the cockpit.

The boat charged on at full speed. George called "Prepare to jibe," and the foredeck guys scrambled forward.

Someone said, "Look, there's the Photo Boat"

"Vultures! They come out here and wait for us to crash."

"Where are they?" George looked to the left for the photo boat. "I sure hope they get a good picture of my new boat."

WHAM!

The burble hit us while we were still traveling at absolute max speed. The spinnaker overpowered the rudder and pulled the boat in a circle. We were broaching. George frantically tried to steer down, but with no result. The boat no longer responded to the helm. It continued to round up. We were totally out of control.

Click.

The boat lay flat over on beam's end, pinned down by the wind still in the spinnaker. We hung on for dear life and just tried to stay on the boat, scrambling in every direction. The boat lost forward momentum. On its side, keel to the wind, the boat was dragged sideways across the water by the still-full spinnaker. Everyone stood on something that a moment ago had been vertical.

Click.

Chapter 12

Pinpoint Navigation

The 70-mile Windjammers Race from San Francisco to Santa Cruz is one of the best-attended races of the summer. Occasionally, the biggest boats finish before the wind dies, just after sunset. Most of the boats, however, don't finish until the morning breeze sets in.

Gary, Bill, and I were already halfway down the coast to Santa Cruz in Fetish II, my Cal 2-27, when dusk began to fall. We were all familiar with the waters outside the Gate and the navigation for the rest of the race was simple—just follow the coast. Eventually, it would curve east at Davenport into Monterey Bay, and lead to the finish line just outside the Santa Cruz harbor. Our race strategy was equally simple: sail hard while the wind lasted, and do our best to keep the boat moving after the wind died at night.

All afternoon, we had a nice breeze. We worked hard tuning the spinnaker and maximizing boat speed as we sailed south along the coast. The waves were too small to surf on, but they did help us slide south down the course.

Our competition had long since turned into white specks around us. Those particular white specks had then mixed in with the white specks in other classes. We no longer knew which white specks were our competition.

Sometime in the mid afternoon, we passed Half Moon Bay. We could just make out the coast way off to port. The details were lost in the haze. We couldn't identify anything on shore.

We had been maintaining a log and keeping our dead-reckoning position plotted on the chart, so we knew pretty well where we were. When we looked toward land, we could see land, but it was difficult to tell how far off the coast we were.

As the warmth of the day began to cool into evening and dusk faded into dark, our afternoon breeze followed the Sun. As dark settled on the ocean, Bill turned on the running lights. When the wind became light enough we began to reach up to keep the boat moving.

On shore, Pigeon Point Light flashed its ten-second pattern, distinct, but a long way back on our port quarter. With a hand-held compass, I took the bearing and entered it into the log.

At 9 P.M., I sent Bill below to get three hours of rest, while Gary and I continued sailing the boat in the light air—down in the puffs and up in the lulls. We tried to get as far south as we could by keeping the boat speed up, rather than going closer to the desired course.

An hour or so later, Pigeon Point Light looked much smaller and farther away. Before it faded completely, I took another bearing. Below, I advanced the last line of position by our distance run and crossed it with the current bearing for a running fix. It placed us a little ahead of where the dead reckoning said we were, but it had bad parallax. I decided to go with the dead reckoning, rather than the running fix, and I made a note in the log.

As the temperature-dropped in the dark, fog settled over the fleet. It hid the sailboats from each other and from the coastal-shipping traffic. Except for the Moon shining down through the fog, we sailed totally blind. We continued to work south as best as we could, but the light air kept us reaching up for speed.

We heard a freighter in the fog, but not very close. A hundred sailboats must have been racing down the coast to Santa Cruz. I wondered what the radar screen on the freighter must have looked like. I bet they were just as scared as we were.

Eventually, we decided we were getting too far offshore and jibed to angle back in. We logged the jibe and concentrated on getting the best speed and southing out of the boat. For a while, we sailed higher than we wanted. Soon, the boat seemed tuned and moving again.

An hour later, we noticed the Moon had disappeared above the fog. Either the fog was thickening in general or it was thicker closer to shore. The spinnaker hung more limply now.

On the principle there was less wind in fog, we jibed back out.

At midnight, Gary went below and woke Bill. When Bill came on deck, he was carrying a large coffee cup and declared three hours of sleep was not quite enough for his tired body.

The old timers at the yacht club believed this race was won or lost at night. We worked hard to get as far south as we could, but I could feel fatigue sapping my energy.

Toward shore, we heard a lot of fog-horn activity in the distance. I hoped they got it all sorted out okay.

By 2:30 A.M., I was both exhausted and sleepy. My body needed rest, but I still had a half hour to go. I wondered if I could get a fix somehow with the RDF. At least it would be good to move around.

Below, I turned on the light over the counter where I had the chart. I could barely see the chart. At first I thought I was just sleepy. Then, I realized the cabin lights were dim. The battery must have run down.

"The battery is low," I called up the hatch to Bill. "Why don't you start the engine?"

The battery wouldn't turn the engine over, and we only had one battery.

Great! Here we were in the middle of a fog bank, with freighters coming through, the running lights were going out, and the engine wouldn't start.

Bill was pragmatic. "Well, we can't stop here. I guess we'll have to keep sailing," he said quietly from the helm.

I tried to read the chart by the light from a flashlight. The bright spot moved around on the chart and I couldn't follow it with my eyes. I was having a hard time concentrating. At last, I found Point Pinos had an RDF transmitter, but I knew it was too far aft to give us a good running fix. I didn't see any other station to work with.

Fighting fatigue, I did the best I could to get a bearing, and plot the LOP. At 3 A.M., I took the second RDF bearing on Point Pinos and crossed the two for a running fix. The two lines were almost on top of each other. This verified our distance offshore, but not our distance run.

I couldn't label the point a "fix" of any kind. On the chart, where the two lines crossed, I wrote "3 A.M. Guess."

Too tired to do any more, I woke Gary and took his place in the bunk. I was asleep before my head hit the pillow.

Gary checked the log and chart as he went on watch. On deck, Gary told Bill about my "3 A.M. Guess." They laughed. Bill told Gary about not being able to start the engine. They didn't laugh. They couldn't decide if I were too cheap to buy a battery or too weight-conscious to add another battery to the boat. Neither speculation was satisfying. They firmly agreed I should have installed the second battery.

Not long after I hit the sack, they updated the dead reckoning, now based on the 3 A.M. Guess, and observed how far south we were. They decided to jibe back in toward shore, toward the finish line. They settled the boat on the new course and logged the new heading. A quick look at the chart showed the new course would take us in just south of Davenport, on a good approach to the finish line. According to the chart, they had jibed at about the right time.

The running lights eventually dimmed to nothing. Occasional freighters still passed through the fleet of sailboats, but none came close to us.

At 6 A.M., they woke me. I could see the light of dawn out the hatch. They wanted to know where we were. They were tired of navigating from a 3 A.M. Guess.

By the light of early morning, I looked at the chart again. Now I found what I was looking for last night—an AM radio tower north of Monterey—KIDD. The tower was at a reasonable angle from Point Pinos and would show our distance run.

When I crossed the two RDF lines of position, I had a good fix. But, we were in the middle of Monterey Bay—seven miles south of where I thought we were. We had sailed seven miles past the finish line. We would have to beat back upwind another seven miles to the finish.

Bill and Gary weren't happy. To sail 14 extra miles in a 70-mile race would certainly make us last. All our competitors must be in by now. We would have to eat a huge slice of humble pie.

With the big genny and little conversation, we beat for an hour-and-a-half back to the finish line. As the Sun rose and warmed the air, the fog thinned.

Finally, we saw the pier and knew we were closing with the finish line. As we approached, we couldn't see any of our competitors or hardly any other sailboats at all. We knew they were all in the harbor having a cup of cheer and waiting for us to show up. Oh, well.

We sailed through the finish line, just so the Race Committee would know we were no longer out on the ocean.

At the line, the Race Committee gave us a shot gun, not a whistle. A shotgun was typically for the first boat to finish in each class. This didn't make any sense. They must have screwed up. Maybe they lost their whistle. We were so tired.

We couldn't start the engine, so we sailed over to the harbor mouth and into the opening. We would have to dock under sail and we were a little on edge going in. Santa Cruz harbor is small and a little tight, and we only had a little wind to work with.

Inside the harbor, the dock was empty. Instead of scrambling for any possible place we could find, we had our choice of anywhere we wanted. A few of the biggest boats were tied to the wall. We sailed toward the first one, dropped our sails, and coasted to the side tie.

The harbor was empty. I remembered the 1970 Mackinac Race when we sailed into an empty harbor expecting it to be full. It hit me before it hit Bill and Gary. Our competition and the rest of the fleet were still out on the ocean waiting for the morning breeze. The reason we didn't see anyone at the finish line was they weren't there yet. We did GOOD!

I couldn't remember ever getting the advantage on either Bill or Gary. Now that I had it, I wanted to make good use of it.

As the owner and navigator, in my most authoritative voice, I brazenly announced to my lowly crew, "The reason we did so well was my Pin-Point Navigation!"

Chapter 13

Man Overboard Drill

Surprisingly, the first sailboat race from San Francisco to Hawaii was for singlehanders, not for boats with full crews. Two years later, in 1980, the Ballena Bay Yacht Club organized the first race from San Francisco to Hawaii for fully crewed boats. Trying to promote a safe race, the Race Committee specified the minimum amount of food and safety equipment that must be carried. In addition, they strongly suggested each boat conduct a Man Overboard Drill.

Most boats responded to this suggestion by tossing a cushion in the water, and then returning to pick it up.

When the owner of the boat I was going to race on talked to the crew about doing the Man Overboard Drill, I was dumb enough to say, "Well, I have a wet suit."

"OK. Why don't you go down and put on your wet suit," the owner said. "Frank, you take the helm."

This was a practice day. The crew who would race this sailboat from San Francisco to Nawiliwili Bay on Kauai were the only ones on board. We were all excited about this first race across the Pacific. We wanted to know the boat really well before we sailed it at top speed night and day for a week-and-a-half.

We had been sailing near Yellow Bluff when we turned down and set the spinnaker. Headed toward Raccoon Straight with the chute pulling hard against the ebb current, we were ready to start our man-overboard drill. Everyone on board knew when I went down to put on my wet suit.

By the time I returned with my wet suit beneath three sweatshirts and jeans, we had passed through Raccoon Straight and were sailing beside the wind shadow downwind of Angel Island. The wind was a lot lighter, but the boat was still moving nicely under the three-quarter-ounce chute.

Frank was still on the helm, and the owner was forward trying to work out some problem on the foredeck. I went aft and sat on the stern pulpit, poised above the stern wake.

The committee on the foredeck broke up several minutes later, and the owner started aft. As he passed the shrouds, he made eye contact with me and nodded. I rolled over backward and started falling.

Before I hit the water, I heard someone holler, "Man Overboard!" No surprise. Everyone on board knew it was coming.

Splash! I was in the water in the middle of the frigid San Francisco Bay.

When I popped back up, the boat was sailing away under full spinnaker and main, perfectly trimmed, moving fast.

One of the guys had already been assigned to watch me. He stood on the transom with his whole arm extended directly toward me, watching me carefully, just like the book says.

I watched the boat sail away from me and began to wonder why I owned a wet suit.

The first clue I had that something was wrong was when the watcher took his eyes off me. That was definitely not what the book said.

I didn't think much about it at the time. When I saw him look away, I ducked beneath the water and stayed down as long as I could. The wet suit without a weight belt made me pretty buoyant. But I did my best to stay well underneath and out of sight. I laughed inwardly. *It serves him right for taking his eyes off the man in the water. I'll teach him a lesson,* I thought, and I fought to stay down longer.

When I bobbed up, the boat was a little farther away. The people were getting smaller.

The only part of me they could possibly see was my head sticking out of the water. It was a little frightening to realize my head was getting smaller, too.

I watched the boat sail farther away. Finally, the spinnaker collapsed and began to flog behind the main. It seemed like the spinnaker take-down took forever. The boat continued sailing farther away.

I could still make out the boat but, mostly, all I could see was the mainsail. They probably couldn't see my head at all now.

Looking around at San Francisco Bay from two inches above the water, I wondered if I could swim to shore. Well, maybe if I ditched the three sweatshirts and the jeans. The safety of shore looked a long way off.

Eventually, they did get the spinnaker down and the boat turned around. Even the mainsail looked small now. I must be invisible to them. What if they couldn't . . .?

No, don't think. . . .

The hull looked tiny, but I could see the mast was fairly well centered over the bow, so I knew they were headed pretty much toward me.

I didn't have a watch, but I knew it had been a while since I first hit the water. I was thankful for my wet suit. Without it, a half hour of exposure in water at this temperature would lower my probability of survival to 50 percent. My muscles would stop working from the cold. When you can't swim, you can't keep your head above water.

I wonder how far the tide had moved me.

Pretty soon, the boat began to get bigger, but it was headed a little off to my left. Eventually, I could see four people on the bow looking for me in all different directions. None of them moved.

Finally one pointed at me. Then, the rest pointed at me, too. I knew they saw me. The boat changed course a bit to head directly at me.

In a few of minutes I began to hope they would miss me. I had a vision of getting run over by a spinning prop. When they were close enough to shout they wanted to know if I was OK. I decided I would play the unconscious victim.

I put my face in the water and played dead. I could no longer see the boat approaching. I sure hoped they would miss me.

I ran out of air, and I simply had to look. I took a peek and a breath. They had turned away enough to bring the boat alongside me. I put my face back in the water and waited. They were close. I could hear the prop spinning hard in the water as they backed down.

Someone grabbed me. It felt like reuniting with mankind.

They tried to lift me, but I was too heavy. Reaching down from the deck, it was impossible to lift a man in jeans and three sopping-wet sweatshirts.

When my ears came out of the water, I heard a lot of shouting on deck.

"Stop the boat! We're dragging him."

"Get a halyard and clip it to his belt."

"I can't hold him. He's being pulled aft. Stop the boat!"

"I'll get a halyard."

"I don't want to put it back in gear. We're too close to him."

"Stop the boat!"

"The main is still drawing. Ease the main sheet."

Someone else grabbed the back of my sweatshirts and pulled hard.

"Stop the boat!"

"We'll never lift him. Get a halyard."

"Here's the halyard."

"Ease the halyard. I can't reach him with it."

"That's the end of it."

"Easing the main sheet."

"Stop the boat. I'm going to lose him."

"It won't reach him."

"Get a line. Quick! We'll tie it to him and the end to the halyard."

"Right!"

The hands on my back changed position. I wondered if I were being pulled out of their grasp.

"Here's the line. I think it'll hold him. What do you think he weighs?"

"With all that gear on, I have no idea. I can tell you he's heavy. He's full of water."

"Give me the end. I'll pass it through his belt, and then back to you."

"Here."

"Lower him back down into the water. He's lighter there."

"Get ready to hoist him! Get three guys on the end of the halyard."

I was back in the water, still being dragged, but more slowly now. The line was passed through my belt and back up to someone on deck. The line pulled tight and I was unceremoniously hoisted by my belt to well above the life lines. Half upside down, water poured out of my clothes.

"Hi guys. Thanks for coming back for me."

My lighthearted banter wasn't met with any smiles.

On the way back to the dock, we talked about what happened, what went wrong, and how not to do the same thing if and when it really counted.

With one man in the water and one man watching the man in the water, they were short two positions for the spinnaker takedown. Then, in trying to do it fast, they tangled a couple of lines and the knot pulled tight. They finally had to cut one line to get clear. Worst of all, when they cut the line, the other line ran free, and one of the crew got a rope burn on both hands.

When everything went wrong and the shouting started, the watcher on the transom was distracted into looking to see if he could help—a natural reaction. When he looked back to find me and I wasn't there, his heart sank. He knew if we had we been in the ocean with any swells to hide me, he never would have seen me again. He was greatly relieved when I popped back into sight.

After we repacked the spinnaker, folded the jib, and put the boat away, we drove home, glad we had done the drill, but a little sobered. We were all a little concerned about 2,000 miles of open ocean, a third of which would be in the dark.

69

Chapter 14

My First Ocean Passage

In 1980, when Ballena Bay held the first fully crewed race to Hawaii, not many of the owners or crew in San Francisco had sailed across an ocean. Sat Nav, LORAN, and GPS didn't exist—navigation was by sextant. Stan Honey had not yet written Determined by Weather. And the difference between rhumb line and great circle was a theoretical concept understood by only a few.

On this inaugural race from San Francisco to Hawaii, I fell in love with the open ocean.

Officially, it was a race. In reality, it was a parking lot for sailboats.

The Pacific High had moved south over the fleet, capturing all the boats but one in hundreds of miles of dead calm. Only Merlin had the boat speed from the start to outrun the Pacific High as it moved south.

When we left San Francisco on the first crewed race to Hawaii, we sailed into a rollicking beam reach. The high moved south faster than the low moved out of the way. The isobars compressed directly over the fleet. At first, it was exhilarating. Then, it became serious heavy-weather sailing. Of the forty boats that started, eight retired and one boat was lost.

A storm in the ocean is a dangerous, and yet a wondrous, thing to experience. When the storm winds drive the seas into swells and the fetch is long enough, the resulting mounds of moving water look huge to a sailor from the Great Lakes.

The biggest waves I'd ever seen were driven by 60 mile-an-hour winds in Lake Michigan. But these were ocean swells. As large as Lake Michigan is, it simply doesn't have the fetch to create big swells.

But the ocean does.

As each swell loomed up on the starboard side, I wondered how we could possibly sail over such a formidable consequence of nature's power. As the swell slid underneath us, I marveled at how the boat floated up the side of the swell until the boat was lifted over the crest.

Not until much later did I learn about the real danger. When the face of the wave becomes steep enough, the front part of the top slumps and breaks like the top of a wave rolling up on shore. However, most waves rolling up on shore are tiny compared to mid-ocean swells. In the mid ocean, when the top of a swell falls down the face, literally tons of water cascade down across the area where we were floating up. Without knowledge or fear, I was in awe. The ocean was showing me a little of its violent strength and fierce beauty.

The strong winds ended when the low moved away from the high, and the high came south over the fleet. The calm created the parking lot and captured all but one of the boats. Merlin was 76 feet long and very fast. In the storm, she had simply outrun the rest of the fleet. When the high shut off the wind for the rest of us, Merlin was just ahead of the high. She kept moving and managed to get into the trades. She was gone.

The rest of the boats were scattered by the storm. At the daily radio check-in, we knew each other's position by latitude and longitude. Looking out to sea, all the boats were out of sight over the horizon from each other. The sensation of the closeness of the boats, yet knowing they were hidden by the curvature of the Earth, was my first real-life sensation the Earth was not flat.

Without wind, we idled in dying breezes. We watched the sea slowly calm to rolling swells and, eventually, to a flat and oily mirror that continued to flex and distort. We spent hours, and then days watching for cats' paws to announce the first breath of air. Only the water itself had movement—a slow, small swell that still had the power to gently roll the boat. It slatted the main and sucked the limply hanging spinnaker in through the foretriangle and out again. The Sun glinted slowly on the slick, unbroken surface of the water. No waves and no bow wake existed to spoil the reflection of the boat in the water.

Occasionally, a moment of breeze gave the boat some movement, and the spinnaker would fill and move the boat toward the finish line. Other times, it would provide only enough steerage way for the helmsman to get the boat pointed in the right direction again.

When a puff came, it would come from over the starboard quarter, or further aft, making the course to Hawaii a deep run on starboard in faltering air. Very slow going. The resulting boat speeds didn't always transfer the calm under the high into calm in the characters of the racers who were dependent on the wind. Behaviors varied.

"We lost 18 miles yesterday," I overheard the owner tell the navigator. The navigator agreed; we had "lost" 18 miles. I didn't know how anyone could "lose" 18 miles at sea, so while I was getting ready to go on watch, I tuned in on their conversation. As I listened, I realized they were talking about the difference between our daily run and the distance we had closed with Hawaii. Over the last 24 hours, we'd had an 18-mile difference. "If only those miles were toward Hawaii," the owner concluded. "We would have gained on our competition."

No! I thought. *Reaching up in light air to heat up the boat was the right thing to do.* I learned in the light airs in Lake Michigan that the combination of higher and faster in light air was often the longer, but quicker, course to a downwind mark. I tried to explain this to the owner whose experience was from windy San Francisco Bay.

He refused to go north of the straight line to Hawaii. Frustrated, I drew diagrams in my personal log for him, but they didn't impress him. "OK. If you don't want to go north, how about jibing and going south? We have to keep the boat speed up," I proposed.

"No, we'd have to change course so far we wouldn't be going toward Hawaii at all. In fact, we'd be going away from Hawaii," the owner replied. "This is a race and the finish line is Hawaii!"

So, we sailed straight toward Hawaii. Slowly.

We weren't alone under the high. Each day, the boats reported their lack of progress on the radio roll call. It was slow going for all of us.

One night, frustrated with absolutely no wind and the lack of boat speed, I began an experiment. The sailing rules require the boat to be propelled only by the action of the wind and the waves on the boat. Well, I didn't have any wind, but the remains of a swell were still gently rolling the boat.

I couldn't imagine where the swell was coming from. Without any wind under the high, I supposed it must be coming from the other side of the high. Somewhere the wind was blowing and creating waves. And those waves were still rolling the boat slightly as they passed underneath.

Someone on the last watch had centered the main and cranked the mainsheet in tight. I was sure they had done this to stop the slatting of the main. If I let it out, it would slat badly from the rolling of the boat. I wondered if it filled a little on each side as it slatted, would it generate forward motion as we rolled from side-to-side—something like continuous, miniature roll tacks with a 45-foot boat.

I let the main out some. BANG. It filled as the boat rolled. BANG. It filled on the other side. BANG. I watched the main for a while. BANG. I eased the main out some more. BANG. Eventually, I eased the main until the rolling of the boat wasn't enough motion to fill the main at the end of its arc across the boat. The banging subsided, so I trimmed it back in a little. BANG. After several minutes of banging, the boat had a slight forward motion, and I was able to steer a course directly toward Hawaii. BANG. This seemed the most effective trim for the main in the gently rolling sea. BANG.

It wasn't long before the owner came up on deck. Without speaking, he went directly to the mainsheet and tightened it all the way in again. The banging stopped. The owner went below.

I think this was my second mistake.

One afternoon, some of the guys decided to jump overboard for a swim. No doubt the cool water was refreshing to both their overheated bodies and their frustrated minds.

Great idea, I thought. *I'll have someone take my picture,* and I got my camera out of my duffel.

Well, one thought led to another, and I tied a line onto the front of the boat. Then, I swam out in front of the bow and had a crewmate take a picture of me towing the boat across the ocean with the line in my teeth. After the picture, I looked down at my feet hanging in the water. It was an odd feeling to know there were two miles of water beneath my feet. I was glad I could still feel the Sun on my back.

On board, the spinnaker was still up and an arbitrary puff filled it. The boat drove ahead, picking up speed. It's amazing how fast a boat can sail past a swimmer.

I grabbed the line out of my mouth and hung on to stay with the boat. My tow through the water was fast enough to be a thrill, and yet slow enough not to be dangerous. It was plenty fast enough, though, to create excitement on deck, including in the owner.

Oh, well. The ocean loved me.

One morning during roll call, when the communications boat called Gray Wolf to get her position report, she responded but, obviously, something was wrong. All her transmissions were badly overlaid with what sounded like static. Through the static, we could just hear the voice of the navigator giving their location. Then he explained they were having radio trouble and they might be unable to call in tomorrow. They would call in as soon as they got the problem fixed. Then, with a burst of static, they were gone.

The next morning, Gray Wolf didn't respond to roll call.

The morning after that, their radio was loud and clear. The navigator gave their position, now 150 miles south of the fleet. He also reported they were having a fine day sailing in a steady 15-knot breeze, and he wished the rest of the fleet good sailing. The two crew who had made the static noises were now laughing their heads off in the background.

We looked out at the slick water under the high. We listened to the slatting sails. I gave the owner a tiny smile.

The ocean is great! It loved me, and I loved it. We were beginning to get to know each other.

Eventually, the high moved back north and the breeze filled in again over the fleet. With full spinnakers, but still out of sight of each other, we all raced for the finish.

The last couple of days the wind was flat on the transom, and we jibed on every wind shift. The thrill of surfing down big waves got to all of us. I was high on endorphins and wished it would never end. We didn't do well in the race, but I fell in love with the most beautiful water I have ever seen.

Up until then, my longest sail was from Port Huron to Chicago, when we rounded Cove Island light in the fog. This was a new and larger world, vast and beautiful.

The ocean had captivated my soul.

Chapter 15

Teaching Kids

I loved sailing and wanted to share my pleasure with kids just beginning their lives in sailing. Teaching in the Richmond Yacht Club Junior Program was an obvious opportunity.

Holding the attention of 15 year olds, I found, was nearly impossible for a man who never had children. So, I cheated. I created a set of visual aids — a few colored translucent sailboats, black dots for marks, a committee boat, and a wind arrow.

When I pushed them around on a viewgraph, I had control.

"OK. Today, we're going to talk about starting tactics." I set the committee boat, a mark, and a wind arrow on the viewgraph. Last night, I planned my whole lecture. "In a normal windward start, all the boats try to get to the favored end of the line, going full speed, just as the gun goes off." I positioned four sailboats on the viewgraph, approaching the starting line on starboard.

"Yes, Jim?" I shouldn't have looked up.

"Last week, when we were starting, Bill came in from behind the committee boat and almost hit me. He can't do that, can he?"

This wasn't part of my lecture, but I thought I probably ought to deal with Jim's question before going on with what I planned to say. I left the committee boat, the pin end of the line, and two sailboats on the viewgraph. As I removed the other two boats I said, "OK. Let's say you're the green boat. Were you headed for the line, like this?"

"Yeah, I was headed right for it. But I was closer to the committee boat."

"OK. Like this?" I slid the green boat closer to the committee boat.

"Yeah."

"Let's say Bill is the red boat. Was he over here behind the committee boat?" I pushed the red boat over into a barging position.

"Yeah, but back more from the committee boat."

I moved the red boat back a little.

"Yeah. And he came in right on top of me. It was really close."

I slowly pushed the red boat up until it was between the green boat and the committee boat. "So, if he caught you, he was going faster than you were?"

"Yeah. I guess so."

"Was there any contact? Did Bill hit you?" Now Bill looked like he wanted to say something.

"No, we didn't hit. But he was really close."

"Did you have to alter course to avoid contact?"

Bill started to say something, but Jim continued, "No, he was between me and the committee boat."

"Well, if there was contact, or you had to alter course to avoid contact, then he's not allowed to do that. He would have owed you a 720 after the start."

Bill couldn't contain himself any longer. "I never touched him! My dad showed me how to start like that. He does it all the time in his boat."

"Bill, Jim doesn't remember any contact. So, if you managed to squeeze through there, then you pulled off a pretty slick start. If there wasn't room enough, you would have hit either Jim or the committee boat, or forced Jim to change course."

Now Bill was looking pleased and Jim was uncertain. I thought this was where I should jump back into my lecture.

"We have two sailing concepts here. One is barging and the other is room freely given." I was pleased to get started again.

"That's not what I saw," Sue broke in. "I saw Jim turn down, a little bit, and then he came back up."

I tried to suppress a groan. "Where were you at the time?"

"I was behind Jim, back about a boat length."

"Here?" I put the polka-dot boat behind the green boat. I wondered if I would ever get back to my lecture.

"And there was another boat about even with Jim, to leeward."

I added a checkered boat to leeward of the green boat. "Here?"

"Uh huh," Sue agreed.

"Jim turned down toward the checkered boat, and then back up, like this?"

Jim jumped in to explain. "I was going really slow, and so I turned down to get a little more wind. As soon as I got going a little, I headed back up."

"So you were going slow, waiting for the gun." I tried to get everyone's attention back. "If you turn down and the boat below you had to turn down to avoid hitting you, then you fouled him. So, if you're close to a boat below you, you don't want to turn down. Not even a little bit."

Now Jim was looking glum again.

"No. They weren't that close," Sue interjected.

"Jim, I think you were doing the right thing. I call it parking. To do that you sail up to the line and park. You ease the sail out until the boat stops. Well, almost stops. But, be careful you don't turn down on anyone. Keep the boat angled off the wind as if you're beating. Just let the main out until the boat slows down." I turned Jim's boat back to a beating position and pushed the boom to the side as if the main were flogging.

"If you park right next to the committee boat, there won't be any room for another boat to come between you and the committee boat. If you slide sideways while you're parked, you'll let another boat in above you. Like Bill here in the red boat." Somehow, this feels like the lecture I prepared last night. How did I get here?

"If you can park next to the committee boat and hold your position, then you'll have the best position when the gun goes off. If someone is already parked where you want to park, then you can do one of two things. You could go to leeward of the parked boat, sail up close to the line, and then park." I demonstrated this on the viewgraph. "Or, you could park just above the boat that's parked where you want to be and wait for him to slide sideways. If he does, then slide sideways with him. That will put you in his place and give you the start." I slid two boats sideways on the viewgraph to show what happens.

Then I realized I had just about covered my lecture material: barging, room freely given, not turning down on a boat below, and parking.

Was I done?

The words of an old friend came into my head. When you have a stopping point, declare it a success and move on. It must be time to move on.

"So, how long can any of you park?" I looked at the kids to intensify my question and realized I was back in control.

"Today, before we start racing, we're going to practice parking. Here's how we're going to do it. The Race Committee will set an unreasonably short starting line. It's going to be just big enough for two boats to start at a time." That got their attention. "So, only two boats can be on the line when the gun goes off. The rest of the boats will have to follow behind."

On the viewgraph, I pushed the pin end of the line over to the committee boat, leaving just enough room for two boats to sail through. Of the four boats still on the viewgraph, it was obvious only two could start at a time. This was a terribly congested situation.

"When you get out to the committee boat, make groups of four boats. We'll start you four at a time." I set a mark on the viewgraph upwind of the starting line. "After the start, sail up to the weather mark, and then come back for another start. As soon as one group of four is started, we'll start the next group of four."

"Remember, the objective is to get into position and park before anyone else does. Then, hold your position until the gun goes off. If you slide sideways, another boat will come in from above you to get the good starting position. With practice, you'll be able to park longer and longer without moving. If you park first and do it right, no one can take the start away from you."

"Let's go racing!"

Chapter 16

Four Grown Men and a Whale

Dennis, a friend at Richmond Yacht Club, purchased a used Swan 42 in Los Angeles. The first thing he wanted to do was bring the boat to San Francisco, where he would fit it out before sailing it for the next few years.

Taking a totally unknown boat out into the ocean, beating it upwind around Point Conception, and then 400 miles to San Francisco, is an excellent way to find out what doesn't work or is ready to fail.

The four of us who delivered Dennis's "new" boat from Los Angeles to San Francisco thought we were ready for anything.

"Hey! Did you see that?" asked the guy I had just relieved at the helm. "There's a whale over there. I just saw it spout."

"No, I missed it. What happened to the wind on your watch?" I asked, settling in behind the wheel. I was trying to get in tune with the weather prior to my watch.

We were about five miles off the famous Big Sur coast, between San Simeon and Monterey. It was a beautiful shoreline, rugged and majestic, but totally unapproachable from the sea.

"Well, let's see," the previous helmsman thought for a moment. "The wind came up early in our watch, but it's been fairly steady for the last couple of hours."

We talked about the weather and most anything for a few minutes. Maybe he was making sure I was awake before going below to get some rest himself.

"Evening." My watch mate climbed out of the main hatch into the cockpit. With both of us on deck, the previous watch was now free to go below.

"Hey, look! It's closer," the relieved helmsman said, pointing to starboard again.

I spun around to starboard, looking out at the early evening gray and white sea of whitecaps. I was too late to make out the spouting of the whale.

"Yeah, I saw it," said Dennis, who was getting ready to go off watch.

"What's going on?" asked my watch mate.

"There's a whale over there. I saw him spout a couple times. Almost straight abeam."

"Great!" We all waited to see if the whale would spout again or disappear.

After a few moments, it spouted again. This time all four of us saw it. "Wow! That was maybe only a hundred yards off," said the first guy. "He's getting closer."

The next time the whale spouted, he was only 50 yards off. The time after that, he was only a boat length away. Each time the whale spouted, it was straight out to starboard and moving the same direction we were. And, each time, four or five minutes lapsed between the whale's appearances. And each time it got closer.

Thrilled by the closeness of the world's largest animal in its natural environment, all four of us stared at the ocean, hoping to see him spout again.

The next time the whale spouted, he was only six or eight feet from the boat. He spouted just as his blowhole came even with the transom. Then, as he swam past the starboard side of the boat from astern, we watched his back glide past us on the surface and disappear into the ocean just in front of the bow.

When the whale blew the next time, he was only a few feet from the boat. The spray from his blow blew across us and the back half of the boat. It stank like a muddy seashore at low tide. I didn't care; I was amazed to see a whale so close.

"Do you think the bottom of the boat might be shaped like his mate?" someone joked.

"Yeah, what color is the bottom paint . . . Whale Skin Blue?"

"You think this is a courting gesture or a mating ritual?"

Again the whale blew just beside the transom and slid by on starboard, headed in the same direction we were. This time, he was only a foot from the boat. His speed through the water was just a little faster than our boat speed. The top of his head and back were well above water as he slid by. The whale was longer than the boat, and he gave us a good look at his back as more and more of him passed by the cockpit.

"Do you suppose it's territorial?" someone asked. "I mean, each time he's been on the same side and each time he's gotten closer and closer."

"You think he's trying to herd us? Maybe the other way?"

"Do you think he's a she and has a calf over there?"

Suddenly we were jolted out of our mystic love of nature. We each fell quiet as we tried to understand what was going on. None of us had any useful knowledge. Only the Darwinian theory of the survival of the fittest popped into my head.

"You know, the hull of this boat is only about an inch thick. That whale is solid muscle all the way through." The reality of our situation began to sink in.

Again the gray five-story-building in the shape of a whale blew at the transom and slid past us, this time inches from the boat. I looked over the side of the boat to watch him from the helm. From that angle, I couldn't see any water between the whale and the boat. I flashed on all the races I had started and remembered how close some of the boats had been when the gun went off. Now, I was worried about how close the whale was to our boat. I couldn't help wondering whether the whale and the boat might bump, but it turned out the whale was a better helmsman than my competitors. We never did touch.

Again he blew and slid by, just as close as the last time. Again we sat and stared at the closeness, and the mass, of the whale.

"Do you think we ought to go somewhere else?" asked Dennis.

"Well, this is his ocean, not ours," replied one of the crew.

"Yeah, and if he, I mean she, has a calf over there, I don't want to make her angry at us," Dennis added.

One more time, the spray and foul smell covered the cockpit. No one knew what to do. Again, the whale disappeared in front of the boat.

"Dale, steer down. Let's get out of here," directed the new owner. "I don't like this."

"OK," I replied. "But let's wait until I know where he is."

The previous summer, one of the boys I was teaching in the junior sailing program was returning a boat from Hawaii to San Francisco with his father after the Pacific Cup Race. One night, they ran up on a whale sleeping on the surface. They didn't know if the whale responded with a little, "You hit me, I hit you," or just started swimming to get away. As the whale moved, the powerful flukes hit the keel. With one whack, the whale cracked the bottom of the boat the entire length of the keel. They started taking on water faster than they could pump it back out. The Coast Guard flew a diesel-powered bilge pump out to them. With the diesel pump running 24 hours a day, they made it to shore. They took the boat immediately to the boat yard where a boat lift was waiting for them. The yard lifted the boat until the water level inside the boat was higher than the water level outside. Then, the water started running back out the crack.

Don't hit the whale, I thought. *Don't hit the whale.*

I waited until the whale spouted at the stern and passed by one more time. As soon as we were sure he was clear ahead of the boat, we eased sheets and headed down to a broad reach.

The whale came with us and passed us again close aboard on starboard.

"Let's jibe," Dennis said. He really wanted to get away from the whale.

Again, we waited until we knew where the whale was. Then, we turned down and jibed.

Then, the whale came by on the port side for the first time. Still close aboard.

"How about turning on the engine and making some noise? Maybe he won't like that."

"Yeah, and let's hit the fog horn, too. I'll get it."

We tried all of that, as well as slapping the side of the hull. Again and again, the whale covered us with spray and slid by inches from the boat.

We didn't think of it then, but we each could have had a picture of us patting a whale in the wild as he spouted right beside the boat. No, what we tried to do was figure a way out of this situation.

Have you ever seen four grown men sitting around having a serious conversation about how to look unattractive to a whale?

We tried everything we could think of. What finally worked was going dead in the water. We turned off the engine, took down the sails, turned off the lights, and sat quietly. The boat settled in broadside to the waves and rolled. There was no forward motion, no sign of life.

The whale got bored and eventually swam away.

Chapter 17

Doublehanded Tragedy

When sailors don't go sailing all winter, they develop a strong, pent-up desire to get back on the water. The Doublehanded Farallon Race is scheduled in March, just before the normal race season begins.

The 30-mile beat to Southeast Farallon Island, followed by a 30-mile spinnaker run back to the finish line on the city front is a perfect opportunity for a seasoned race skipper and his best crew member to sooth their winter woes.

March weather in San Francisco is usually warm and lovely, making the spring race all the more desirable. But, occasionally, a late winter storm sweeps down across San Francisco, making the waters outside the Golden Gate seriously dangerous for small boats.

"Wow! That one's huge!" Bill looked out across the port beam at the hill of water sliding toward the Southeast Farallon Island. "Let's not cut this too close."

"No, let's round out in deep water," I agreed. "I don't like those waves at all." All the boats we could see seemed to agree.

Bill and I had been on a hard beat since leaving the entrance to San Francisco Bay. The wind had been blowing 30 most of the morning. We were thankful for the heavy weather abilities of the Baltic. Pounding up over the ten-to-fifteen foot waves was wet work, but Giggles had been moving well all morning.

On the long starboard tack after leaving the entrance, we were able to keep Alcatraz Island centered behind the Golden Gate Bridge by working up in the puffs and letting the Baltic do what it did best.

We had only taken one small tack to the right. When the Southeast Farallon Island appeared on the horizon, it was nearly on the bow.

As we came close to the island, we tacked to port and began looking for the lay line across the windward side of the island. Our competition had long since been lost in the maze of boats in the fleet, but we felt good about our position as we closed with the island. This was Baltic weather!

Now, sailing along the side of the island and looking at the swells breaking on the north face, we no longer had any thoughts of our competition. Those huge swells commanded our entire attention.

The size of an ocean swell is dependent on wind velocity and how long the swell has to gain energy. Upwind of the Farallon Islands lay a thousand miles of open ocean. When a low parks in exactly the right place in the North Pacific, storm winds drive the swells hundreds of miles over the deep ocean before they attempt to roll over the Farallon Islands.

Fifteen miles to weather of the Southeast Farallon Island, the ocean is still at full depth, some five to six thousand feet deep. The ocean bottom then rises abruptly to the continental shelf. In the last five miles before the Southeast Farallon Island, the bottom rises from three thousand feet to zero at the shoreline.

As the bottom comes up, it has the effect of compressing the water movement in the bottom of each ocean swell. As the swell passes into more shallow water, the energy from the bottom of the wave pushes the rest of the water up into higher and steeper mounds.

When swells in the open ocean are well formed by storm winds, and then trip over the rising bottom, the resulting mounds of water approaching shore are similar to steep hills - hills that move sideways and end up washing the rocky side of the Southeast Farallon Island before the energy gathered over hundreds of miles is spent in one enormous crash on the shore.

"I wonder how much mass is in that thing?" Bill asked no one in particular. Bill was an engineer in his day job and, sometimes, on races as well. "I don't have any idea how many cubic feet would be in that . . . it's too big to call it a wave . . . or even a swell. It's . . . it's gigantic."

I agreed, but I didn't think Bill heard me. They were gigantic. I didn't know what to call them either.

Theoretically, Bill and I were on a port beat looking for the lay line on the right side of the course—in this case, the line that would take us just to weather of the island on starboard tack. Looking out to port, the weather side of the island was already a little aft of the beam. We should have been able to tack at any time and lay the island. Unfortunately, if we tacked now, our course would take us across the area where the hills of water tripped over the rising bottom before meeting the solid rock of the island.

To us, it was not time to tack.

We held on port tack a little longer. The boat just ahead of us tacked to starboard and took up the course we were leery of. She was the first boat around us to tack to starboard. Apparently, the skipper thought he could make it.

"I think he's early," Bill mumbled, more to himself than to me.

"I don't think he's very smart," I answered in the same tone.

We held course on port and slowly overstood more and more. The windward side of the island was now almost back to the quarter.

I was watching the mounds of water, trying to figure out where the deep water must have ended. Bill was watching the boats around us to see when they would tack.

"There goes another guy," Bill noted. "I don't think it's time yet. About ten more boats are still on the same tack with us."

"I don't want to sail across the face of anything like that," I agreed.

We stayed on port and sailed on north to get beyond the stacked-up swells approaching shore. Our progress took us further away from the island.

The only mark in this race was the Southeast Farallon Island. The race circular said to leave the island to port and return to San Francisco. Clearly, cutting the weather mark close would shorten the distance in the race. The danger, of course, lay in riding the top of a hill of water onto the side of a rock island.

The race rules say if you hit a mark, you must re-round it. If we hit this mark, re-rounding might not be an option.

So far, only two boats had tacked. The rest were going the same way we were, looking for a safe line.

"How deep is the water under those waves?" Bill asked.

"Well, an underwater shelf continues out from the point on the northwest corner. I think a quarter mile from the point, it's still only 25 or 30 feet deep. After that, it's not so shallow." I was glad I'd studied the chart before the race, not because I could answer Bill's question, but because rounding would take us close to the shallow area. "Check the chart—it's the top one in the nav station. But, I'm pretty sure that's right."

"Only 25 or 30 feet?" Bill stared at the boat to port, and then at me. "Look at the height of that wave. It's higher than that guy's mast." Bill was now pointing at the first boat that tacked. "If the water depth is 25 feet without a wave, then in the shallow spot there wouldn't be any water at all under the trough. How deep is your keel?"

I remembered a 35-foot boat that sailed over the bar into Tomales Bay in calm weather and set her keel down on the sand on the way in. When the boat bottomed in the gentle trough, the sand bottom tried to push the keel up into the main cabin. They had to haul the boat and repair the bottom before they could sail it home. And that was with almost no wave action at all.

Sometimes, being an engineer is OK.

"Yeah, we'll have to find deep enough water, so we don't bottom out," I said to Bill, wondering just how to judge that from the only part of the wave I could see.

Another boat well ahead tacked to cross the face. "What do you think?" I asked Bill.

"I don't know. I don't think I want to be inside his line." Bill wasn't as negative as before. "He'll cross in front of us. When we cross his line, we'll be able to see where his course will take him."

I wasn't eager to cross a hill of moving water and, now, I was also worried about bottoming out in a trough. We held on port a little longer.

When we crossed the track of the boat that just tacked, we looked at his course. He was going to miss the island by a good margin, but we weren't sure how much surge was in the top of a swell that size just before it broke on the shore. We decided to play it safe.

The first boat that tacked was now tacking back to port. Apparently, he didn't like where he was going and he decided to get out of there.

Then, we noticed he barely had enough wind to tack. Bill understood it a moment before I did. Right now, the boat was in a trough. The huge wave just upwind of the boat was blocking most of its wind. Slowly, the boat came around onto port tack. Then, the swell slid underneath the boat and lifted it up into the wind. Exposed to the wind, the boat heeled over and began driving.

While we were watching that boat, another boat tacked to cross the island. This time, we thought we ought to go, too. We waited until he crossed us, and then we tacked into a conservative position just outside of him.

We watched all the boats inside us for signs of trouble. When we sailed into the big swells, we noticed we lost sight of the first three boats to tack. They were on the other side of a swell and had completely disappeared behind it. They reappeared when the swell lifted them up, slid beyond them, and crashed on shore. We were glad they were still there.

As a swell passed beneath us, the water movement in the top of the swell pushed the boat sideways toward the shore. Then, as the swell slid away, the boat was pushed sideways back away from the island. It was nervous going.

We watched the depth sounder for shallow water. So far, it wasn't a problem. But, just as we approached the shallow area, an alarm went off. Scared, I instinctively headed up, starting an unplanned tack. Then we realized the sound was only the GPS arrival alarm, not the depth-sounder shallow-water alarm. We still had plenty of water below us.

Bill went below to turn off the GPS alarm and to reset the GPS to the Light Bucket. When he returned, Bill told me what he had heard on the VHF. A 31-foot trimaran had turned over somewhere near the Southeast Farallon Island. Apparently, it was in the doublehanded race. No one seemed to know where or have any other facts.

We scanned the water for an upside-down tri, but we didn't see anything. We kept looking, not sure what we were looking for and not wanting to find anything.

In another five minutes, we cleared the shallow area, cracked sheets, and headed down to finish rounding the island. We made it! We were past the most windward part of the island. Now for the blast back to the Golden Gate.

As we headed south along the west side of the island, Bill saw something bright blue and yellow in the water, way in near the shore. The part at the surface looked like it might be two or three feet long, but Bill couldn't tell what it was. Without any discussion, we decide if it were a man in the water, we had to go back for him.

I put Bill on the helm and went forward to pull down the jib. Bill turned on the engine and we powered back upwind toward the place where he saw something in the water.

I tried to call the Coast Guard on VHF to see if they had any knowledge about the tri that flipped and, more importantly, the doublehanded crew that sailed it, but I couldn't raise them. The Coast Guard was in San Francisco on the other side of the rock called Southeast Farallon Island. Because we couldn't raise them, we went in.

Even though we were well south of the shallow area where the swells were rolling up on the island, there was a strong surge in the water. The boat was being shoved all over the place by the remains of the swells that glanced off the side of the island. As we got close, Bill asked me to take the helm, and went forward to act as lookout.

Closer and closer, we powered toward shore with no knowledge of any rocks or shallow spots below the waterline. With one eye on the depth sounder, I was more worried about the surge slamming us sideways against a rock than about driving straight forward onto one. The bow was pretty strong, but the sides of the hull were much more vulnerable.

Bill spotted the blue and yellow object, and he began hand signaling to me. I steered to follow his directions.

Soon Bill turned and ran aft. "Get out of here!" he hollered. "It's a gear bag, not a man. Turn around and get away from here."

All too willingly, I agreed, and spun the boat around. Then, I tried to get back on our inbound track. If I didn't hit a rock on the way in, maybe I wouldn't hit one on the way back out.

Soon we had the jib back up, and started the roaring reach back to San Francisco.

After we cleared the island, we had a good VHF line-of-sight to San Francisco. We were relieved to hear from the Race Committee the two men who were sailing the overturned tri were both rescued. We were glad we had tried to help and we were relieved to get back out without mishap.

On the way back to the Gate, the seas were steep and fast. They would have made great surfing, but if we steered down enough to surf, our course would take us south of the Gate. On the other hand, the need to stay high would keep the lightweight boats from surfing away from us. Baltic 38s aren't competitive in a surfing match.

We traded off the helm on the way in, trying to keep our fatigue down. The exhilaration of the high-speed blast more than made up for the exhaustion. We were both on a high.

After we passed the Light Bucket, I took the helm again, while Bill went below to get some cookies and check the chart. About five miles from the Gate, a big wave hit Giggles on the quarter and pooped water up onto the deck in front of the cockpit. I was astonished. I had never seen green water on the bridge deck before. Some of it rolled below.

"Hey! Cut that out!" Bill called from below. "I've got water all over the charts."

"Sorry." I realized we must be crossing the bar outside the San Francisco entrance. When the bottom came up at the bar, the waves got bigger and steeper. *Some wave,* I thought.

Half an hour later, we heard a VHF call from Razzberries. Back about where Giggles pooped the wave, a catastrophe was unfolding. Razzberries was the closest boat and stopped to help. The Coast Guard had been standing by near there because of the rotten weather and was on scene immediately. No one could help. The tragedy struck too fast.

Two men, both tethered to the boat, were sailing a low freeboard 29-foot boat in the race. They pooped a wave just as Giggles had, but the wave literally washed over the back of the much-smaller and lower boat. Both men were instantly washed off the boat into the water.

The 35-mile-an-hour wind pinned the main flat against the leeward shrouds and continued to drive the boat forward at full speed.

The man who had been on the high side was pulled up short just outside the boat when his tether pulled tight. He grabbed the life lines and started to climb back onto the boat. He was attempting to climb back onto the boat *over* the life lines, but he had been washed off the boat *under* the life lines, which meant his tether was wrapped around the lifelines. He couldn't get far enough back onto the boat to feel safe about unclipping his tether. So, he climbed back outside, and then back in under the lifelines.

Back on the boat, he discovered his sailing partner, who had been steering, was now being dragged six-feet astern of the boat by his tether. Face down in rushing water with nothing to hold onto, he had no way of righting himself. He died before the Coast Guard, or Razzberries, or even his friend on the boat could do anything.

Chapter 18

I Can Navigate Better Than You Can

In San Francisco, I joined the Oceanic Crew Group, which rewarded organizations working for the vitality of San Francisco Bay by taking them out sailing on the Bay.

Most of the sailors in the Crew Group were quite capable. Their boats were comfortable and well-maintained; however, by racing standards, the boats were filled with the comforts of life. Few of the Crew Group ever raced. They preferred to enjoy life in a different way. At the same time, they were knowledgeable, skilled, and interested in good seamanship.

As happens in volunteer organizations, the members create the activities.

Back in the days before GPS, Loran, and Sat Nav, I raced on Lake Michigan in many of the port-to-port races across the lake. Crossing the lake, we always maintained a log and plotted out track. After being out of sight of land for several hours, the challenge was to see if we made landfall where we thought we would. With different winds and wave conditions, sometimes we were close and sometimes not.

When I moved to California and began racing on San Francisco Bay, I was forced to learn about tidal currents. Tide was a huge factor in getting to the end of the race before my competitors.

For my new friends in the Oceanic Crew Group, *sooner* wasn't important. *Skillful seamanship* was. Somehow, *skillful*, not *sooner*, played in my head with the dead reckoning I did years before on Lake Michigan.

I became obsessed with the concept of *skillful* sailing. What did it mean to sail skillfully? How could anyone tell if they were more or less skillful than the next person?

Many people would probably say racing was *the* test of skill. My new friends didn't want to race, yet they were able seamen. What would be a challenge for them?

Could navigation become another test of skill, *the* test?

I began work on finding a way to turn navigation into a friendly competition. I wanted a challenge where the requirement for high skill would select the best, and the people could get together afterward and talk about their experiences—something that would make for a good day on the water.

Modern navigation, using a GPS and a laptop computer, seemed far too precise for competition, so I shut them from my thoughts. Now what? How do you navigate without electronics? Well, how did they navigate before all this stuff was invented?

Then, it started falling into place. Dead reckoning! An on-the-water competition in dead reckoning!

Dead reckoning is low tech. It only requires the use of the ship's compass, paper charts, a pencil, dividers, triangles, tide tables, and a good head. OK, but how could we measure speed without electronics or the boat's speedometer?

In the days of the British Admiralty, speed was measured with a chip log, an extremely low-tech device. As the old sea story goes, a *chip log* was a small piece of wood attached to the end of a line with knots tied in it at regular intervals. When the wood was dropped into the water, the line unwound from a spool as the ship sailed ahead. A sailor would feel the line as it spooled out and count the knots as they passed his hand in a measured period of time. And, of course, he would report the speed of the boat in "knots."

An hourglass would have been too inaccurate for use with a chip log, so I relented a little on the "no electronics" ban. A wrist watch and a stop watch were added to the acceptable equipment list.

Just to make sure it was truly a dead reckoning contest, I disallowed "eye ball" navigation and all lines of position (visual, equal depth, electronic, or any other kind). Speed was to be determined from a chip log, course from a compass, and time from a wristwatch or a stop watch. The only technique of navigation was to be dead reckoning.

Now, how to set it up and run it like a contest? First, I named it the Chip Log Navigation Contest. The body that ran the contest was, of course, the Chip Log Navigation Contest Committee, an ugly mouthful.

At the next Oceanic Crew Group meeting, I explained how the contest would work. The Chip Log Contest Committee would define three or four legs, each starting at a buoy at a known location. The end point of each leg would be defined as a range and bearing from the starting location, or as a latitude and longitude. The finish of one leg would be near the buoy at the beginning of the next leg. The last leg would finish near the raft-up party.

The objective of the Chip Log Contest was to sail the legs while navigating via dead reckoning and to be more accurate in arriving at the end points than the other boats. Because this was a sailing contest, motors couldn't be used for propulsion.

Even though the end point of a leg might be defined as a range and bearing from the starting point, sailing might require tacking upwind or sailing around a point, an island, or shallow water. The navigator would want to consider the effects of tidal current, wave set, and side slip as the boat sailed along. At the same time, the crew on deck would be sailing as straight and steady as possible, while keeping track of the course made good and measuring speed with the chip log.

Knowledge of how your boat sails in various conditions, how to estimate the current over the sailing course, and skill at dead reckoning were all major factors in accurately arriving at the end point.

All boats would sail the same course but, obviously, not at exactly the same time. They could start whenever they were ready, sail as fast or slow as they decided, and follow any course they chose. If a boat wanted, it could start a leg a second or third time, but it could only finish each leg once.

The total distance for each leg would be long enough to allow small errors to creep into the sailing and navigating. The total length would be short enough to allow for a good party at the end.

While sailing the legs, a GPS would be turned on and set to show present latitude and longitude. The readout would be kept covered while sailing the legs. An "official observer" would be assigned on each boat to maintain the Answer Sheet. When the navigator tells the official observer "the boat IS NOW AT the end point," the official observer would quickly uncover the GPS read out, write down the present latitude and longitude on the Answer Sheet, and recover the GPS.

The Answer Sheets would be turned in to the Chip Log Navigation Contest Committee at the party. The committee would then calculate the "Distance Off" error at the end of each leg. The winner would be the boat with the lowest cumulative error.

Some of the navigators at the Oceanic Crew Group saw this as an opportunity to practice dead reckoning. Others saw it as a way to test their navigation skills against their friends in a structured competition. Still others, I believe, saw it as a raft up and afternoon party where the contest was secondary. Everyone was looking forward to a good time.

The inaugural Chip Log Navigation Contest was held on April 24th, 1999. *Latitude 38* magazine candidly reported on the event:

> Navigating from a known point to a destination without electronics or sightings is never easy. But when the winds are gusting up to 45 knots and there's a 3.5 knot ebb, it's a good bit more difficult. Add a little nausea that comes from working below while the boat is bouncing around in the chop, and the challenge begins to meet the limits of human ability. That's the way it was for the inaugural Chip Log Navigation Contest sponsored by the Oceanic Crew Group.
>
> The Contest Committee chose a day with a big ebb just to make the navigation more interesting. But they claim to have had nothing to do with the weather. The course contained three

legs, all inside the San Francisco Bay, for a total of about ten miles.

With nine OCG boats signed up for the first-ever Chip Log Contest, each navigator knew the challenge was to be the best. The boats gathered near the start of the first leg, and when they were ready, started off one by one.

The first leg was a heavy beat from buoy R2 near Treasure Island across the face of Angel to the end point near Belvedere. The second leg was from G2 at Belvedere Point through Raccoon Straight to a point north of South Hampton Shoal. And, the final leg was from South Hampton to near the party at Treasure Island.

Following the navigation contest, the boats rafted up in Clipper Cove for libation and boasts, while the Contest Chairman tried in vain to make his old handheld-navigation calculator compute the navigation error for each boat at the end of each leg. After total failure, one of the contestants had to determine the winners by the age-old art of charting.

Meeting the challenges of both navigation and weather, Cindy Norman on a Baltic 38, posted the best navigation accuracy for the day. At the awards ceremony, Cindy explained a little about her navigation technique. 'Well, when I couldn't stand it below any more, I took the chart out on deck to get some fresh air and started navigating there. The first leg was a heavy wet beat, so it wasn't long before I found a pencil won't mark on a totally soaked chart. But after the first leg, I did better. The second leg was downwind, and the charts dried out a little.' Cindy's total distance off for the three legs was only a mile and a quarter.

The second place navigator was Hugo Landecker, on a Westsail 32. Hugo was close behind Cindy with a mile and three quarters total error. He also turned in the most accurate leg for the day, only two-tenths of a mile off. (That's like navigating from the Golden Gate to the Santa Cruz pier with nothing but a pencil and paper, and only missing it by three miles. But, to make it a fair comparison, the ocean would need a current that varies from 3.5 knots this way to 1 knot that way!)

Even though the weather took its toll on both people and equipment, everyone learned more about navigation, their boats, and tides in the Bay. 'I've studied piloting in the books, but having a real situation to deal with makes all the difference,' mused Mike Skinner. Hugo got several serious nods of agreement when he pointed out, 'Having short legs and tacking upwind sure keeps the navigator busy!' But, Louis Benainous cut straight to the chase, 'I want a re-match!' A sentiment shared by all.[3]

In fact, a rematch occurred on San Francisco Bay on September 25th, 1999. And in 2001, the Chip Log Navigation Contest was held on San Diego Bay on one of the strongest tide days that could be found.

All in all, the Chip Log Navigation Contest was fun to create. And, for those with dead reckoning knowledge, it was fun to do. But it never caught on. It never became *the* test of sailing skill.

(Complete Chip Log Navigation Contest Rules and information on how to run or participate in a Chip Log Navigation Contest can be found at www.CaptainDale.com.)

---

[3] *Latitude 38* magazine. Sausalito, California. June 1999.

Chapter 19

Atlantic Perils

Most of my blue-water experience has been in the Pacific, which has a much nicer reputation than the Atlantic.

A few years after "Four Men and a Whale," Dennis traded his boat for a used Swan 53 in Newport, Rhode Island. Before delivery, he ordered new sails and improvements to the cabinet work in the interior.

Dennis wanted to keep the boat in Florida. The first passage would be to deliver the boat from Newport to Charleston.

Selecting dates for the passage ran the risk of bad weather on both ends. Departing Newport in fall ran the risk of encountering an early winter storm. Arriving in Charleston before the ocean water began to cool off increased the possibility of encountering a late hurricane.

In the end, the timing was determined by the boat yard, as the work ran a little late.

"Here it is. I don't know why we didn't think about this before." Dennis had just returned from the hardware store with an electric heater.

"I think we were all so cold our thoughts froze," replied Harry, as he looked for the 110 outlet in the main cabin.

The thermometer had been dropping the last two days while the boatyard finished the cabinetry rework in the main cabin. Now that the work was done, we were trapped in port by an approaching cold front.

We waited. And we shivered.

The boat had been launched the day before I arrived, and we were staying on the boat until departure. Inside, it seemed freezing and I now had the beginning of a roaring head cold. So, I both shivered and blew my nose.

The weather map on TV showed Newport was about to receive its first winter storm. It was an easy decision not to leave until the storm cleared. Twenty-four hours later, the heater was trying desperately to keep the boat warmed up to cool as a freezing rain turned to ice on the deck.

Cold front, in the lexicon of the northeast, is a term not fully understood by warm-blooded California sailors. When I left San Francisco, I brought all my warmest gear and thought I was ready. The cold snap showed me I was ill-prepared to stay in port next to the heater, let alone go out on the ocean. Adjusting to reality, the six of us went to the local marine clothing store and purchased the warmest thermal underwear they stocked.

"I just heard from the weather service the local fishing guys use." Dennis put his cell phone back in his pocket. "They told me that after this storm, we should have several days of clear weather. The longer we wait after that, the worse our chances are for getting out of here until spring. November really is the beginning of winter."

We all agreed about it being winter. We could feel it in the air, even inside the boat.

"They thought we ought to leave either tomorrow or the next day," Dennis continued, "but no later." We were all getting cabin fever and agreed sooner was better than later.

In the morning, Dennis returned to the boat as I was getting dressed. He was obviously more eager to get started than I was. In fact, I didn't feel all that well. "Take a look at this morning's newspaper," Dennis said. "Lots of pictures of last night's ice storm." He was right. The winter landscapes were beautiful, but only if you were reading the paper in front of a roaring fireplace.

After breakfast, I grabbed my camera as we prepared to leave. I took pictures of the sheet ice on the dock and a picture of a leaky faucet with an icicle that was pretty descriptive. Handling the frozen dock lines reminded me of frostbiting in Chicago, but there was no way to get a picture of the frozen lines.

My cold had turned into something that permeated my body. I ached all over. The idea of ice on the docks loomed as a major deterrent to going sailing. Our departure either had to be now or next spring and we were here now.

Away from the dock and powering out of the harbor, we were about to receive our worst warning. As we raised the main, the water that had frozen over night in the folds of the main fell on the deck as ice. I scraped enough together to take a picture and we headed out to go sailing.

Going down the river, we put two reefs in the main as we raised it. We didn't know the boat; we thought being a little conservative was a good idea. A double reef and the small jib were okay in the river. When we sailed out into the ocean, it turned out to be plenty of power.

As we sailed away from the shoreline, the ocean took on an ugly attitude. It didn't care if we were the recipients of its sullen behavior. The wave structure was still being driven by the wind behind yesterday's storm, producing steep faces. It was the only time I've ever seen a roiling, dark-brown ocean.

The Swan weighed nearly 50,000 pounds and had enough sail area to drive her well. The seas tossed those 50,000 pounds around like a dinghy. Fortunately, our course was downwind, angling across those big brown waves. Even so, the motion of the boat was terribly uncomfortable and the cold was brutal.

When the boat was on top of a wave, it sailed great. The sail area and water-line length combined to give us a fast and exhilarating ride. Then we screamed down the face of the wave, gaining speed from the downhill slope. In the trough, at maximum speed, the boat stuck her bow into the bottom of the next wave and stopped. The water closed over the bow, covering the foredeck with a foot or two of water. The whole bow of the 53-foot boat disappeared into brown water, with only the jib sticking up out of the wave. Laboriously, the water poured off the foredeck and the front of the boat rose out of the water. Then, we climbed to the top of the next wave and accelerated again. And again, and again, and again.

For me, the motion of the boat was awful. The lurching forward, pitching, and stopping were more than my inner ear could deal with. My stomach sympathized with my inner ear. Together, they told the rest of my body it was too hot and too cold at the same time.

Thank goodness, we didn't have to change headsails. We never could have stood on the foredeck. Crawling on hands and knees would have presented more surface area for the next wave to pound. A sail loose on the deck would have been dragged off the boat by a single wave.

Someone mentioned the *The Perfect Storm* had taken place just a hundred miles or so east of our position. It, too, was during the first big winter storm. If this was the aftermath of a storm, I couldn't imagine what the real thing would be like.

I stood all my watches, but this was definitely not the fun part. I'll never forget my introduction to the Atlantic.

A few days later, the storm was farther behind us both in time and distance, and the weather improved. We began to have a relatively nice sail. But the Atlantic wasn't finished with us.

South of Rhode Island, the coastline curves to the west and then back east to Cape Hatteras. South of Cape Hatteras it falls away to the southwest toward Charleston.

Cape Hatteras turns the Gulf Stream out into the ocean, where the Gulf Stream and the Labrador Current collide, creating unstable conditions, storms, and sea swells. The dangers to ship traffic have caused this area to be called the Graveyard of the Atlantic. Cape Hatteras is the eastern corner of the Bermuda Triangle.

Cape Hatteras, which boasts the tallest lighthouse in America, is the point all coastal traffic must round.

Sailing a straight line from Newport, we were approaching Cape Hatteras from somewhat out in the ocean. We hadn't seen the shore since leaving Newport, but our GPS told us we were right on course. Cape Hatteras lay directly ahead.

I was asleep in a bunk when the parade to the nav station started. Someone came below and turned on a light over the chart table. "It's on the chart. I'll look," he said, loudly enough to be heard on deck. Then, a minute later, he hollered out the main hatch, "Twenty-four miles—that's the maximum distance in clear weather."

"Well, then, I don't understand why we can't see it. It's pretty clear tonight," said a faint voice from on deck.

"Maybe there's fog or haze over Cape Hatteras. Maybe it's in the fog. We don't know," the voice at the navigation station shouted out the main hatch.

"I hope not. I don't want to close with the shoal at Cape Hatteras in the fog," said a second faint voice on deck. "The deep water is to the left of the light, and it's all shoals to the right. We have to find the light and go to the left."

I was beginning to wake up, but I really wanted to stay asleep. I rolled to face the center of the boat and put my back against the hull. Then it was quiet again, all except for the footsteps going up the ladder to the cockpit. I drifted back to sleep.

"This says it's a flashing light—every seven seconds—not a steady light. So that can't be it." The voice was back at the navigation station.

"Well, it's the only light out here. That's got to be it," came the reply from on deck.

"If the light we're looking at is actually on shore, then Cape Hatteras Light is over to the left somewhere," said the second voice on deck. "That would mean we're headed to the right of Cape Hatteras Light. It's all shoals to the right of the light." That voice must be Dennis, the owner. Owners are always worried about things like running their boats up on the rocks.

"If it isn't flashing, then that isn't it! It can't be." The voice at the navigation station grew louder. It got quieter as he climbed the ladder and went out the main hatch.

"And another thing," the conversation continued on deck, "that light is too small. The Cape Hatteras Light is huge! The light we're looking at looks like a hundred-watt bulb in someone's bathroom window."

"Well, then you tell me where Cape Hatteras is."

"Yeah, I know. It ought to be right in front of us. I don't understand it either."

I felt like I should get up, but I didn't want to. Maybe I still had a little of whatever masqueraded as a cold and seasickness during the first part of the passage. Officially, I was off watch. I rolled to face the hull. *We're just not there yet,* I thought. I tried to drift off again.

"Well, we've been steering right on the light, whatever it is, and the GPS bearing is changing as if we're going to leave the Cape Hatteras to port. If this light is to the right of Cape Hatteras, then it has to be on shore. And we're headed towards the shoals." The second voice was now at the navigation station with the first.

"Yeah, I agree, the bearing from the GPS is getting smaller. If we were headed right at it, the bearing would stay the same. That means the way point is moving to the left, relative to the boat. Or, the boat is moving to the right."

"But that doesn't make any sense."

"I agree."

"I don't really believe this, but, well, aren't there all kinds of weird stories about the Bermuda Triangle?"

"No."

"Come on. Be serious."

Now I really needed to get up and join the party at the navigation station. I rolled away from the hull and pushed my unwilling legs over the edge of the bunk. Dennis beat me to it. I never got out of the bunk.

"Let me sit down, please," I heard Dennis say. "I have an idea. What if the light is out . . . for maintenance or something?"

"Are you kidding?" said the first voice. "That's the most important navigation light on the East Coast."

"US Coast Guard. US Coast Guard. US Coast Guard. This is the yacht Razzamatazz. Come in please." Dennis was obviously on the VHF.

"Razzamatazz, this is the Coast Guard. Over," came the immediate reply from a young man.

"Yes. We're approaching Cape Hatteras Light and we can't see it. Is it operating tonight? Over."

"Sir, the Cape Hatteras Light is burning as reported," came the reply from the young Coast Guard man.

This reply might have seemed a little unclear to Dennis, so he tried again. "I mean is the light on? Is it working right now? Over."

Again the reply was, "Sir, the Cape Hatteras Light is burning as reported."

Dennis stared at the VHF, not sure what to say next.

Then a tired and gruff voice blared through the VHF, "I can't see it either!" The finality in the voice suggested he was used to giving orders and being followed. He never bothered to identify his boat. His one statement simply ended the conversation.

"So the light really is out," said one of the voices at the navigation station.

"OK. But why does the GPS say we're passing to the right of the light? We can't do that."

"Darned if I. . . ."

"I see it!" came a shout from on deck. "There's the light. I mean I can see the tower. Wow, we're close! I'm going to fall off some." Everyone at the navigation station scrambled up the ladder to help.

On deck, the structure of the Cape Hatteras Light House was just visible in the dark. It was definitely time to fall off a little, but not dangerously close. The crew eased sheets, and we passed to the left of Cape Hatteras Light in deep water.

The hundred-watt bulb turned out to be in the stairwell, not a bathroom. In the morning, we unraveled the GPS problem. The GPS way point was four miles out to sea from the light. When we were steering on the light in the stairwell of the lighthouse tower, we were passing four miles to the right of the waypoint, not the lighthouse.

Personally, I chose to blame it on the Bermuda Triangle, not illness and fatigue.

Chapter 20

The Disaster Passage

Every once in a while, you hear a sailing disaster story. On one of my return trips from Hawaii, we truly had a disastrous passage. The list of broken things and personality disorders was so long, I knew I couldn't remember it all. I started making a list in the back of my personal log.

"OK, you get the dinners and we'll get the rest," the delivery skipper nodded at me as we walked into the Honolulu Costco. We were provisioning the boat for the delivery trip from Hawaii back to Los Angeles after the Transpac Race. "You know what works, cooking at sea. You've done a lot of it."

True, I had cooked at sea on my cruise to New Zealand and back. During that year-and-a-half, I had created a loose-leaf cookbook of everything that worked for me in the galley.

Before leaving home for this trip, I asked the delivery skipper if he wanted me to bring any of my recipes. "No," he said, "we'll just cook the same things we did on the race to Hawaii." At the time, that sounded reasonable, so I left my at-sea cookbook at home.

Now, standing in the Costco entrance, I realized cooking "the same thing" wasn't going to work. For the race, the wives of the racing crew had pitched in to make casseroles and other dishes. Now the race was over, the silver had been awarded, and the race crew and their wives had gone home. On this passage, we wouldn't have any precooked casseroles from a home kitchen to serve.

Twenty-two-hundred miles from my cookbook, I suddenly needed to create enough dinners to feed six guys for two-and-a-half weeks out of an unknown boat galley at sea. I didn't even know what pots and pans were on board. Not much, I'd bet. They would have taken everything off the boat to save weight.

"How many dinners should I get?" I started calculating, thinking about the length of the passage. Every time I'd done this trip before, it had taken between 16 and 19 days. This was a bigger and faster boat, so the passage would probably be a little quicker. But I didn't know how many extra dinners the delivery skipper wanted to carry as a safety margin.

"Oh, probably 12 or 13," he replied, and pulled his cart around to get started.

The delivery skipper had been part of the crew that raced the boat to Hawaii, so he knew the boat. I thought he should have a good idea of how long the passage home would take.

He also was responsible for expenses and presenting them to the syndicate. If the expenses ran too high, they would have to assess everyone in the syndicate . . . long after all the fun was over.

I'd never made the passage in 12 or 13 days, but I'd always been in smaller boats. I did remember a story of one boat that made it back in 12 days. They'd had an unusual weather pattern and sailed directly toward San Francisco the entire time. "But doesn't the trip take more like 15 or 16 days?" I countered out loud. "What are we going to do for the rest of the meals?"

"Oh, well, we'll catch fish for the rest." He was ready to start shopping and probably thinking about his list.

"Uh, well, I think we ought to take enough food to get home. Just in case we don't catch enough fish." I wasn't a very good fisherman and I didn't like the idea of being dependent on what seemed like luck.

"Well, I guess we could. Why don't you get 15? That should get us there." His cart was in motion.

"OK." If this boat really was fast enough to reach Los Angeles in 13 days, then we'd have a couple extra dinners.

I started thinking of the large entrees in the frozen section, and then remembered a conversation between two of the delivery crew earlier in the day. The owner's boat guy had been riding one of the two college kids about being a vegetarian. It struck me as a poor way

110

to start a friendship when we were all going to live in close quarters for two weeks.

At least I had learned one of the crew was vegetarian. I'd hate to discover that two days out on the ocean. I had no idea what a vegetarian could eat—probably not the entrees with meat in the frozen section. Maybe I could find one or two that were meatless, but I couldn't imagine the rest of the crew eating meatless dishes for two weeks. Certainly not the owner's boat guy.

I turned to the vegetarian and asked, "Why don't you come with me? I'm going to need some help."

The vegetarian and I headed toward the frozen entrees with one cart. The delivery skipper and two more crew headed toward the canned goods and the paper goods with another cart.

It turned out the vegetarian knew exactly what to substitute for our entrees. He'd been making those substitutions all his life. He picked up veggie-burger patties and a variety of heavy snack foods. Well, they looked like snack food to me. The vegetarian insisted they were fine for him. For the rest of the crew, I selected several fresh meats, seven or eight frozen entrees, canned ham, shrimp, and roast beef. We both counted to 15 as we put meat and meatless into the cart.

We arrived back at the checkout counter just ahead of the delivery skipper and the guys with him. They now had two carts loaded full of all kinds of things for breakfast, lunch, and snacks.

I hoped we had enough. I tried to imagine the volume of a meal for a hungry guy. Then, I tried to multiply that by six guys, three times a day, plus snacks, for two weeks. How big a pile of food would that be? How much bigger would the pile be while it was still in its packaging? Were three shopping carts of packaged food enough? Even the Costco-size carts?

We made it through checkout and back to the boat with all our supplies, and carried everything onto the boat. Before we started stowing everything away into the lockers and cupboards, the bunks and the sole in the main cabin were stacked high with groceries. Just for fun, I got my camera and took a couple of pictures of the grocery piles when they were the biggest. I took a few pictures of the crew, too.

111

The owner's boat guy wheeled around to me. "What're you doing?" he jabbed. "Taking pictures for your family album?" His tone definitely wasn't nice. "Is that what you keep for family heirlooms?" he sniped rather bitterly.

Oh, brother, I thought. *Well, I have pictures from a lot of trips. I guess I don't need any more from this one.* I lowered my camera and, eventually, put it back in my sea bag where it rode the whole way home.

"When are we leaving?" I asked, as we began emptying grocery bags and stowing everything into lockers.

"Tomorrow at 5 A.M.!" announced the delivery skipper, more to everyone in the cabin, than just to me. "We need to get the boat back ASAP."

The owner's boat guy mumbled something like, "I'm ready. All I want to do is sail this mother back." He went aft to his bunk and started unpacking his personal gear.

The owner's boat guy had been racing on the boat for the last year. When the syndicate got together for the Hawaii race, the crew pitched in enough money to cover expenses. The owner's boat guy wasn't able to come up with any cash, so he didn't get to make the race. In place of racing to Hawaii, the owner had promised him the trip back.

"Anything need repair before we go or is the boat ready?" I queried. I thought if things needed repair before we left, we would have to work fast or delay the departure until the work was done.

"Well, the boat is pretty much ready to go. We just raced it over here, so we ought to be able to sail it back," said the delivery skipper. "We did a lot of work on it before the race, so we ought to be OK."

"What's with the binnacle guard?" I asked. We had all seen the yellow and black construction-area tape wrapped around it.

"Well, the binnacle guard isn't bolted to the cockpit sole very solidly. If you grab it, you'll find it's loose. Don't lean on it or you'll break it. We tried to fix it before the race, but we ran out of time. We put the caution tape on as a reminder not to use it."

112

With the boat beating upwind through the big waves in the trades, it seemed to me we might like to have the primary cockpit handhold. *Well, we aren't racing,* I thought. *I guess we'll manage OK.*

Two of our crew were still in college. The vegetarian was a senior and the ethics major had just graduated. They were both going on for master's degrees.

The vegetarian and the ethics major were making good progress stowing all the food supplies. The piles on the bunks and cabin sole were showing signs of getting smaller. I hoped the rest of us would be able to find everything while beating home. Well, if we had to ask where something was, there were only six of us to ask.

"Also, something's wrong with the head. It works, but not well," the delivery skipper added. "I tried to clean it and I did free it up a bit, but I haven't had time to rebuild it or anything."

"Do we have the rebuild kit on board?" I figured if we had to, we could rebuild it at sea. It's hard to work on a boat bouncing over the waves, but it could be done.

"No. I didn't have time to get to West Marine to pick up one."

The vegetarian was stowing snack foods in a locker over the nav station. "Oh, the latches on those two cabinets over the nav station don't work exactly right," the delivery skipper explained. "They opened on us during the race and spilled everything on the cabin sole. Don't put anything in those two."

"Anybody find the diesel starting fluid yet?" the delivery skipper asked. "The engine starts OK with it, but it won't start without it."

"Yeah, I put it over here."

"Well, let's put it here on top of the engine compartment. Then, we'll always know where it is when we want to start the engine."

"Sure, here."

"Hey, anybody on board?" came a call from the dock.

The delivery skipper looked up through the port window. "Yeah. Come on board," he shouted out the main hatch. Then, more quietly to us in the cabin, he said, "That's probably our last crew member. I thought he was going to be here earlier."

Thump. Thump. Something hit the deck. Two somethings. A moment later, the head and shoulders of the boatyard worker appeared in the main hatch. "Here, let me hand these down to someone," as he passed first one suitcase, and then another, down the main hatch.

Suitcases? I thought. *Who is this guy? Has he ever been sailing before?*

"Well, we're all on board now," said the delivery skipper. "We leave at 5 A.M. tomorrow."

An hour or two later, the piles of groceries were all stowed. The two cabinets over the chart table remained empty, and the excess bags and boxes were in the dumpster on the dock. We tried to fix a few little things, topped off the water, made sure the spare water jugs were safely stowed, and then stowed our personal things where they wouldn't fall.

By the time everything in the boat was stowed and ready to go to sea, it was too late to go out to eat, so the delivery skipper had a pizza delivered to the boat for our last dinner in Hawaii. We had plenty to eat, but I was a little concerned about sleeping on a stomach full of pizza and starting on a heavy beat early the next morning.

As we handed pizza around the cockpit, the delivery skipper introduced us to each other. I was named second-in-command because I had already made this trip four times, and I owned and raced a 38-foot sailboat in San Diego. This was the first trip for the vegetarian and the ethics major. They didn't have much big boat experience, but they both raced small boats at a lake sailing club in San Francisco. Neither the owner's boat guy nor the boatyard worker had made the trip before, but they sounded eager. At least the owner's boat guy knew the boat, having raced on it for a while around Los Angeles. I hoped the boatyard worker would have experience repairing whatever might go wrong on the passage, but his sailing experience was uncertain. He said his reason for signing on was to get free passage back to the mainland.

The delivery skipper assigned bunks for the passage. He and the two college kids were in the main cabin. The owner's boat guy, the boatyard worker, and I were in the aft area under the cockpit. This was a 50-foot boat, so the six of us had plenty of space.

The delivery skipper announced the watch schedule: three hours on and six hours off. Two people would always be on watch at a time. Each man had his own three-hour watch schedule and overlapped an hour or two with the person before or after him in the rotation.

The watch sequence started with the delivery skipper, followed by the ethics student, the vegetarian, me, the owner's boat guy, and the boatyard worker. We were all most interested in who came just before and just after us in the sequence. These were the people we would be on watch with. I would share the first two hours of my watch with the vegetarian, and the last hour with the owner's boat guy.

Bringing a new person on every hour or two would keep the on-watch people more alert. The delivery skipper made it clear this was a big boat and, with only two people on deck at a time, callouts would happen any time extra hands were needed. Any time at all.

Sleep came later than we wanted. No matter, the delivery skipper woke us at 5 A.M., saying, "Let's get going. We gotta get the boat back."

At breakfast, we were each assigned a glass to use for the trip and we wrote our name on it. By not sharing our glasses with anyone, we wouldn't have to wash them. By using paper plates, we'd have minimal clean up after meals.

I decided during the two weeks, I'd wash my glass. Maybe I just wouldn't tell anyone.

With too little sleep and a cold breakfast on top of last night's pizza, we backed the boat out of the slip and headed out to sea. Outside the harbor, we turned downwind and south around the island. Fortunately, we had to buy diesel and the gas dock was in the next harbor to the west. I was pleased we were spared the hard beat up through the Molokai Channel.

After topping off the diesel, we continued on around the island enjoying the flat water in the lee of the island. When we could see the last point of land and knew we were about to sail out from under the lee, we switched to a smaller headsail. It was nice to make the change in the lee, instead of in unprotected waters.

In preparation for the sail change, the delivery skipper implemented a rule for the trip I've only seen in racing, never in cruising: he assigned everyone a fixed position. The two who knew the boat best were assigned to the foredeck, one man was a floater normally stationed at the mast, two more were stationed in the cockpit, and I was placed on the helm. He explained we were *not* to change positions all the way home; we were always to go to the same job. His reasoning was simple and right on. After we did our job a time or two, we would learn it. Then, if we had a callout in the middle of the night, we would all go to jobs we knew.

When we finally did come out from under the lee of the island, the wind came up and we reefed the main. The first reef went in with no problem. The boat was still overpowered, so we started to put in the second reef. But the second reef point at the luff was torn and couldn't be used. "The plan was to get it fixed in Los Angeles after the delivery, so we didn't try to get it fixed in Hawaii," explained the delivery skipper.

So, we went to the third reef. The boat was underpowered, but it was clearly a better choice than being overpowered. We were going to miss the second reef during the next week or two.

We tried to put the main sheet in the self-tailer on the main sheet winch, but the main sheet was too small in diameter to lock in the jaws. We had to lead the tail across the deck to the closest horn cleat and cleat it there. A little awkward, but it didn't slip.

The controls for an autopilot were mounted in the cockpit, so I asked how to turn it on. I figured during the next two weeks we might like to have some relief from steering.

"Naw," replied the delivery skipper. "We can't use the autopilot. It's too hard to connect below."

Six guys on board and it's too hard to connect? I thought. *Well, I guess we're all going to get a lot of time on the helm.*

"I don't think we ought to go up too high on a beat," the delivery skipper cautioned. "The boat slams too much. We'll never get any sleep."

Well, that'll make the trip home longer, I thought. *It's upwind to Los Angeles.*

Little by little, we learned the boat. Up on a beat, it did pound too hard, no one could even begin to fall asleep. We all willingly chose to fall off 15 degrees to allow the off watch to sleep or move about in more safety. Unfortunately, falling off from 45 to 60 degrees would add hundreds of miles to our passage, maybe two or three days. Then, I remembered we only had two "extra" meals on board for a safety margin.

"Anyone know anything about fishing?" I asked. "I think it would be great if we could have some fresh fish for dinner." And so the fishing expedition started with many claims of expertise and accomplishments. Spirits were high.

Later in the day, we did catch a nice Dorado, which delighted me. If we were going to catch fish, we needed to do it now. I had never heard of anyone catching fish in the high. Dinner that night was fresh Dorado steaks and vegetables.

Even with the sails cracked off and the boat on a close reach, the boat kicked up a lot of spray. The front half of the boat was constantly wet with running water. Inside, it soon became obvious we couldn't use two of the bunks in the main cabin. Leaks had already soaked the mattresses. Another leak at the mast, where the mast came down through the cabin top, had soaked the seat cushion on the forward end of the dining area.

After dinner, while the two college kids were getting ready to wash pots and pans, I fired up the ham radio. I could hear other stations, but everyone I tried to talk to said I was too faint for much of a conversation. I asked the delivery skipper if the radio had worked on the race to Hawaii. He didn't know. They didn't have anyone with a ham license on board during the race. Not to worry, we had an Iridium phone on board, which would be our means of communications with the folks back home.

The delivery skipper also told us he didn't know what was wrong with the VHF. It would transmit on 16, but wouldn't receive on 16. All the other channels seemed OK. It was just the general calling channel we couldn't receive on. "It probably wouldn't make any difference," he said. VHF was line of sight, and we probably wouldn't see any other boats after we got away from shore. We'd probably never use the VHF on the way home.

What about when we're close to the shore off Point Conception? I wondered. A lot of outbound freighter traffic from Long Beach would go right past there. But, then, freighters don't normally talk to sailboats. They only call sailboats in emergencies.

"Hey, how do we get water out of the faucet in the galley sink?" asked the ethics graduate. He seemed comfortable starting with basic concepts.

"Oh," replied the delivery skipper, "I guess when the boat is heeled like this, the pump is too low to lift the water that far. Take a bucket and wash the dishes in sea water."

"OK." Off the college kids went to get a bucket and dip it into the ocean at the rail.

The previous predictions about being unable to start the engine without starter fluid proved true. But it did start just fine when we sprayed starter fluid down the air intake. The batteries took a charge, and they ran the running lights and electronics all night. So, twice a day, we started the engine with starter fluid. Maybe not perfect, but it worked.

When the Sun went down, we learned about the stern light. By regulation, stern lights are supposed to be visible aft across 135 degrees, or from dead aft to 67.5 degrees forward of aft on both sides. This one was twisted to one side in such a way that it shone white light directly into the cockpit, making it impossible to maintain any night vision. This also meant a boat on our port beam would see our stern light when they shouldn't. They would think we were headed away from them when we weren't. On the other side, a boat approaching from the starboard quarter would never see a stern light at all. Well, if he got close enough, the skipper might see the instrument lights in our cockpit.

The night watch is always a time when people get to know each other. The first two hours of my watch I shared with the vegetarian, which was a nice experience. The boat delivery was at the end of his summer vacation. When he returned to the mainland, he would go back to college as a senior.

The vegetarian wanted to see what an ocean passage was like, so he had signed on as crew. Like all of us, he was on an expense-free adventure. He wanted to learn to steer a big boat better, so he wanted all the helm time he could get. I was missing the autopilot already, so I graciously agreed he could steer as much as he wanted. This worked out well. The only time I steered was when he lost his concentration and couldn't find the groove again. Then, I would steer until he relaxed and wanted the helm back.

The other hour of my watch was shared with the owner's boat guy. Life has many challenges. When a person makes a few mistakes, sometimes they seem to be on the road to a few more.

This was his first ocean passage, but having raced on the boat, the owner's boat guy considered it somewhat his boat. He was able to come on the return trip because the race syndicate was paying all our expenses. He was unhappy about not being allowed to sail in the race. "After all," he said, "I was the one who prepared the boat for the race. It just wasn't fair." His personal concept of ownership and expenses seemed to parallel his way of life.

He chattered continuously. When I went off watch an hour later, I found my head was full of fragments and confusion. As I went off watch, I was replaced by the boatyard worker. I couldn't help but wonder how these two would get along. Confusion, disorientation, and outspoken defensiveness on one hand, matched with aggressiveness and few people-handling skills on the other. Both had made their way in life with a physical orientation.

I was glad to get away below. I knew every watch would be the same, all the way home. The same overlap of people and the same unresolved issues.

The next day was the second day of beating north toward the high, up through the rolling swells driven by the trades. We were still in the tropics, so the Sun was high and hot, and the temperature inside the cabin was equally hot. We had spray on the foredeck, and swimsuits and sun tan lotion in the cockpit. The wind was brisk, the boat was responsive, and the sailing was good.

I came off watch in the late afternoon, and began organizing dinner preparation. No fish tonight, so I figured we'd heat a frozen dinner from the freezer. I lit the oven to preheat it.

When I opened the cooler and began moving things around to get to the freezer section, things didn't seem very cold; in fact, they barely felt cool. Maybe the cooler/freezer didn't have enough insulation for the tropics. Either that . . . or someone had left the lid open.

When I got into the freezer area, the thermometer, hidden well down in the "frozen" packages, read 65 degrees. And that was the coldest part of the box.

Obviously, the cooler area was warmer than the freezer area. No wonder it didn't feel cold. And, just as obviously, all our frozen dinners weren't going to last very long at 65 degrees. Well, maybe if they thawed slowly, and we ate the one that was most thawed each day. . . .

The dinner on top was a frozen chicken and vegetable casserole. It was only partly thawed, but because it was on top, I figured it was more thawed than the rest of the stack. I pulled it out and checked the cooking instructions while the oven heated.

"Hey man! Turn the oven off!" called the delivery skipper from his bunk in the main cabin. "It's too hot."

"Well, the frozen dinners are for the first part of the trip. The freezer isn't cold enough to keep them frozen, so we have to eat them," I tried to explain.

"I know. I know. We had trouble with the freezer on the way over. We figured it needed Freon or something," he acknowledged. "But it's too hot in here to have the oven on. I can't sleep, it's so hot. Turn the oven off. Use canned goods or something for dinner."

The package on the "frozen" dinner said one hour and 15 minutes at 325 degrees. I thought because it was mostly thawed, I might be able to cut 20 minutes or a half hour off the oven time. Well, maybe. The delivery skipper's tone of voice suggested having the oven on for even 45 minutes was unacceptable.

I turned off the oven and put the frozen dinner back. "Hey, you guys," I hollered up the main hatch. "You were pretty good with fishing last night . . ."

The only fish we had for dinner were the leftovers from the night before, supplemented with canned goods.

After dinner, while the college kids were cleaning up with a bucket of salt water, I noticed the owner's boat guy raiding the cooler for something to eat. I must have left the chicken casserole on top, because that's what he came up with. Normally, I would've been outraged at a person eating the provisions for the whole crew. In this case, the frozen foods probably wouldn't last long enough to be cooked anyway, so I figured if he were that hungry and could eat it uncooked, then fine. At least it would do someone some good. I'd just have to remember to give him bigger portions tomorrow.

When tomorrow came, we had a new problem to deal with. The delivery skipper had sounded the one water tank to see how fast we were using up our supply. The tank was almost empty.

The single water tank was located under the settee berth on the starboard side of the boat. When the boat was on a hard starboard beat, heeled to port, the water tank was about the same height as the hand water pump in the head on the port side of the boat. The hand water pump had two check valves in it to keep the water from flowing backward when pumping water. When there was a positive pressure from the water tank side of the check valves, they opened and water flowed freely past them. The water flowed past the check valves, out the spigot, into the wash basin, and down the drain into the ocean. Every time the boat heeled a little extra, from a puff of wind or from rolling on a big wave, the water tank was lifted above the spigot, and emptied a little more water into the ocean.

The delivery skipper closed the ball valve to the hand pump to prevent losing any more water and took inventory. We had about 15 gallons in the tank, three five-gallon jugs of emergency water in the forward locker, and quite a bit of bottled water, sodas, and beer in the galley. To refill the water tank, we would have to sail back to Hawaii—two full days. If we went on, we would have to sail about two weeks to the mainland—short of water.

The delivery skipper called the head of the racing syndicate—the guy who had been the skipper on the race—and explained our situation. He was concerned, but agreed we could try to continue with the water we had, if we wanted to.

"Well, I think we can make it," the delivery skipper said. "It's going to be close, but if we're careful and only use the water we have for drinking, we should be OK."

"Besides, we have to get the boat back to Los Angeles. After beating all this way, I hate to give up all the distance we've come. We're going on. We'll make it."

We started mild water rationing. No fresh water baths. Wash dishes in salt water only. The two college kids looked at each other, but no one could tell what they were thinking. The delivery skipper monitored the remaining water the rest of the way home.

We were 15 percent of the way home and on water rationing. Spirits took a dive. This, of course, gave the boat owner's guy and the boatyard worker an opportunity to explore previously hidden wrinkles in their personalities.

Slowly, we beat our way north. Each day, we put as many miles between us and Hawaii as we could. Each day brought us closer to the North Pacific high.

The problems with the boat continued. On deck, the bolts attaching the boom vang to the boom broke. A call came for all hands on deck, but we quickly learned we couldn't repair it until we were back on shore with a better-equipped work bench. Losing the boom vang wasn't a problem while we were on a beat, as the main sheet and the traveler could be used to pull the boom down. But, if we ever got off the wind, we would need the boom vang to keep the top of the main from twisting off.

Below decks, the head wasn't working quite right. It worked, but grudgingly. You had to pump, and pump, and pump.

Back on deck, the port lower lifeline broke. We bent the end of the remaining lifeline double, tied a line to it, and then tied it to the bow pulpit. The result was a loose life line the rest of the way home.

No one trusted it. For that matter, we had concerns about the rest of the life lines. They probably had all been installed at the same time. We wondered which one would be next, how much weight it would take to break it, and whether it would happen in daylight or dark.

Occasionally, I tried the ham radio, but whenever I did make contact, my signal was too faint to have much of a conversation. It was far too weak for a phone patch. I began to realize I wasn't going to be able to use the ham radio to contact anyone at home. My signal weakness seemed constant and I became suspicious of the ground plane being too small. I couldn't do much in the middle of the ocean about the installation of the radio.

As we sailed north out of the trades and into the winds around the high, the wind eased up a little. With all hands on deck and everyone in their assigned position, we shook the reefs out of the main. We were making progress on our passage home.

The overlapping watches with two guys on deck continued like clockwork. My two hours with the vegetarian were usually quiet and thoughtful, with lots of helm work for the vegetarian. Slowly, but with certainty, he was developing a much better touch on the helm. It was gratifying to watch him develop a good feel for it.

The hour with the owner's boat guy continued to be a challenge. He came to believe I had the ear of the delivery skipper. So, he started working on me to work on the delivery skipper. Whatever his cluttered mind came to believe was necessary, he laid on me to pass along. When I agreed, it confirmed he was right in getting me to talk to the delivery skipper. Most of the time he wanted to switch to a bigger headsail or do something to drive the boat harder and faster. If I'd remind him of those below and their need to sleep, or dress, or cook, then I was arguing with him. Almost immediately, I'd be in contention with a self-centered, childish ego that badly needed to be told he was right. When he talked, I quickly developed the habit of nodding wisely and saying little.

As the days passed, I began to notice the boatyard worker was becoming more and more quiet when he relieved me. The two hours he spent with the owner's boat guy seemed to be wearing on him. Somehow, the quiet didn't seem like the kind of quiet that would stay quiet.

Or, maybe I'd had enough of the owner's boat guy, too. At one point, I rolled over in my bunk to see him heating the pressurized can of engine-starting fluid over the stove. He proudly responded to my obvious question with, "Well, I'm not sure we have enough cans of this stuff on board to get us to California, so I'm trying to get one more start out of this can before I throw it away."

I really did try to shut my eyes again and fall asleep. I really did try.

As we sailed north, the wind got lighter and the seas settled down. With everyone in position, we changed to a bigger headsail. The owner's boat guy was certain I had taken his idea to the delivery skipper. Now, he had a flood of new ideas and half ideas I must pass along.

When we left Hawaii, the high had been located far enough north that we expected to tack just to the south of it, assuming it stayed in the same place. We wanted to tack as we approached it while we still had enough wind to sail by, not after we got into the high and lost the wind. It was time for an update on the location of the high.

The delivery skipper got out the weather fax machine to receive the weather data. It should give us a current map showing where the high was located, how it was shaped, and where it was expected to go in the next day or two. But, the weather fax had "stopped working." We never got the weather map.

The high was somewhere up there ahead of us, but we had no idea of how far or where. Would our track take us straight into it, or to the right or left? Should we tack now, or hold on for a day or two more, and then tack?

We sailed north into the dying breeze. When the wind got "light enough," the delivery skipper said, "It's time to tack." We tacked to an eastward heading, not knowing where the high was. We lost the wind for a while, but not so long that lack of fuel became a problem.

Now we were headed toward the California coast and spirits rose. Even the boatyard worker and the owner's' boat guy seemed to get along better.

The boat was now on the opposite tack and heeled the other direction. Now the starboard side was the low side of the boat. The galley sink, which had been on the high side, was now at the level of the ocean. Water ran back up the drain into the bottom of the sink. We had no way to get the last of the dirty water out of the sink. It just sloshed around in the bottom, waiting for the bottom of the sink to rise above the level of the ocean.

With the boat on the new tack, it was torqued in the opposite direction. The sliding cabinet doors over the refrigerator/freezer would no longer open, so we couldn't get to the food in those two cabinets. Of course, the guy who noticed this first was the owner's boat guy, who was always scavenging for more to eat.

The head, which had been working if you pumped a lot, became more cantankerous. Sometimes pumping and pumping would work, and sometimes not. So I kept pumping. I figured the flap valves on the inside were either worn out or full of salt water corrosion and hardened crud. The head needed to be torn down, cleaned, and rebuilt with new valves and O-rings.

One night, two hours after I went off watch, the owner's boat guy was relieved from watch and came below. He was never a quiet or timid guy, but this night, he seemed more agitated than normal. I had been asleep and figured if I feigned no awareness of him, I could get right back to sleep. Just as I convinced myself I could do it, I became aware of the sweet smell of a cigarette not made by one of the major manufacturers.

The aft compartment was big enough for four bunks and the engine. The whole compartment was underneath the cockpit and had a low overhead. The entire area didn't have much volume, so the smoke got thicker as it filled the available space.

On my return to San Diego, I was scheduled to take a medical test for my Captain's license. The Coast Guard had a zero-tolerance policy. I had no idea how much free smoke I would have to breathe before I would show positive on the drug screening. I decided not to risk it and took my pillow up on deck to sleep in fresh air.

The delivery skipper, who had just relieved the owner's boat guy, asked me what the heck I was doing with a pillow on deck. After a short discussion with me, he went below and had a longer discussion with the owner's boat guy. When he came back on deck, all he said was, "You can go below now." As I descended the ladder, the owner's boat guy was carrying his sleeping bag and pillow forward to the sail locker in the forepeak. His comment was an unfriendly, "I'm going to sleep forward. I don't want to be around you anymore." I wondered what our next watch together would be like.

The boatyard worker had been on watch with the delivery skipper when I took my pillow up on deck and had watched the whole thing. When he came off watch, he decided to befriend me. I was awake again, and the owner's boat guy was forward, so we talked for a while in the aft quarters. It seems he was pretty frustrated with the outspoken, overbearing attitude of the owner's boat guy and he needed a friend himself.

The boatyard worker told me how his watches with the owner's boat guy had been going. I had guessed right, just not severe enough. He went on to say how the owner's boat guy had been on "ice meth," and had come off it just before the trip started. He was going through withdrawal on the sail back to the mainland. All he was on now was a little grass. The boatyard worker explained that while a person is on "ice meth," they're never hungry, so they never eat. But, when they come off it, they're hungry all the time. That's why he'd been raiding all the food stores.

At this point, I began to think of the owner's boat guy as the druggie. In my mind, "druggie" became his new nickname. Every time I saw him looking for more food to stuff in his mouth, his new name was confirmed.

Eventually, I mentioned my conversation with the boatyard worker to the delivery skipper. He said he knew. He had been trying to defuse the whole thing for a long time now. The best he could do was listen, and listen, and listen.

Over the next few days, as we sailed toward California, the wind shifted forward. Slowly, it caused us to change course from east to southeast. Without a weather fax, we couldn't tell where the high was, but I was certain it was the cause of the continuing wind shift.

Eventually, we were unable to lay Point Conception, but we were headed well to the south of it. When our course became more than 45 degrees south of Point Conception, we tacked back to starboard and established a course with more east in it than north.

The new course felt wrong. It felt as if we were going north, away from Point Conception. Both the compass and the GPS told us this was the better tack, but they were hard to believe.

The druggie was unhappy. He thought we ought to be sailing toward Point Conception, not away from it. No one wanted to try to explain to him this course was closer to Point Conception than our previous course. Sometimes rational conversations are a lot of work.

The delivery skipper was calling the head of the race syndicate on the Iridium phone every once in a while to update him on our progress. He called again just after the tack.

The druggie decided he was the boat owner's guy and the boat owner needed to know what was going on. He started calling the owner directly, with his own personal version of updates. From this point on, I'm sure our situation created a lot of confusion on shore.

After tacking back to starboard, one good thing was we could get the two cabinets over the refrigerator open again. The druggie found new territory for his pleasure.

By now, the head wasn't pumping solids out at all. It seemed no water was coming in, so I brought a bucket of sea water into the head and poured some of it into the bowl. It did pump the solids out, but just as the bowl got empty, it belched brown water back up out of the bowl onto the floor. I gave up. I left the half-full bucket on the floor in the head. I think others tried it, too, but nobody said anything. None of us ever went in there again without sea boots.

A couple days later, the wind began to back into the northeast. As soon as port tack was favored, the call came for all hands, and we tacked back to port.

Just after the tack, the delivery skipper hollered from the foredeck for me to steer the boat down as low as I could for a short while. They had a problem and needed to put the jib in the wind shadow of the main to take the strain off the jib sheet for a moment.

We eased sheets and I steered down to a run. Running before the wind with only a main, a wave picked up the back end of the boat and we started surfing. On only one wave, I saw the knot meter climb from 6 to 12, with the jib blanketed. It must have been some ride for the guys on the race under spinnaker!

A few minutes later, they solved the problem. The foredeck crew was happy again and started coming aft. The delivery skipper signaled for me to steer back up. Reluctantly, I started turning up.

The boat went broad side to the waves just as the druggie walked past the main hatch. When the boat rolled, he fell face down onto the deck and started sliding across the deck, head first toward the low side. Everyone saw him sliding. They ran to grab him, but no one was close enough. He continued to slide until his head was outside the life lines on the low side, over the ocean.

Just as the top of his shoulders passed under the lower life line, he managed to get a hand on a stanchion and stop his slide into the ocean. His face was only inches from the water. He held on and two pairs of hands grabbed him. The student who had just graduated from college in philosophy, with a major in ethics, was in the cockpit handling lines. In a quiet voice, he said, "Darn it. I thought we were rid of him." *Well,* I thought, *I guess I'm not the only one.*

On the new tack, the wind shift continued, and we were let up until we could lay Point Conception. We were on our way home again. It felt good.

About this time, the delivery skipper gave us a pep talk. It seems we had been doing well with the water consumption, but we were still several days from shore and we needed to be careful. With no other option, we took his advice seriously.

Later, the delivery skipper found a private moment below and asked me what I had heard from the druggie or the boatyard guy. Was trouble brewing? Did I know anything about what was going on between the two of them?

"No," I responded, "the druggie has been pretty hostile toward me ever since he moved into the forepeak." I wasn't on watch with the boatyard worker, so I hadn't heard much of anything.

Then, the delivery skipper unloaded. He had been holding together a fragile truce between them for most of the trip. But his sense of trouble had just been escalated. The boatyard worker had told the delivery skipper to get the druggie off his back. He had taken all he was going to take. He had a gun in his suitcase and, if the druggie got on him one more time, he was going to get him.

Stunned, I promised to listen to both of them. If I heard anything, I'd let the delivery skipper know. Clearly, the druggie was making more enemies. And not all his enemies were kind and gentle.

The wind filled some more and we reefed the main, to the third reef again. In the process, the whole reefing mechanism, the shives and stoppers in the forward end of the boom, broke away. We jury-rigged a way to keep the reef in, but it complicated reefing and unreefing.

Every once in a while, I tried the ham radio, but the result was the same—not a strong enough signal for a phone patch.

In the middle of the night, when I came on watch, the two guys on watch were hollering back and forth from the helm to the bow pulpit. The bow-light mount had broken. In the dark, one was trying to hold the boat steady and not send spray over the foredeck. The other was making a temporary repair with duct tape.

The next morning, I got up and started dressing to go on watch. The delivery skipper was sitting on the lower bunk in the main cabin staring at the cabin sole mumbling, "They ate it all. They ate it all."

"They ate it all what?" I asked pulling on my sweatshirt. It had seen too many up-wind watches, and it was full of salt and condensation.

"They ate all the food."

129

"They ate all the food?" I repeated dumbly. I was just waking up. My mind wasn't fully in gear.

"It's all gone. We don't have enough to get home."

"Food?" I asked. "What do we have left?"

"I don't know, but we have five more days to go." He was looking at me now. I knew I had to do something.

I hollered to the two college kids—the vegetarian and the ethics student—and asked them to help me. "Go through all the cabinets, all the bins, and all the storage lockers. Get out all the food. All of it!" I sat down on the cabin sole. "Bring all the food here and set it on the sole with me. And see if you can find some plastic bags."

Pretty soon, the cabin sole had all of our food spread out on it—mostly odds and ends—nowhere near the piles that had lined the floor and bunks before we started.

I looked at the vegetarian, "Make sure you have enough food for the next five days." His supply was intact. It was the rest of us, the meat eaters, who were going to be short.

Out of the pile of food on the cabin sole, I was able to put together five dinners. For three of the dinners, I was able to put together enough canned meat and canned vegetables to make a meal for five people. The fourth dinner was a little creative, but it would provide nourishment. The fifth dinner, however, was a pretty bad hodge-podge of left-over canned goods. By the last day, I figured we might not be too picky.

I put the five dinners into five plastic bags, numbered them 1 through 5, and stowed them in an empty cabinet in the main cabin where everyone could watch them. I told everyone that no one, absolutely no one, was to pilfer these plastic bags. They got the idea.

The rest of the food on the cabin sole was put back into the normal cabinets in the galley, available for breakfasts, lunches, snacks—and pilfering.

The delivery skipper decided to call the head of the race syndicate with yet one more update. Unfortunately, when the Iridium phone had been used the last time, it had been left on the wet cushion by the mast. It was now sopping wet from the water leaking down the mast. The phone simply wouldn't work. The druggie decided he needed to go back on deck for a while.

That evening, I tried the ham radio again with little hope of replacing the dead phone. I couldn't raise anyone on the western side of the US. But, I was surprised to hear a loud clear voice saying, "Go ahead N6OMD. I'm in New Jersey, and I read you loud and clear." Dumb luck provided me with a freak atmospheric bounce and my signal was good enough for a phone patch. Yes, he had one, who did I want to call? I gave him a San Diego number and told him to call collect.

By now, the list of things that had gone wrong filled a whole page in the back of my personal log. But the major problems—food and water—were clear in my mind. By the time my friend answered the phone, I was wondering how long the freak atmospheric condition would last.

I tried to start with "No one is hurt and we aren't in any immediate danger. The Iridium phone doesn't work and the ham radio only works on a freak bounce, so you won't hear from us until we get to shore." As fast as I could talk, and as fast as my friend could take notes, I ran down the list of problems starting with food and water, and then worked my way through the things that had broken or didn't work.

Freak atmospheric conditions aren't dependable. I lost the bounce into New Jersey. I didn't even get to say thank you to the ham who helped us.

I found out later, my friend, who had been receiving phone reports from the head of the race syndicate, called him back with my report. They tried to fit this information into what they already knew, and then piece together just how serious our situation was. With all the conflicting reports, they couldn't put much certainty to anything.

We continued to sail the boat straight toward Point Conception. We were strongly motivated to get to Santa Barbara as soon as possible.

The five dinners turned out to be less filling than desired, but they gave us five days. Unfortunately, on the third of those five days, we ran out of CNG (Compressed Natural Gas) for the stove. The last two dinners we ate cold, but we were glad to have them.

We made landfall at Point Conception. At least our open ocean navigation was good. When we looked for the charts to begin coastal navigation, none were on board. "Well, we all know this coast line pretty well. We don't need charts," explained the delivery skipper. That was true for him; he knew the area well.

We certainly didn't need the charts to tell us where the freighter lanes were. We could see the line of outbound freighters for miles ahead. Thank goodness the night was clear.

Shortly after landfall, we ran totally out of water. We wouldn't have another drink until we got to shore. In the previous five days, the six of us had drunk a total of two five-gallon emergency jugs of water. Actual average consumption had only been a little over a quart a day.

When we sailed in under the lee of Point Conception, the wind died. The delivery skipper and the druggie tried to start the engine one last time. No matter how much spray they aimed down the air intake, it wouldn't start. They decided the fuel filter must be dirty and changed it. The engine refused to start. They decided they needed to bleed the fuel lines, but the user's manual wasn't on board. They had to guess which ports on the injection pump to open in the bleeding process. Still, the engine wouldn't start. Now the battery was beginning to turn the engine more slowly.

The delivery skipper voiced his exhaustion and decided to get some rest before doing anything more. At least some battery power would be left to work with when he was fresher. He went to bed, but the druggie continued working on the engine.

The on-deck watch sailed the boat in the dying breeze as far as they could. When it died completely, the boat stalled and the sails began to slat. Local knowledge was that, under Point Conception, the wind always came up around noon. All we had to do was wait.

Our expectation of "five more days" turned out to be wrong. Dawn of the sixth day found us under Point Conception still a half-day's sail west of Santa Barbara. We were totally out of food and water. Well, not totally. Later that day, I found a nearly empty jar of strawberry jam, which I'm afraid I didn't share.

With the commotion of trying to start the engine and the slatting of the sails, I couldn't sleep. Maybe I just wanted to get to shore and get off the boat. Maybe I had cabin fever.

I was dressed and ready to go on deck when I heard the druggie say, "Oh, it broke." I turned to see the druggie sitting by the engine with a pair of pliers in his hand. In the pliers was about an inch-and-a-half of the copper tubing that, up until a moment ago, had carried the diesel to the injection pump on the engine. The rest of the tubing was still in place on the engine. We had no way to repair the fuel line without new tubing. Without the engine, we were forced into sailing to Santa Barbara. Well, the wind was supposed to come up in the afternoon.

The delivery skipper got up and called the Harbor Master at Santa Barbara on his cell phone to see if they would come get us. They said they would help us once we got to the Santa Barbara breakwater, but they wouldn't come any further.

The delivery skipper called a tow service. They would come, but it was a three-hour run to get to us, plus the time to tow us to Santa Barbara, and two more hours to return home. The rates were high enough to make the delivery skipper get off the call without having the service come get us.

Finally, we got a tow from another sailboat bound for Santa Barbara. They dropped us at the harbor entrance. The Santa Barbara Harbor Master came out and pushed us into a slip, 16 days after leaving Hawaii.

Showers and a nice lunch made a big difference in our outlook. The delivery skipper wanted to get emergency repairs and be off for Los Angeles as soon as possible. One by one, the boatyard worker, the vegetarian, the ethics graduate, and I each explained we would get off here rather than continue to Los Angeles. Only the druggie helped the delivery skipper make the last leg.

After lunch, the four of us who had left the boat were walking down the dock together. I asked the ethics graduate, "Well, Mr. Ethics, after all your studies, are we justified in jumping ship?"

"Yes," he answered. "Implicit in a verbal contract today is the concept that humane conditions will be provided. They failed to do that."

Chapter 21

The North Pacific High

The endless sunny summer days in California are a result of a high-pressure system that forms a thousand miles west of Seattle. As the ocean warms in the summer, the high gains in size and strength, and it becomes the dominant weather feature in the north Pacific. Low-pressure systems traveling across the north Pacific from the Orient to the States are diverted to the north by the strength of the North Pacific High.

Sailing along the southern edge of the high in light winds and flat seas, the majesty of the ocean takes on a mystical beauty. Sailing for a few days in such astounding beauty changes the souls of men.

"I just got the weather map," said Harry, as he stepped from the cabin into the dark of the cockpit. "The high is in almost the same place it was yesterday. Still just as strong."

I'd been looking up at the stars. Harry looked up, too. With no man-made light for hundreds of miles, the stars seemed much bigger than anywhere else on Earth. The Moon shone down on the water. The light shattered into a thousand tiny sparkles on the slowly undulating sea. The boat sailed gently over the dark blue ocean, making two small lines of bright sparkles behind us.

For the last two days, the wind had been easing off. Until yesterday, we had just enough wind to sail by. The boat was moving well, but more slowly now. If we slowed down much more, we'd have to turn on the engine to keep a fair boat speed. As the waves diminished, the boat took on a more gentle motion. The silent stillness of the ocean seemed in as much awe of this place as Harry and I.

Yesterday afternoon, a few small clouds occasionally spotted the sky overhead. At the horizon, the even height of the scattered cloud bottoms made them appear overlapped and close together. The sensation of a ring of clouds all around the horizon and a clear overhead gave me the feeling of being exactly in the center of the high. I felt I could look up into the face of nature.

I tried to shake the feeling and looked north over the rail toward where I knew the center of the high was located. The calm water seemed to go on forever. I had the sensation I could see over the curvature of the unbroken horizon and on to where the center of the high truly was. Intellectually, I knew I couldn't see that far, I knew the calm water under the high continued for hundreds of miles. It was just a feeling.

The beauty of the calm in the high was overpowering for me. The tricks my senses played on me added to the strength of my feelings. If ever a sacred place on Earth existed for me, this surely was it.

Maybe the calm, reserved power of the ocean made this place feel so special. Or, maybe the difficulty of the heavy beat coming north from Hawaii through the Trades made this quiet part of the ocean so intense. Or, maybe the reason was knowing this place was so hard to get to that few people ever experience it. Or, maybe just being alone in one of the most beautiful places on Earth brought Harry and me to a state of wonderment and awe.

"Harry. . . ." I didn't know how to say what I was feeling. We both stared at the giant stars a while longer and felt the small waves pass gently under the boat. The night was warm and comforting.

"It's beautiful, isn't it," Harry helped me out.

"Yeah." I tried again. I still couldn't find the words.

Finally, I realized I didn't have the words. Even so, I wanted to share this place with everyone who felt beauty in the world. Staring up into a million sparkles, I asked Harry, "How do you explain this to anyone?"

Across the cockpit in the dark, Harry answered, "You can't."

Part III

The New Zealand Trip

The New Zealand Adventure

Sometimes sailors get crazy ideas. And some crazy sailors try to follow their ideas. My first ocean passage was the race from San Francisco to Hawaii. When I returned home from that race, I began to dream of sailing the ocean on a longer adventure. It was just a dream, but it wouldn't go away.

Seven years later, I sailed out beneath the Golden Gate Bridge bound for the South Pacific. It would be a year-and-a-half before I returned.

The following are from the New Zealand adventure.

I Am a Sextant

I am a sextant.
Carefully made, accurately scribed, all silver and black,
fitted with filters and lenses and a micrometer screw.
Carefully held, I do a function not understood.

I hold the sextant.
Alone on the boat, eight days out on a blue and white ocean,
working quickly with steady hands at twilight's end.
I am driven, but where I must go, I do not know.

Chapter 22

Getting My Leave Approved

In the late 1980s, my employer had a policy called "Once in a Lifetime." The idea was to permit an employee to pursue an opportunity big enough and spectacular enough to happen only once in that employee's life.

The policy allowed an employee to take a year off without pay to pursue the opportunity, and then to return with no pay cut. On the other hand, if the employee didn't report for work on the first day after the leave, he automatically resigned.

To an avid sailor, this sounded like an invitation to go sailing.

"No. There isn't any form. Just write a letter." My boss was rather unclear about how to apply for a "Once in a Lifetime" leave. He did agree sailing to New Zealand was certainly an unusual opportunity. My proposed departure was over a year away. He had more immediate concerns on his mind. In fact, I could feel his desire to return to the problem he was working on before I popped into his office with my question.

Unfortunately, I hadn't even told him the worst part yet. To sail to New Zealand and back, I needed the year's leave, plus all the vacation I could save before departure, plus two extra months—which no corporate policy covered—unless I wanted to sail during hurricane season somewhere along the way. Two extra months for which I had no way to apply.

Well, if they would grant 12 months without pay, maybe they would grant 14 months without pay. Or, maybe they wouldn't.

I only had one way to find out. My boss said write a letter, so I did. In the letter, I requested the one year "Once in a Lifetime" leave. I proposed my plan for saving my vacation days and combining them with the leave. I outlined the hurricane season off the Mexican Coast and in the South Pacific. And, I requested two extra months of leave without pay to avoid the hurricane season. I wanted to be away from April 1, 1987 to October 1, 1988—one year of leave, four months of vacation, and two months of whatever they wanted to call it.

I had no idea what management's response would be to the extra two months, but I wanted to sail to New Zealand. The idea of sailing in a northern hemisphere summer, a southern hemisphere summer, and a second northern hemisphere summer was just too good. I could sail for a year-and-a-half, and skip winter.

My hopes for a quick response weren't satisfied. New product announcement dates were established long before my request was submitted. They were the most important thing on my boss's agenda. I had no response to my request.

I had a 45-foot cruising boat built—a Norseman 447 with a center cockpit and an aft stateroom—bigger and more complex than any boat I'd ever owned. This boat was big enough to live on and carry all the things I wanted to take along, as well as big enough to sail in all the conditions I expected to find between San Francisco and New Zealand. And small enough to be sailed short-handed.

When you have a boat built, you get to choose a great many things. By this time, I'd had a variety of experiences on many different boats. I'd worked with lots of things I did and didn't like. In ordering the boat, I chose the things I liked, decided how to resolve the tradeoffs, and wrote an eight-page letter of specifications to the builder.

Some of the normal choices were a cutter rig, an oiled teak interior, a dining table that would seat six for dinner, a three-burner stove with oven and broiler, and a refrigerator/freezer. The refrigeration system had two compressors: one was belt-driven by the main engine and the other ran on 110 provided by the boat generator or dockside power.

The boat was built with rod rigging, removable staysail stay, break-away forward lowers, stairs on the mast, 13 winches, hydraulic backstay and boom vang, and a windlass/wildcat on the bow.

Not all my choices were perfect. When I chose brown for the boot top and sail cover, I made a mistake. Later, when I was talking with the boat designer, he asked me what color I'd chosen for the boot top. When I told him brown, he declared in a huff, "Brown? Brown's got no place on a boat!"

Norseman 447s were normally built with three opening ports in the hull on each side. In a bad storm, I was afraid of the boat falling off a big wave, slamming down on the low side of the boat, and punching the entire frame and window right out of the hull, leaving a big hole in the low side of the boat. So, I specified an unusual thing, no opening ports forward or amidships. By not having opening ports, I could have more storage lockers installed and lay out the forward head for better access from the fore-cabin.

When the boat was delivered, I berthed her at the Richmond Yacht Club and started fitting her out for short-handed, long-distance cruising. Now that I actually had the boat, I wondered if management at work would let me have the two extra months and allow me to sail to New Zealand. But no word came down from on high.

I had a long list of things to buy and do to get ready. I ordered sails: big and little jib tops, a big staysail, a storm staysail, a big reacher/drifter for off wind, and a main with three reefs. I installed the electronic navigation equipment, the ham radio, the VHF radio, and a cassette player.

The deadlines at work kept me at the office with no letup in overtime. Whenever I wasn't at the office, I was working on the boat. I installed 400 amp hours of battery power, a battery charger, and a 3.5 KW generator. I rebuilt the space under the master bunk in the aft stateroom to hold an inflatable dinghy while at sea. And, I bought a medium-size dinghy with hard floorboards and an eight-horsepower outboard.

I tried smiling at my boss and watching his face for any hint of trouble or success. He must have had troubles. I decided it mustn't have anything to do with me.

I sailed the boat for fun and sea trials. I wanted to know what worked and what didn't. The boat seemed solid, but the small storm jib didn't have a good sheet lead. So, I added huge pad eyes on the side of the dog house and big turning blocks.

I ordered an eight-gallon-per-hour desalinator in unassembled form and installed the parts in the aft cabin wherever there was space. Then, I wired the motors, plumbed the pumps and filters, and piped the fresh water output to the ship's water tank.

I reviewed my old celestial navigation book, bought a sextant, and practiced with a simulated horizon in the backyard. I found I could get within a ten-mile radius if I didn't make any mistakes in the sight reduction. However, my mistakes were so frequent, I bought a handheld engineering computer with a programming chip for reducing star sights.

Summer was nearly over when upper management moved a few lower managers around and split up my department. When I reported to my new department, my new manager knew I'd put in a request for a leave without pay, but never mentioned whether it would be granted. And not a word about the extra two months!

It was still nine months to departure. I had to assume I would get the time off.

I added twin poles to the foredeck, a radar reflector at the second spreader, cushions in the cockpit, and pots and pans in the galley. I had a stern ladder built with a release that could be pulled from the water. I strengthened the transom and mounted a wind vane. The sea trials with the wind vane turned out to be extensive. I spent a lot of time experimenting and learning how to make it steer the boat.

Working on the boat only at night and on weekends made for slow progress. Summer was gone and winter was in full force in San Francisco. Still no word on my leave.

My departure date was only seven months away. I had to finish getting the boat ready, but I was beginning to worry about my leave. Am I doing all this work and spending all this money on a pipe dream that will never happen? Had the change in managers somehow messed things up?

I installed a below-deck autopilot and it worked like a champ. I had a dodger and a bimini installed. Then, I had a side panel made that would close off the windward side of the cockpit from the dodger to the aft end of the bimini. I borrowed a sewing machine and made a sun awning that would cover the whole boat at anchor. Then I modified it to collect rain water. I installed safety lines and pad eyes in the cockpit so I'd have something solid to clip my harness to in a storm. I bought a two-step boarding ladder, which made getting from the dingy up onto the boat much easier. My doctor helped me put together an extensive medical kit, taught me how to give shots, and gave me information on how to tie sutures.

Still no decision on my 18-month request. In five months, I was personally committed to leaving on a grand adventure. I was going to go, even if I didn't get the two extra months! I had no idea where I would go if I didn't have time to sail to New Zealand and back. I just had the fever.

I mounted a four-man life raft in hard canister on the aft deck, which served as a small cocktail table between two low lawn chairs. I hoped I'd never need it for its primary purpose. I made and installed a rack for 120 cassettes, and as many feet of bookshelf as I could squeeze into the boat. I installed a barometer and even a pencil sharpener. I had two long deck bags made for the two jib tops and tied them along the rail on both sides of the foredeck. Sail changes became a lot easier when I didn't have to push the old sail below and carry the new one up on deck. I studied for and obtained a General Class ham license.

For the better part of a year, I'd been working on the boat every spare moment. It sure would be nice to sail off into the sunset. With only four months left before my leave I couldn't understand why management hadn't responded to my request.

In January, the new plant accounting calendar was published showing the holiday schedule for the new year. I'd carried a few more unused vacation days into the new year than I expected, so my previous request was no longer quite right. I wrote a new letter to my new boss laying out my new plan.

In for a penny, in for a pound, I thought. I added my extra saved vacation days and the new movable holidays to the 18 months in my last letter and said I planned to leave six work days earlier. I wondered if I would get a response to this letter or from this manager. They *had* to say something pretty soon, I was leaving in two-and-a-half months.

What if they didn't give me the extra two months? Should I try to go to New Zealand anyway and risk the hurricane season to get back? Should I change the plan and go somewhere else? Where? Stay in the Northern Hemisphere? Japan? That would be a big change, but it might be a possibility.

I'd added so much stuff to the boat, she was already down on her lines. When I repainted the bottom, assuming I was leaving in two months, I painted the water line up an inch-and-a-half. When I loaded the cruising anchors and chain, the extra bottom paint disappeared into the water. I built a table for the cockpit that was just big enough for two dinner plates and silver.

Six weeks before departure, I still hadn't heard about my request for a leave. So, I invited my manager, his manager, and their families to go sailing on a Saturday afternoon. Ostensibly, I wanted them to know how I would be living for the year-and-a-half while I was gone. We had a nice sail, and I reminded them I was planning on leaving in a little over a month. They were sociable, but no one mentioned the status of my leave.

I built high life lines and installed them. I bought charts of New Zealand waters and all the places on the way from San Francisco to New Zealand. I made rat guards and put them on board. I bought canned goods and varnished the cans. I rubbed Vaseline® on six dozen never-refrigerated eggs. I made arrangements to rent my house to a friend who was getting divorced. I left the furniture and paintings, but started moving all my other stuff into storage. About the only thing left was my guitar, which would go with me on the trip.

About three weeks before departure, the third-level boss, the guy everyone looks up to, appeared in the door to my office. "Tell me again why you need the two extra months?" he asked flatly.

I was sick.

In my surprise, I started trying to explain about the distances and the speed of the boat. Inside my head, I wondered if I could find a copy of my first letter. Verbally, I fumbled around about the hurricane season. I knew I wasn't explaining it well. I couldn't even remember what I'd just said, but I had a strong need to keep talking.

"Oh," he said. "You're doing it for safety." He smiled and disappeared.

Itinerary

During the trip, I wrote a newsletter every two or three months to my friends back home. The first letter, written before leaving, carried this itinerary, a result of coordinating with my friends who would be joining me for their vacations.

DENOUEMENT
SAILING ITINERARY (quite tentative)

	miles	time
March 30:		
SF to Nuku Hiva, Marquesas Islands	2,900	19 - 31 days
Early May:		
Nuku Hiva to Hiva Oa	85	Overnight
Late May:		
Hiva Oa to Manihi, Tuamoto Islands	500	3 - 4 days
Manihi to Rangiroa	100	1 day
Early June:		
Rangiroa to Tahiti, Society Islands	225	2 days
Late June:		
Tahiti to Moorea	12	Morning
Morea to Huahine	80	Overnight
Huahine to Raiatea	25	Morning
Raiatea to Bora Bora	25	Morning
July 22:		
Bora Bora to Niue	1,050	6 - 9 days
Niue to Vava'u, Tonga	225	2 days
Vava'u (via many small islands)	170	???
August 13:		
Nuku'alofa to Suva, Fiji	400	3 - 4 days
October 21:		
Suva to Auckland (?), New Zealand	1,200	8 - 12 days
(Fly to Australia for a month of sight seeing.)		
April 5, 1988:		
New Zealand to Tubuai, Austral Islands	2,200	15 - 22 days
Tabuai to Tahiti	330	2 - 3 days
Tahiti to Rangiroa, Tuamotu Islands	225	3 - 5 days
July 5:		
Rangiroa to Hawaii	2,300	15 - 25 days
Hawaii to SF	2,100	19 - 28 days

Chapter 23

The Cast Party

Richness and complexity are necessary parts of every grand adventure. If the adventure is grand enough, the complexity will involve many more people than those on the boat anchored in a tropical lagoon.

I knew I wanted to have the bills paid and the rent collected while I was gone. And April 15th would come and go before I'd return. Something on the boat might break or wear out. Various people wanted to take vacation and join me for a passage. As I sailed from island to island, I wanted to write a newsletter for my friends back home.

All in all, I needed a staff back home.

"Butch, meet Joe. Joe is going to pay my bills while I'm gone. He's the guy who'll bring you the year-end statements, so you can file my taxes next spring." I turned to Joe. "Joe, this is Butch. He's my accountant and he'll be doing my taxes." We were standing in my living room and the doorbell rang again. "Butch, if I owe anything on my taxes, Joe will write the checks. You guys need to get to know each other." I could hear voices outside. "Excuse me, I have to get the door."

As I turned toward the front door, I could hear Joe explaining I'd already gone through last year's taxes and made a list of the statements they'd need for the next year. It ought to be easy, he'd just watch for the statements. . . .

I opened the door for Rick and Sandy. They were going to crew on the Tonga to New Zealand passage. Rick was one of the best sailors I knew and I was grateful to have him sail with me. "Rick! Sandy!

153

Come in. Great to see you." I was looking forward to our passage to New Zealand and their good company.

In addition to crewing on the Tonga to New Zealand leg, Rick was going to act as my repair coordinator back home. If I broke something on the boat and needed a replacement part or materials, Rick would go shopping for me and ship it . . . assuming we could figure out where he should ship it.

"Hi," Rick said, sticking out his hand. "I looked through the copies of all the boat manuals you dropped off. You must have spent hours in front of the copying machine. I can't believe it. Parts explosions of the engine, technical manuals on all the electronics, everything."

"Yeah. I hope we never need to dig into any of them," I replied. "But, if we do, I'll have a copy on board and you'll have another copy here. Come in, come in. You need to meet Joe, he's the bill payer. I hope you won't have any bills, but a year-and-a-half of hard use . . . you may need to see him before I get back."

As Rick and Sandy stepped past me through the door, Rick said, "You know, Dale, you sure have come a long way since we were frostbiting in Chicago. This is going to be a great sailing adventure."

"Well," I replied, "You got me out of Chicago." *With the help of a little cold weather,* I thought, as Rick and Sandy headed off toward Joe.

I turned to pull the door shut, but Paul and Suzette were coming up the front walk, introducing themselves to Connie. "So, you're going to sail with Dale in French Polynesia. That's great!" replied Connie.

"Yes, we're looking forward to it. A private yacht in French Polynesia. Are we lucky! Are you going to sail with Dale?" Paul asked.

"No, I'm doing the newsletter on this end. Oh, hi, Dale! I think it's neat you're going to write about your adventures. And I'm glad I get to read the newsletters before anyone else does. I have the mailing list you gave me all set up in my computer."

"Hi, Connie . . . Hi, Paul . . . Suzette . . . come in," I said. "Connie, you need to meet everyone. They'll probably all end up in the newsletter, one way or another. Paul and Suzette, you need to meet Rick, he's the boat-repair expert. Joe will get the mail, pay the bills, and make a bundle of mail to forward to me. When you fly down, get the most recent bundle from Joe and bring it with you. That's probably the best way for me to get mail. I hope I won't need any spare parts from Rick, but get to know him anyway. We've sailed a lot of miles together."

As they stepped inside, I saw Jerry had just parked his car and was getting out. I couldn't seem to leave the doorway.

"Hi, Jerry. Glad you could make it. Come in."

"Thanks, Dale. I'm glad this is working out. I'm kind of at loose ends right now."

"Yeah, I know. I'm glad you're going to be here, too. This way, the house won't stand empty while I'm gone. And you'll have a place to call home for a while. Maybe it'll let you get settled a little." Jerry was just starting through a divorce and his life was pretty much up in the air. "Let me introduce you to Rick, the guy over there. The two of you have sailing in common. He sailed in the 1970 Mackinac Race, the one I told you about with the bad storm. Maybe you can get him to tell you what happened on his boat."

"Thanks for leaving the furniture. I don't have much right now," Jerry said.

I was on such a high, and Jerry, obviously, felt miserable. Well, I was glad he showed up tonight. "No problem. In fact, it saves me having to move everything into storage, and then back into the house again. You might want to meet Joe, too, the one over there. He's the one you'll send the rent checks to."

Bruce, Lina, and Nick were walking up the drive. Apparently, they had driven together. "Hi, Bruce. Hi, Nick," mumbled Joe, and then he went inside.

"Hi, Jerry." They all said, but mostly to Jerry's back. "Hi, Dale."

"My loyal and dedicated crew!" I replied. Bruce and Lina were going to crew the first leg, from San Francisco to French Polynesia. And Nick was on the return leg back from Tonga to Hawaii.

Bruce had named his boat Razzberries, and he remained true to form. "There's an old British sailing custom called 'mutiny.' I think you might want to read up on it a little." Then, more seriously, Bruce asked, "How's Jerry doing? I heard the news."

"I think he'll be all right," said Nick. "He's just going through the bad part right now. He has a lot of friends who'll give him support as soon as he can deal with everything again."

"Come in." Once again, I went through my list of who they might want to meet and why.

By now, the front room and kitchen were full of such questions as, "How do you know Dale?" and "Well, I know what a lot of these people are going to do for Dale. What's your job?" and "Let's trade phone numbers. We'll need to talk while he's gone."

Hey, Everybody! Can I have your attention for a second?" I called out. "Terry phoned and said he couldn't make it. Terry is the ham radio guy. I have a ham radio on the boat, and Terry and I will be in touch occasionally. Terry will be glad to relay messages from anyone, so take down this phone number."

I had no more than given out Terry's number, when someone asked, "Hey, Dale! What're you going to do with all this wine in your liquor cabinet?" Some of my sailing friends were less shy than others.

"Uh, nothing. I'm going to be gone for a year-and-a-half. Help yourselves."

They did.

The boat I chose to sail to New Zealand and back was a cutter rigged, center cockpit, Norseman 447. It would take me on my greatest sailing adventure.

I wanted to give it a name that reflected my relationship to sailing and this trip. To help everyone at the christening party understand the name, I displayed the dictionary definition.

De·noue·ment

(Fr. dā'·nōō'·män')

1. The revelation or sudden understanding that occurs when the threads of a plot come together at the end of a drama or a story.

2. The point in the plot where this occurs.

3. The untying or unraveling of a knot.

Chapter 24

The Circle of Water

Shortly before our departure to the Marquesas in French Polynesia, Island Magazine reported in its feature article: "The Marquesas are, in fact, the most remote islands on the face of the Earth: the island group that is farthest from any continent."[4]

3,500 miles west of Peru

2,500 miles southeast of Hawaii

3,000 miles southwest of San Francisco

On our passage from San Francisco to the Marquesas, Denouement sailed at about the same speed I jog. But, as they say, getting there is half the fun.

The boat was ready. Well, almost. I stowed the last few projects on board to do "along the way." All systems were "go," so, by definition, the boat was ready.

Bruce and Lina had taken a month's vacation and were eager to experience their first ocean passage. They would sail from San Francisco to French Polynesia with me on Denouement. They loaded their personal gear on board and we sailed out under the Golden Gate Bridge on March 31, 1987. It would be 18 months and 15,000 miles under sail before I would sail back in beneath the Golden Gate.

Finally, I was off on my grand sailing adventure to New Zealand. After leaving the US, the Marquesas Island chain in northeastern French Polynesia was the first place I could drop anchor. The ocean was "bottomless" for the 3,000 miles from San Francisco to Hiva Oa.

---

[4] *Island* magazine. P.O. Box 210, Sandy Bay, Tasmania 7006 Australia. August 1985.

When the shoreline disappeared into the haze behind us, we stopped looking back. Other than the boat, the only thing we could see was water and a few clouds. We knew we were on our way!

I set watches using the Swedish watch system—six hours on and six off during the day, and three on and three off at night. The transition from sleeping eight hours at night in a bed to sleeping less than three hours at a time in a moving bunk left us all a little blurry-eyed.

Thank goodness for the five hours of sleep in the daytime. I could almost catch up. As the days and nights passed, my mind adjusted to the new pattern. Rest came more easily in short periods. Or, maybe I just got more tired and slept better.

Once we were on the passage, I joined the roll call on the Pacific Maritime Net on the ham radio. These ham operators are dedicated to making daily contact with sailboats on passages in the Pacific. The late afternoon is devoted to general calling and conversation. But, each evening, the net turns formal and calls the roll of all the boats that have joined the net. Roll call starts with the boat that has been at sea the longest, and ends with boats just beginning their passage. When a boat arrives at its destination, it drops off the roll call and the boats lower in the list move up.

The best thing about roll call was the weather information. The boats on roll call were scattered all over the ocean, and reported the weather and sea conditions they were experiencing. One or two boats always seemed to be somewhere ahead of us, giving us a glimpse of what we would sail into, so I listened every night with great regularity. When my turn on roll call came up, I reported my weather, hoping someone headed my way would find it interesting.

The name of my boat turned out to be frustrating. Everyone on the net wanted to know the name of the boat. I guess I should have been glad they were interested. Time and again, they asked me to spell the name. I did: Delta, Echo, November, Oscar, Uniform, Echo, Mike, Echo, November, Tango. They had just as much trouble after I spelled it as before. No one on the net ever had any idea what the name of the boat was or how to pronounce it. Never again will I pick such a sophisticated name for a boat.

After our first few days, time began to suspend. Our orientation became the boat and the water around us. Our old orientation, where time was important, began to fade from consciousness. Little by little, we stopped relating to time. Time was a number I copied from a device on the bulkhead into the log. It didn't have meaning like wind strength and direction, which I also copied into the log. I suppose this must have been the psychological beginning of my cruise.

Location also began to suspend—no buildings, no trees, no hills, and no landmarks passing by. All I could see outside the boat was an unbroken circle of water and a flat horizon. Seated in the cockpit, with my eyes about six feet above the water, I could see waves for a few miles. Beyond the horizon, the waves were behind the curvature of the Earth and the sky reached down to hide them.

The boat sailed in the center of the circle of water. The horizon always stayed the same distance away. The water rushed by under the hull, and the numbers on the Sat Nav changed. But the circle of water didn't.

About a hundred miles offshore, just before entering the waters off Mexico, the Coast Guard flew over us in a jet. A few hours later, a 150-foot Coast Guard cutter came steaming into our circle from astern. Because they were obviously pursuing us, Lina, Bruce, and I looked at each other and wondered what they wanted, and how serious they were. As they came along side on port, I could see they had an armed boarding party ready. Their inflatable tender was hoisted, over the side, and ready to drop in the water.

We had visions of emptying all the lockers to prove we had no drugs. Denouement was so heavily loaded, it would have created a havoc of canned goods, flour, toothpaste, and spare parts . . . all in the middle of the boat as it rolled and bounced from wave to wave.

From their deck, they used an electric bull horn to ask questions. I tried to shout answers back. What port were we out of? When did we leave? Where were we bound? I asked if we could do this on the VHF radio, but they flatly refused and continued asking questions. Then, without explanation, the cutter dropped back a few hundred yards, and followed us for a while. About half an hour later, they came alongside again with a few more questions. The last question was a request to spell the name of the boat. I guess they figured if I could spell the name, then everything was all right. They thanked me and departed.

Our circle of water was empty again.

Two days later, a storm overtook us. When I looked out at the water, the waves all had white caps. When it rained hard, the circle got smaller. When the rain stopped, the circle returned to its original size and continued to hold us in its center.

Sailing south in the northern trades was sailing at its best—wind on the quarter, warm weather, and 180 miles every day. The wind held all night. We plunged along just as fast at night as in the daylight. After the Moon set—with only stars in the sky—the darkness was nearly complete. Only the navigation lights provided any illumination. I could see my way around on deck a little, but nothing out to sea. Only blackness existed where the circle of water had been all day. I felt a mild surge of concern about plunging forward at full speed, while not being able to see anything in the total darkness ahead. Even though I knew nothing lay in front of me for thousands of miles, my mind and my emotions weren't in the same place.

The numbers on the Sat Nav changed continuously. At noon each day, the person on watch would go below and write the noon numbers in the log. The Sat Nav, not the circle of water, measured our progress. I wasn't sure whether to trust the numbers on the Sat Nav or my own senses.

The winds dropped off as we approached the Doldrums. Then the light-to-nothing breeze was punctuated by blasts from infrequently passing storm clouds. In a windless and drifting day, the occasional storm winds were highly exciting. Bruce started watching the clouds as they appeared over the horizon behind us, watching for a cloud that would pass close by the boat.

When a cloud looked like it would be close, Bruce would steer the boat way off course, trying to drift over in front of the cloud. When he made it, the wind would come up, and the exciting ride would begin again. Then, Bruce would steer back onto the course to French

Polynesia and the boat would rush along in front of the storm. If he didn't manage to get in front of the approaching cloud, the boat would drift in the wrong direction for a while. All in all, we figured we were making better time to Hiva Oa by trying to get in front of any cloud we could. Maybe we were all just bored and needed a little excitement.

The best clouds had rain in them, enough rain for a shower if you were quick. And I was quick! If I weren't quick enough, the rain would stop just as I got all soapy, usually with some soap in my eyes. Then, the rain shower would suddenly be over and I'd have to do a salt-water rinse.

At the equator, Lina summoned the rest of us to King Neptune's Court. Lina had lived in South America and declared herself a shellback. The rest of us were lowly polliwogs. After a proper ceremony, including certification and champagne, we were all declared shellbacks and the feasting began.

The GPS told us we were in south latitudes now, but the water and sunshine looked just the same. When we had absolutely no wind, we fired up the engine and powered south in our still-unmoving circle of water.

Just south of the equator, the reacher/drifter halyard broke. The full hoist 155 percent nylon reacher/drifter went over the side into the water—all except the tack and clew. With all hands on deck, we pulled the sail back on board and looked at the halyard. It had frayed through a couple of feet from the shackle that attached to the head of the sail. This suggested the exit box or the block at the top of the mast was involved. In any event, we needed the sail. The only thing to do was relead the halyard.

With all of us pulling on the halyard, I went up the mast. At the top, I couldn't take my eyes off the circle of water. It was huge, bigger than anything I had ever seen! I felt I could see forever but, even so, nothing was in the circle.

The gentle rolling of the boat on the small swells was multiplied by the lever arm of the 60-foot mast. The men who sailed square riggers were much tougher than I. I came down as quickly as possible.

When the southern trades filled in, they were lighter than the northern trades had been. Now the Sat Nav changed more quickly than in the Doldrums, but more slowly than in the northern trades. Oddly enough, the circle never moved and never changed. I began to feel we were standing still and would never see land again.

On the 26th day, the Sat Nav told us the island of Hiva Oa was just a day's sail ahead. We might see land before dark the next day. It would be close.

The next day, the circle of water looked just like the day before and the day before that. We sailed all day, watching the clouds to see if we could spot a single cloud standing still over the island. No luck. They all seemed to move downwind with the trades. And none stood still in our circle.

Bruce and Lina decided it was my responsibility as navigator to produce the island from the sea. As navigator, I hadn't been able to make the circle of water move for the last four weeks. I had no way of making it move now or of making an island rise up into it.

Just after sunset on the 27th day, Hiva Oa began to climb out of the sea, showing a dark shape over the horizon, just beyond our circle of water. The dark shadow against the red of the dusk in the tropics was incredibly dramatic. We celebrated! When the island crossed the horizon and entered our circle of water, I declared myself a magician.

I measured the angular width with my sextant and plotted our distance from it. With a compass bearing, I had an exact location based on physical evidence. We were exactly where the Sat Nav told us we were.

We had dragged our circle of water from the northern hemisphere to the southern hemisphere. We had brought it to Paradise.

Chapter 25

Red Sky a'Morning

The ocean has moments of staggering beauty. Being on watch at sunset is often breath-taking, but the transition at dawn can be equally inspiring.

The passage from Hiva Oa to Nuku Hiva was a wonderful overnight sail. It blew 10 to 15 on the beam all night long under a bright, starry sky. Until it set, the Moon led us across the ocean, leaving the stars all the more brilliant against the black sky.

I followed Denouement's dimly lit compass card across a peaceful, dark, gently rolling sea. The running lights seemed swallowed by a black blanket of night. The movement of the boat on unseen waves gave me a feeling of comfort and belonging.

Slowly, ever so slowly, the sky in the east lightened and turned red. The strengthening red in the sky mirrored itself across the water to the boat. Just before the Sun broke the horizon, the strength of the crimson climaxed. The red in the water was so intense, I felt I could walk on it back out to the horizon. As the upper edge of the Sun peeked over the red sea, sparkling rubies were scattered from the horizon to the boat.

In that flame red ocean, two silhouettes stood in black contrast: one was the tropical island of Ua Huka; the second was the elegant four-masted schooner, Sea Cloud.

Sea Cloud and Denouement were both bound for the same port on Nuka Hiva. The two boats sailed side-by-side in beauty and awe over a cherry red sea as it lightened to soft pink, and then to a blue-white morning.

Chapter 26

Galley Goulash

Cooking at sea is definitely not why I go sailing. I'd far rather be steering the boat, trimming the sails, or having a beer and watching the stars.

Cooking in a galley has all the challenges of cooking at home, and then some. Some problems are related to the work area—its limited size and erratic movements. Other problems are related to how long you've been at sea when you're trying to decide what to cook next. Still others relate to what country you're going to enter next and what you must eat before you get there.

All in all, every adventure has new experiences.

The second day out was always a struggle. My last off-watch period was six hours long, but after making my entry in the log and getting ready for bed, I only had four and a half hours to sleep before it was time to get dressed, cook, and go on watch again.

Intellectually, I knew I'd feel better after I adjusted to the new awake/sleep pattern required by the watch system. Right now, I was still in the transition between bed and bunk, and I was groggy.

I'd been through this transition before, and I planned especially easy meals for the first two days. The first meal had been roast chicken and premade potato salad picked up at the grocery store at the last minute.

Now, searching the cooler, I found a precooked stew and started heating it on the stove. I poured a package of spring mix salad into a bowl and dug the dressing out of the miscellaneous cooking supplies locker. The bread was still sitting out on top of the cooler because we had absolutely no space anywhere for the last three loaves.

Salad, stew, and bread. Voilà! Chef Denouement serves another outstanding gourmet dinner at sea!

My success was really dependent on the rest of the crew being as sleepy as I was. It worked. No one made the transition from an onshore routine to an at-sea routine easily. I was a culinary genius!

Over the next few days, I continued to pull magic out of the hat or at least precooked meals from the cooler—pregrilled steaks, chicken, and bratwurst. I never once used the word "leftovers."

It wasn't long before we fell into a pattern. Sleeping, personal grooming, navigating, reading, and cooking were all rearranged by the watch system. Living on board a boat bouncing over ocean waves was just tiring enough that everyone ended up doing what was easy.

On Denouement, we typically made our own breakfasts: cold cereal, hot instant cereal, breakfast bars, or coffee cake, and fruit, while it lasted. Coffee was normally made just before the end of the watch and placed in a thermos for the oncoming watch. If someone made sandwiches at lunch, usually they made enough for everyone who was awake.

At dinner, we all ate together, sharing the memories of the day. Normally, someone on watch would cook dinner before the change of watch and serve it at the change, bringing both watches together for a while. After dinner and the change of watch, someone on the new watch would clean up.

As we ate the precooked meals, small amounts of space began to appear in the cooler. Whenever the space became big enough, a loaf of bread or something that had been standing out found a new home in the cooler. Whenever we wanted something from the cooler, we would lift out the things on top and dig through the pile remaining in the cooler until we found it. Digging around, and then piling everything back on top created a jumble in the cooler. The contents began to look like a tossed salad of Tupperware®, bottles, and plastic bags.

The last of the fresh meat was a vacuum-packed irradiated beef tri-tip. Because the beef was irradiated, it lasted longer than all the other fresh meats. When the USA was three weeks behind us, the sell-by-date on the tri-tip was still in the future.

Eventually, the precooked meals and the irradiated meats were all eaten, and we had to switch over to canned and dry foods. Provisioning for this part of the trip had been similar to setting up a small grocery store, based on expected usage. I made a list of comparisons: I liked green beans about three times as much as corn. I didn't like beets at all. And so on. While this wasn't very accurate, it did give me a ratio of vegetables, and everything else, to buy.

After we left the USA, I thought we wouldn't find a grocery store until we arrived at Papeete, about three months into our cruise. For safety, I used the provisioning ratio to stock four months instead of three.

Four months meant 120 dinners and, I assumed, 120 vegetables. I applied the provisioning ratio to determine the number of each kind of canned vegetable, meat, fruit, and dessert. These I rounded up to the next case lot and headed off looking for a special deal at Costco. The calculations were crude, but it did put a small grocery store on the boat.

After the fresh and preprepared foods were all eaten, cooking required going to the boat grocery store to get the ingredients for the next meal. Canned goods were stored here. Dry goods were stowed there. Eggs were stored next to the hull below the water line where they would stay the same temperature as the water. It really was just like a tiny onboard grocery store.

The eggs had been wiped with Vaseline® to prevent dehydration. I removed the labels from all the cans because of stories about labels being washed off by bilge water. So I wouldn't serve a surprise for dinner, I marked the cans with an indelible pen, and then brushed them with varnish to prevent rusting.

After two or three weeks at sea, the remaining fresh fruit and vegetables were showing obvious signs of old age. The softer vegetables were gone and the roots were just beginning to wilt. The oranges and lemons were still doing pretty well.

The apples and oranges had started the passage on deck in a plastic lattice-work box. They had burlap wrapped all around the sides and over the top. Every watch, we poured a bucket of seawater over

171

the burlap and prayed evaporation would be more effective than the tropical Sun.

The soft fruits we stored in a hanging hammock in the main cabin, so they would be in the shade and have plenty of air while they ripened. And ripen they did. We still had a good supply left when we noticed the strings of the hammock were cutting into the bottom fruit. Fresh fruit juice was leaking from every cut and dripping from the bottom of the pile. The hammock bounced and swung as the boat rolled and pitched on every wave, while the strings cut deeper and deeper into the fruit. The swinging hammock distributed the juice evenly across the cabin.

During the first passage or two, I would go to the onboard grocery store every day to pick out the ingredients for the next dinner. While the boat rolled and pitched, I would rummage around below through the many lockers and bins to select the canned meat, vegetables, starch, and dessert for that evening's meal. Sometimes, as the boat rolled and pitched, saliva would begin to run in my mouth and I would have to hurry my search. My carefully selected dinner didn't always seem to taste like it should have.

Finally, I got smart enough to have a staging locker. Before each passage, I would dig through the canned goods at anchor, rather than in a rolling sea, and stage the things I expected to cook on the passage.

After a few months, I noticed some of the soda and beer cans weren't full when I opened them. And what was left inside was flat.

Stowing aluminum cans right-side up caused them to wear on the bottom as they slid a tiny bit with the movement of the boat. The wear created pinholes in the thin foot. A fine-looking can of beer only reveals how empty it is when it's picked up, its contents having long since been pumped overboard by the bilge pump.

The solution was to stow soda cans and beer cans on their tops, not their bottoms. The rolled seam at the top takes much more wear before developing a hole.

Canned meats provided good nourishment, but frozen meats were a treat we all looked forward to. The freezer on Denouement was filled to the brim, mostly with meats. Truly, frozen meats were a treasure in the "land" of no grocery stores.

About two weeks into the first passage, I dug into the freezer to select the prize for that night's dinner. When I opened the freezer, my nose told me all was not well. To my horror, the packages next to the front wall were soft, not frozen solid as they should have been. Slowly removing packages and checking each one led me to the terrible act of throwing almost all the meat overboard. Only the packages directly next to the cold plates were still frozen. The rest failed the squeeze-and-sniff test.

When the refrigeration system was installed, I tested the freezer. The thermometer hovered at around 20 degrees. Pretty good for a boat freezer! Then, on a weekend trip, I carried a frozen chicken for three days. Proof positive! Now, throwing spoiled meat overboard, I absolutely couldn't figure out what had gone wrong. I was sick at the loss of my prize dinner stash.

Eventually, greater knowledge replaced what I learned during my sea trials. For the passage to New Zealand, I had filled the freezer absolutely full. With the freezer full, the packages next to the cold plate acted as insulation for the adjacent packages, which acted as insulation for the next packages. The packages on the side opposite the cold plate were well insulated from the cold plate and slowly warmed to above freezing. No matter how much I ran the refrigeration, the cold plate never got any colder and neither did the packages opposite the cold plate.

Long before we arrived in Tahiti, the oranges and lemons were consumed, leaving the plastic lattice-work box without a current purpose. When I figured out the freezer problem, I made a liner for the freezer box from the plastic lattice-work box and some small blocks of wood. The liner kept everything in the freezer an inch-and-a-half away from the walls and bottom of the box. The air space provided good ventilation between the walls and the packages inside the liner. The circulation of cold air from the cold plate reached all around everything in the freezer. From that time on, we had less usable space in the freezer, but everything inside the lattice-work liner stayed frozen. In fact, on the return passage from Hawaii to San Francisco, we celebrated the halfway point with ice cream from the freezer.

I always thought I'd be able to catch fish and live off the ocean. At sea, I normally dragged a meat hook, a one-eighth inch Dacron line tied to the transom with a hundred-pound leader, and some kind of feather over a large hook. Not very sporting, but supposedly effective. Even so, fish for dinner was a rare treat, rather than a staple.

One time, I caught a tuna at sea. I dragged it until there was no fight left in it at all. Completely exhausted and not swimming, the tuna was still big enough that dragging it through the water at sailing speeds put quite a load on the eighth-inch line. To bring the fish up to the side of the boat while sailing, I had to wrap the eighth-inch line around a winch and crank it in. When the tuna was along side, I gaffed it and managed to swing it up over the life lines, onto the deck. After I killed the tuna, I wanted to carry it to the leeward rail to dress it out. By then, my excess adrenaline had worn off and I could no longer lift the fish. The best I could do was drag it across the deck.

This was the freshest tuna I'd ever had and I treated myself to a fine morsel. To my surprise, tuna in the supermarket tasted far better. However a few hours later, the sashimi was excellent. It was clear my taster was conditioned to aged fish.

We only ate a quarter of the tuna. We gave a quarter to the mayor of Ahe, a quarter to the owner of a mooring I used temporarily, and the rest to a boat with a pet cat named Tippy. The cat ate more tuna than I did and fell in love with my meager fishing abilities.

My meal planning called for sandwiches each day. I carried enough flour to bake all the bread we'd need. However, lying at anchor in French Polynesia, each morning I woke to the smell of fresh French bread being pulled out of the oven at the local *boulangerie*. French bread was baked fresh in every village and it was far better than the Irish Fisherman's bread I knew how to make on the boat.

My assumption of not being able to buy fresh bread led me into bad planning. Eventually, I threw away 15 pounds of flour.

When I left San Francisco, I wasn't concerned about the agriculture regulations in New Zealand. They seemed far away. In Tonga, with our next port of entry being New Zealand, the agriculture regulations seemed much more immediate. When we were walking on the beach, some young kids tried to sell us some shells. I remembered we couldn't take honey into New Zealand and wondered if they would bargain with me. I told the kids to wait and took the dinghy back to the boat.

When I arrived back where the kids were, they had been joined by their mothers, a neighbor or two, and a few more kids. I asked if they knew what honey was. They all nodded yes.

As a negotiating technique, I unscrewed the lid and stuck my finger into the honey, and then into my mouth. Then, I passed the honey jar to one of the mothers. She repeated my finger tasting. Her face lit up like a sunrise at sea.

Suddenly, she began speaking in Tongan and all the kids scattered. Moments later, they returned on the run with far-better shells. It doesn't pay to plan the provisioning too closely.

One time, while anchored in a lagoon just off a small village, a copra boat arrived under the hot noonday Sun. The boat was rusty from stem to stern, and it seemed to chug in from some Michener story just over the horizon.

The copra boat had barely come through the entrance to the lagoon when the village people started climbing into small boats and rowing out. By the time the copra boat had its anchor down, the small boats were converging on its starboard side, where a boarding net was being lowered.

The head man of the village told us everyone always went out to the copra boat to buy things. So, we decided we would, too. We didn't need anything; we just wanted to see a real copra boat.

After climbing up the boarding net, we followed everyone else without knowing where they were going. In a few moments, we arrived at the commissary on a lower forward deck. Commissary? What did we need? I had provisioned for everything I could think of. What did we need?

Ice cream!

Of course! So, we ordered ice cream.

What? It only comes in gallon cartons? Well, OK. Vanilla.

What do you do with a gallon of ice cream in the tropics? Sometimes, things just work out.

Chapter 27

Coral

Atolls are hardly islands at all. After volcanic action forms an island, sometimes the island slowly sinks back into the sea from its own weight. As the island sinks, the coral grows up to the surface of the water—first, around the shore of the island, and then around the outer perimeter of the coral. If the island sinks completely, the coral may form a ring around a lagoon where the volcanic island originally stood. Sometimes palm trees begin to grow on the coral perimeter, sometimes not.

Coral without vegetation presents the greatest danger to ocean sailors. From the deck of a boat, telling the difference between a wave with a white cap and a wave breaking over a coral head is nearly impossible. A large area of the Tuamotus is so infested with awash coral that no one dares go there.

Nuku Hiva lay three days behind us. The first atoll on the northwest end of the Tuamotus lay ten miles in front of us, in the black of night. Or, so the glowing numbers on the Sat Nav said.

We were bound for Ahe, a ring of coral about six miles wide and thirteen miles long. Inside the coral perimeter, the entire center was a lagoon, spotted with a few coral heads. In the dark, we couldn't see anything ahead of the boat—no trees, no lights, no nothing.

When the Sat Nav gave you a fix, it had a normal working error of a couple of miles. After that, the dead reckoning continuously introduced more error. With nothing closer than a few hundred miles, the Sat Nav was fine for open ocean navigation.

Approaching an unlit coral ring in the dark requires much more precision. It wouldn't do to verify the error in our navigation by driving the boat up onto something hard, which our dead reckoning said was still a mile ahead. In an hour-and-a-half, we'd be there. It was still pitch black.

Fear disguised itself as prudence. We altered course and sailed back out to sea to stand off for the night.

The detailed chart of the pass showed we would be heading southeast when we entered. If we entered early in the morning, the rising Sun would be nearly ahead of us. The Sun's glancing rays and reflections on the water would hide any coral heads in our path. Entering the pass later in the day would be better—with the Sun behind us. Then, the Sun would be shining down into the water at the same angle at which we'd be looking into the water for coral heads.

About halfway through the night, we turned around and headed back toward Ahe. At 8 A.M., we first saw the palm trees rising from the horizon. The atoll itself was low enough that the land didn't come into view until the palm trees grew to full height. Then, the low tropical growth connected the base of the trees and drew a green line at the water's edge.

From the chart of Ahe and Charlie's Charts[5], we knew the pass was a little south of the northwest corner of the island. Charlie's Charts even noted the exact latitude and longitude of the entrance. Our dead reckoning showed the latitude and longitude of our position, but this was based on the last Sat Nav fix. The Sat Nav was good enough to find the atoll in the daylight, but it wasn't good enough to find the pass. We'd have to find the pass by sight.

As we sailed past the northwest corner of the atoll, we gave the unknown coral shore a fair berth. Sailing what we hoped was a safe distance offshore, we began watching for the pass into the lagoon.

Sailing southwest along the western edge of the atoll, we watched the low tropical island slide by. The land barely rose up from the water and looked as though it might wash away at any time. The palm trees seemed more substantial than the land. Certainly, they rose higher above the water. The lower vegetation grew right down to the

---

[5] *Charlie's Charts of Polynesia,* by Charles E. Wood. Surry, BC, Canada: Charlie's Charts, 1983.

water. In a few places, though, the tropical vegetation had never obtained a foothold and raw coral could be seen between waves rolling up on the shore. In one place, a big stick had become stuck upright in the coral. It was a classic tropical island, a band of brilliant tropical greens with a few palm trees, trapped in time between a dark blue ocean and a light blue sky.

We continued watching for the pass and sailed slowly southwest. We had read some entrances were identified by range markers. Instead of big navigational lights like in the US, the upper-range marker might be a church halfway up a hill across the lagoon from the entrance. And the lower-range marker might be a large cross in front of the church down by the edge of the lagoon. The two structures would define a line that crossed the lagoon and passed through the middle of the entrance. We didn't see any buildings at all, but we kept looking.

More coral atoll and green vegetation drifted passed us on our left. We were now off the middle of the western side of the atoll. I thought we should have seen the entrance by this time. We began wondering all kinds of things. Were the charts right? Did the Sat Nav have more error in it this time than normal for some reason? Had the coral grown back, closing the pass since the charts were drawn?

We had no idea what was wrong. We just stared at the entire western side of Ahe and asked ourselves stupid questions. As we tried to create some answers, astern of us and to our left, where we had just sailed by, a fishing boat came through the palm trees and out into the ocean.

It's amazing how long the human mind can hold onto two absolutely contradictory concepts. There was no pass there; the fishing boat came out of the pass.

With absolute disbelief, we headed back to where the fishing boat had come through the trees. Sure enough, the break in the coral was big enough to allow boats to enter.

To see the break in the coral, we had to be close to the shore and exactly in line with the entrance. Even then, the palms on the other side of the lagoon camouflaged the break in the coral on this side. The big stick we had seen was, in fact, a South Pacific navigation aid, marking the pass into the lagoon. We *had* seen it, but we hadn't recognized its significance.

The pass was quite narrow and the chart showed a shallow spot in the middle of the entrance on the inside. From just outside the pass we could see through the pass and into the lagoon, but we could not see any markers indicating the shallow spot. We had to judge the depth of the water by its color. The best way to see the variations in color was by looking down into the water, rather than at a shallow angle across the top. With the Sun still a little in front of us, this was especially true.

In the lee of the atoll, just outside the pass, I lowered the main, climbed the mast, and sat on the first spreader with my arm wrapped around the mast.

We approached the pass cautiously under power, watching for the telltale light green or yellow indication of shallow water over coral. As we approached the entrance, our progress slowed to a stop. The water was going by the boat just as fast, but our progress toward the pass simply stopped. We were barely holding our position over the bottom with a current setting us back as fast as we powered forward.

We increased engine speed until we crept into and through the pass. In the middle of the pass, we estimated the current at four knots and thanked the San Francisco Bay for all the good training in tidal currents.

This current wasn't tidal. Atoll passes have an unusual current effect: a lot more water runs out of the pass than in. All along the windward side of the atoll, the ocean waves and swells are driven up onto the reef by the prevailing wind. At each low spot in the coral, the waves wash or seep over the low spots into the lagoon. Inside the lagoon, very little wave action occurs, nowhere near enough to wash over the low spots in the coral on the leeward side. The water that builds up in the lagoon has only one place to run back out into the ocean . . . out through the pass.

Once inside and away from the adverse current, we quickly powered away from the pass. Inside the lagoon, several large coral heads had grown up from the bottom to just under the surface of the water. I stayed aloft and called directions to the helmsman as we motored around them to the small village of Tenukupara.

We met the mayor of Ahe and spent an afternoon learning about the black-lipped oysters and the black pearls grown there.

We also learned about the typhoon that hit Ahe in 1983. Every building on the atoll, except the town hall, was destroyed by the gigantic ocean waves as they washed over the atoll. The people survived by standing knee-deep in water in the town hall, the only building constructed with cement block.

In total, we spent nine days at anchor in Ahe. Most of the time we spent in rest and recovery, shelling and board sailing.

Ahe was our only port of call in the Tuamotus. Next, would be Tahiti, in the Societies.

To get to Tahiti, we had to sail between two atolls, 18 miles apart. With a two- or three-mile error in the Sat Nav, we would know our location within a six-mile circle. Even at night, we ought to be able to move our six-mile circle through the eighteen-mile gap. Both atolls had vegetation on them, so the palm trees should be visible.

To give ourselves an advantage at night, we timed our passage for the full Moon. The first night after departing Ahe was a beautiful moonlit sail across a glistening black-and-white photo of a tropical ocean.

The second night, we had to thread our way between the two coral atolls. Everything was going fine at dusk. When we first saw the atoll Arutua in the fading light, I took a visual fix with bad parallax from two ends of the atoll.

Just as I finished plotting the fix, a tropical storm swept over us. Rain, wind, wind shifts, cold, and more rain. The sudden wind shifts in the storm forced just as sudden course changes. Our dead reckoning quickly developed more and more error. At night, in the middle of the storm, we went through the gap without ever seeing land on either side.

Everyone knows coral heads below the surface of the water are invisible. But, it never dawned on me that, given enough water *in* the air, coral atolls above the surface are also invisible.

Chapter 28

Niue to Vava'u

Navigation has always been one of my strengths. I liked it, I studied it, and I worked at it. At sea, I religiously kept a log. Not so much because I thought the electronics would ever go out, but more because I enjoyed making my navigation work out with reality.

As navigator, I made Hiva Oa and every other landfall rise up from the sea on the appointed day. I liked being right.

Niue is the smallest land mass to achieve the distinction of becoming a separate country. Perhaps because Niue is so tiny and remote, no one but the Kiwis knew it was there.

In the British Admiralty charts, Niue didn't even get a chart of its own. The island of Niue was shown as a small insert on the Suwarrow Island chart. The insert showed Niue about as far west as could be. Any further west and Niue would have had an east longitude.

It wasn't surprising no one knew about it. Niue didn't have a harbor, just an open roadstead on the side downwind from the trades. Unfortunately, the roadstead was open to any western rollers driven by a storm. Whenever a storm blew in, no boat could anchor there, and all the transient boats were forced to leave the anchorage. The native boats, however, were small enough to be pulled up out of the water, so they were kept on land when not in use.

The anchorage at Alofi was tenuous at best. The bottom in the anchorage area was solid limestone, impossible to anchor on. Sand collected in the low spots and, where the sand was deep enough, it would hold an anchor.

After we dropped our anchor on what looked like a sandy spot from the bow, we backed down to see if it would hold. On the third try, the anchor seemed to hold, so I went for a swim with mask and fins. I wanted to verify the anchor was well dug into a good spot of sand and not just caught in a small crack of the limestone under a thin layer of sand.

Swimming back to the ladder, I noticed five or six small snakes swimming with me. It was a huge ocean, but I got back on board as quickly as possible. Later, one of the citizens of Niue laughed as he told me, "Yes, the snakes are highly poisonous. But they can't open their mouths wide enough to bite you." I tried to be sociable and not let my fear show.

Checking in was more fun than formal. When we anchored, Customs launched two small fishing boats and motored out to Denouement. We were the eighth boat to call there that year. I think they wanted to see our boat more than they wanted to do government work. They processed us with many friendly stories and an invitation to come see them play soccer on Saturday. On their return to shore, the two boats had a water fight. Would that all government officials took their work so seriously!

We soon learned the island itself was a nine- by twelve-mile lump of limestone and coral which had been lifted up from the sea in three stages. Back when the island was only a shallow place in the ocean, coral grew from the submerged limestone to the surface of the water. With the first lifting, this shelf became an island. Then, over time, coral grew from the new shallow spots of limestone to the surface of the water, creating the second shelf. The second lifting pushed limestone and the new coral up, creating a bigger island with two levels. After the third lifting, the island was 200 feet high with three tiers.

The higher land had been exposed to plant life and weather deterioration the longest and had collected the most dirt. The lower tier had some dirt in places, but was mostly the same maze of coral shapes that grew under water before the last uplifting. After drying in the air, the surface contours had become gray, jagged, cinder-like clinkers, from two to twenty feet high. Walking or crawling on all fours around, over, and through them felt a lot like we were still under water. Only knowing we were still breathing helped us believe we were above water.

Amazingly, we were able to rent a car from a local resident. By driving and hiking, we visited some of the more unusual places around the island . . . bathing pools of the ancient kings, natural bridges, and caves hollowed out by both sea and rain.

If not for the trail marks left by the Niueians, we would never have found our way in or out. Not only had they left trail marks but, in two places, they also left heavy climbing ropes to enable others to repel down the steep faces. And, in one very rough area on the way to a spectacular blowhole by the ocean, they had packed in cement and made foot-sized flat places for people to walk.

The Niueians are wonderful people. When we asked why they made the footsteps, their answer was an innocent "For others to use. It is difficult without." Indeed, they were as genuinely warm and friendly as any people we'd met.

We stayed for the soccer game and cheered our friends from Customs. Soon after, we began getting ready for the short, two-day passage to Tonga.

Both Niue and Tonga are very Christian, so we knew to avoid leaving or arriving on Sunday. We didn't expect any government services on Saturday either. Eventually, we planned to leave on Wednesday and arrive two days later on Friday, accommodating both countries.

Our soccer friends at the Customs office in Alofi stamped our passports, and bid us farewell and safe passage as we checked out. We deflated the dinghy, stowed it and the motor, and made the boat ready for the ocean. Right on schedule, we raised the anchor and headed out to sea once more.

The passage itself was an easy, downwind rollick in the trades. I posted our progress and the distance yet to go. When the Sat Nav changed from west to east, I duly entered it in the log, pleased with our progress.

I'd planned our departure from Niue, so we'd arrive at Tonga at dawn on Friday, and set our departure time accordingly. The strong trades delivered us a few hours early. We arrived close aboard Tonga in the middle of a moonless night. Too dark to see anything, we stood offshore, waiting for the first light of dawn.

As soon as we could see in front of the boat, we raised our yellow quarantine flag and headed toward Vava'u. The entrance, between two small islands, was wide and clear, not at all like the narrow entrances through the coral we'd seen in Polynesia. We accepted its beautiful invitation to sail in.

The Sun was well over the horizon when we approached the Customs dock. We turned on the engine, lowered the sails, and broke out the dock lines.

Just as we reduced power to slow our approach to the Customs dock, another sailboat came by and gave us a friendly, "Hello! Where are you in from?" They had obviously seen our Q flag.

"Hello! We just came from Niue."

"Well, if you're looking for Customs, you'll have to wait 'til Monday. They don't work on Saturday."

"Saturday?"

"Yes. When you sailed from Niue, you crossed the International Date Line. It's Saturday here."

Chapter 29

The Pacific Maritime Net

The Pacific Maritime Net is a group of hams, some of which are sailing across the Eastern Pacific, and some of which are on land, thinly scattered from Alaska down the western coast of America, through Hawaii, to French Polynesia and New Zealand. Those on land have excellent equipment and great signals.

Sailboats at sea, on the other hand, often have poor transmission capability. Their transmissions are limited by low-battery power, electrical terminals corroded by salt air and water, weak ground planes, and nothing but a backstay for an antenna.

For those on shore, communicating with sailboats is a challenge they enjoy. For those on boats, the shore operators are often their only contact with the outside world.

A German picnic in Tonga may not seem likely, but that's where I was when my sister, Dorothy, called. Dorothy knew I was somewhere in the South Pacific Ocean, but she had no idea where. Our mother had suffered a stroke and Dorothy wanted to tell me what happened.

Preparing for the trip, I had obtained a ham license and installed a ham radio on the boat. When I departed from San Francisco, Terry, a friend of a friend offered to be my stateside ham contact. An experienced ham operator, Terry knew about the Pacific Maritime Net.

I had given Terry's number to everyone at the Cast Party. Just before leaving, I put his phone number in the first newsletter. Anyone who needed to get in touch with me could call Terry and he'd try to get a message to me.

This was all theoretical—just a name and a phone number in a newsletter. When our mother was admitted into the hospital four months after I set sail, Dorothy had no idea where I was. She did the only thing she could. She found Terry's phone number and called him. "Yes," he said, "I'll try to find Dale." My sister was doubtful; the South Pacific was a big place. The most recent news she had from me was the second newsletter about a month before. It said I'd be headed to Tonga soon, which wasn't very helpful.

Terry had his ham radio turned on even before he hung up the phone. It only took him a moment to find the Pacific Maritime Net. Unknown to my sister, the timing of her call was perfect. The net was just preparing to start roll call. At the beginning of each roll call, they always made general announcements and asked if there was any emergency traffic.

When Terry answered with his call sign, the net manager recognized him. When the net manager heard what was wrong, he explained the net had me arriving in Tonga about three weeks ago, with no contact since then. The net broadcast my call sign to see if I would answer.

I was at a picnic and could not answer. They put out a second call, a long call. It was clear I wasn't on the air that night. My friend Sam, on Pinwheel, was anchored halfway across Vava'u and was absentmindedly listening to the net. He knew my call sign. When Sam heard the net was trying to reach me during the emergency messages, he answered on his ham radio and asked if he could help.

The net manager explained the emergency and said I should call my sister, and gave Sam her phone number. Sam was anchored too far away to do anything himself, so he turned on his VHF and asked if anyone anchored in front of the Paradise Hotel was on the air. A boat anchored near Denouement answered. They wrote down Sam's message, rowed over to Denouement, and taped the note on the main hatch.

About an hour later, I came back to the boat from the picnic and saw the note. Immediately, I fired up my ham radio and tuned in the net. Roll call was over, and most of the land-based operators had signed off. A few were still on, but no one knew any more than I did.

The obvious thing to do was call my sister. I was at anchor and not at sea. If I were at sea, one of the hams would have given me a phone patch, but phone patches aren't allowed when the boat is at anchor.

Just then my VHF called out "Denouement. Denouement. Denouement." The boat next to me was calling me on the VHF. They, too, were still listening after roll call and heard me on the net. They understood why, at the moment, I wasn't thinking exactly clearly. Calmly, they offered the solution to my not being at sea.

The Vava'u Communications Center was manned 24 hours a day. Why didn't I go up there and call on a land line?

Fifteen minutes later, I was in the Communications Center. In a few more minutes, the phone rang.

"Hello."

"Hi, Dorothy. How's Mom?"

"They found you? A third of the way around the world, in all of the South Pacific, and they found you? It's only been two hours since I called!"

189

Chapter 30

Map and Compass

Tonga is a storybook island paradise. 450 miles upwind from Fiji, and 1200 miles northeast of New Zealand, the 171 dots on the map are scattered across 500 miles of the tropics. They are loosely grouped into four chains. The Ha'apai group lies between the Vava'u group—our port of entry—and Nuku'alofa, the southernmost group, and closest to New Zealand. After many years of being closed to cruising yachts, the King of Tonga had, for the first time, declared Ha'apai open to tourism.

On Lifuka Island, in the Ha'apai chain, I met Brother Chris, who was halfway through a five-year contribution of helping the people of Tonga. When Brother Chris accepted my offer for dinner on board Denouement, I was delighted.

"They are truly wonderful people, but they're not aware of the outside world at all," Brother Chris said, over a dessert of canned sweet brown bread and canned Bing cherries. "They really have no concept of the things that are commonplace in more advanced countries."

"Is that what you're trying to do? Introduce them to the rest of the world?" I asked.

"Well, no. Most of them have been here all their lives and they'll never leave Tonga. To introduce them to what goes on in the rest of the world is probably unnecessary. In some ways, it would even be unkind." After reflecting a moment, Brother Chris continued, "On the other hand, a few things available in the modern world would be useful and reasonable to introduce here in Ha'apai. Of course, a very small few might leave Tonga and see more of the world—so they would need to be prepared in ways the others shouldn't."

"How do you do both? Teach and not teach?"

"There seems to be no single good answer to the situation. My work here is to make the decisions about what they're exposed to and what they're not. Mostly, I've been setting the curriculum at the high school, but it comes up in all kinds of ways.

"When I came to Tonga, I brought a high-frequency radio with me, so I could talk to my friends in New Zealand. I also listened to the weather forecasts from New Zealand about our area of the Pacific. When the New Zealand weather service expected an atmospheric disturbance to come this way, I passed the forecast along to the Tongans.

"Many of them had no idea what a radio was or weather forecasting either. Their natural assumption was that I was conjuring up bad weather for them. From their view, I was bringing punishment down on them because of something they had done. Being a man of the cloth isn't always an advantage.

"Needless to say, I stopped passing along weather forecasts. I still think they are valuable, but we'll have to work up to that. Right now, I'm trying to get the concept of maintenance across to them.

"Throughout all of Tonga's history, the Tongans have lived at a subsistence level. In the tropics, that's not a bad way to live. The land and the ocean provide plenty to eat. Banana leaves serve as plates and are biodegradable. Their garbage is natural, also biodegradable. So, they did the obvious thing and it has worked fine for generations. Nothing was ever saved. Their society has been centered around caring for the young and feeding everyone.

"Now a few somewhat more modern things are coming to Tonga. More so in Nuku'alofa than here, but it's starting here, too. Cement-block construction, electricity, and outboard motors to name a few."

"And radios?"

"Yes, radios, too."

"A new kind of awareness must now be developed in the people—the concept of maintaining. The idea of needing to maintain machinery must be accepted before they can focus on the process of changing the oil. They must learn that bicycles shouldn't be used and thrown away like banana leaves.

"I've had more success in the high school than outside it. We still teach all the old topics. But, now, every boy is required to study the basics of electricity, cement-block construction, and plumbing. I think these are basic to the social growth of a society, even in a hand-to-mouth existence. If girls want, they can take the same classes, but it's not mandatory.

"Math is taught, of course. This year we started teaching 'Map and Compass.' I managed to get a few compasses donated. We use a measured stride length as a practical unit of measure."

Map and Compass, I thought. "I have maps. Well, charts and compasses on board to navigate with. Perhaps I could help in some way? How about a practical exercise? On the water?"

Brother Chris was delighted. Soon we agreed Denouement would host a field exercise in Map and Compass in the lagoon.

Three days later, four high-school age Tongan boys and two instructors introduced themselves as they came aboard. "Now everyone remember to speak English," reminded one of the instructors. "This is courteous to our host." Everyone nodded in agreement.

Once we were underway, I asked the boys about their Map and Compass course. It turned out they understood bearings, deviation, and lines of position. But they had never seen the kind of tools used on most sailboats for dead reckoning. So, I went into lecture mode. Anyone who could successfully navigate from Niue to Vava'u was an expert and had the right to lecture.

They understood the basics well and quickly grasped my points. Then, I posed my first question: "Where are we on the chart?" I barely had to show them which line drawings on the chart represented which islands around the lagoon. They leapt into the navigational problem.

To no one's surprise, they thought in Tongan. To the instructor's chagrin, they began talking rapidly among themselves in

Tongan. They were working on a problem and couldn't help but solve it in the most expedient manner. Very quickly, they took bearings and crossed two lines of position drawn from two islands and marked an X on the chart, all the while chattering away in Tongan. "Mr. Parshall, we are right here," one of them said politely in English.

"Very good!" I praised them. "Now what course should we steer to go to the point marked A on the chart?"

Again a flurry of Tongan, followed by a polite, "132 degrees."

"Here at the helm, I only have a magnetic compass to steer by. Is your course in Magnetic or True?"

Another quick conversation in Tongan, and then "That is 132 degrees magnetic, Mr. Parshall."

So, I set a course for 132 degrees by the ship's compass and off we went.

"Now, please tell me when we arrive at A on the chart." I tried to match their politeness.

At this point, two boys dove for the chart and parallel rules, one grabbed the hand-bearing compass, and one stood by me to see if I'd ask more questions. The air was filled with Tongan as the boy with the compass called bearings to the two at the chart.

In a little while, the boy closest to me said, "Mr. Parshall, we are almost there." I throttled back and let the boat coast. As we slowed, he said, "The lines of position are now crossed at the location marked A."

"You guys are really good!" I meant it.

They did just as well navigating to Point B. As they worked, they settled into more of a team. Before heading to Point C, I asked them to make sure I didn't get off course. "If I did," I asked, "would they please tell me which way to steer to get back on course?" I did steer off course, and they easily handled this problem, too. Clearly, they had been taught well and knew the material. More importantly, they knew how to think in problem-solving mode.

As we returned to the anchorage, I went below and made popcorn for everyone. I doubt they had ever seen popcorn, or a man in the kitchen, before. The concept of a man in the kitchen was politely and quietly ignored. It was clear they liked the popcorn better.

Teenage boys the world over have a universal instinct for what to do with things that taste good.

Now, years have passed. I am still uncertain how Brother Chris should have answered the question of what to teach the Tongans. Was introducing popcorn a good thing? What if they couldn't get any more? Would navigation skills ever have any value? Anywhere around Tonga, you could tell where you were just by looking at the island silhouettes on the horizon. Did they need knowledge about electricity on a tropical island? Would plumbing and sanitation be valuable? Well, maybe if the population grew. And cement-block construction would certainly stand up to a hurricane better than sticks and thatch.

Perhaps one young person might grow up to be the navigator on a copra boat. But do you teach navigation to them all?

What did they really need to know, and what was an unkindness?

Chapter 31

A Sailor Goes to Church

There's just something about crossing an ocean in a sailboat that makes a sailor go to church.

In Tonga, the sermon was always in Tongan, which didn't do much to improve my cosmic connection or my seamanship. I went to church anyway, hoping it might tip some balance of spiritual forces and make up for any lack of forethought I might have going into the next storm on the ocean. After the service was over, it was clear the real draw for me was the choir.

Tongan church choirs are astounding. They seem to collect the most wonderful singers and blend them together to produce great choral effects. In terms of pitch, balance, and emotional content, they're excellent.

Most music was passed on verbally, person-to-person. What was written down was written in a notation unique to Tonga. Because the Tongan notation is so different from the western system, the Tongans could not read the works of the great western composers or share their Tongan works with the West. Four-hundred years of the best music ever written, available to both Tonga and the West, couldn't be performed by the other.

The "Class of '87" refers to the sailboats traveling before the trade winds through the South Pacific that year. We were all driven by the need to be out of the Tropics before hurricane season started in the summer. A few boats would head north to Hawaii, but most would go to New Zealand. Harmony and Denouement were two boats in the Class of '87 heading to New Zealand.

Jack and Eve named their boat Harmony for Jack's musical interest and talent. Every island village we stopped at, Jack would seek

197

out the local churches in search of an organ to play. Playing the local organ in every village church was part of Jack's way to get to know and interact with the people.

Jack knew the richness of western music would never be available to Tongans as long as they continued using their Tongan music notation. He also knew changing to a new notation would be challenging for a nation that loved its music.

In Nuku'alofa, Jack sought and obtained an audience with the King of Tonga. He proposed the idea that Tonga should change from their old musical notation to the western system.

Jack was quite thrilled to share an hour with a reigning monarch in today's world. He was enormously gratified to discuss a topic he loved so deeply. Jack proposed to the King that the accessibility of western music would be worth the difficulty of change. Both Jack and the King agreed changing a country takes time.

Jack continued playing local church organs, and I continued listening to church choirs.

One Sunday, I attended church at the Free Wesleyan Church of Tonga. I admit my craving for the music was my strongest motivation, and I brazenly tried to find a seat in the middle of the congregation where I could hear the choir well.

After I sat down, the Tongan lady just in front of me became rather agitated. She couldn't speak any English and I couldn't speak any Tongan. Without any explanation, she motioned for me to follow her, got up, and went to the aisle. She seemed absolutely upset because I was sitting in the pew right behind her. It was her church and her country and I wanted to be a good guest. Without any idea of what I had done, I followed her.

When I got to the aisle, with more motioning, she led me to the nearest door, and ushered me outside. Baffled, I followed her. Outside, she led me around several corners of the church, and then motioned me to enter in through a different door. She would go no farther, but she insisted I enter. Still in the dark, I did as she motioned.

Once inside, and up a few steps, I immerged in plain view of the entire congregation. I had been led to the right wing of the transept. Surprised, I looked around, but I was already exposed. The only thing I could do was sit down on a pew and face the chancel.

The main body of the congregation was then looking directly at the left side of my face. If my left eye so much as closed a tiny bit or my head tipped forward even the slightest, everyone in church would know. I knew the sermon would be in Tongan. I hoped the choir would be good.

Gaining a little security for the next passage was always a good idea. I simply wasn't certain I wanted to be the guest everyone watched when they got bored.

When I looked out at the congregation, the lady who had led me to this exposed position was just returning to her seat. She saw me looking at her and broke out in a big smile. Later, I found out I'd been ushered to the pews reserved for honored guests.

The choir was seated in the first few pews. They, too, were facing me and, between songs, they might not have anything else to look at. Oh, well. At least I had a seat where I could hear the choir.

In front of the choir, on the floor, sat all the small children. The girls each had on their Sunday best, an amazing collection of lace and ribbons. The boys were all dressed formally, including the traditional Tongan pandanas mats worn around their waists in respect to the Queen. They were truly darling. I wondered if Tongan children were as prone to making simple, honest statements about sleeping guests as American children were. I felt the pressure increase.

For a few minutes, nothing happened. I watched the children, all dressed up in their finest. I waited for the first sound from the choir. I tried not to look at the congregation.

A few more minutes passed. I wondered why the service hadn't started. I reminded myself they weren't used to running their lives by American clocks.

Then it happened. The King of Tonga and his family entered the transept wing directly across from me. They sat in a pew facing the chancel . . . and me! I vowed to stay awake, no matter what language the sermon was in.

The choir rose and the first powerful chord resounded throughout the church.

Chapter 32

Arrival in New Zealand

Rick and Sandy flew into Nuku'alofa, my last stop in Tonga, and boarded Denouement for the passage to New Zealand. I was delighted and grateful for their excellent help and great company. Rick had sailed across the Atlantic, but this was Sandy's first long passage.

Toward morning, on our seventh night at sea, we were approaching the New Zealand coastline and expected to be talking to Customs by mid morning. All we had to do was find the right place to enter the Bay of Islands.

"Look! There's Cape Brett Light," Rick said, pointing over the port bow into the dark.

"How can that be? We're too far out to see the light." I began working it out in my head as I looked at Rick in the near-dark cockpit. "The last Sat Nav fix was about 3:30 A.M. At that time, we were 32 miles from the entrance to the Bay of Islands. And, in the last hour-and-a-half, we'd have gone about ten or eleven miles. We should still be 20 miles from the entrance. And a little more from Cape Brett."

Over in the Tasman Sea, a storm was building and moving our way. It would probably cross the northern tip of New Zealand and overrun us in a few hours. "Cape Brett is only a 17-mile light . . . in perfect conditions." I stumbled along, not sure what was wrong. "Where did you see it?"

We were charging along on a pitch-black ocean, hoping to make Opua, or at least the protected waters in the Bay of Islands, before the storm battered the boat. It wasn't raining, but the building night wind felt like the storm wasn't far behind. The waves under the boat were gaining force and size.

"Up there," Rick said, pointing forward on the port bow. "I can't see it now. Wait 'til we get back up on a swell."

In the eight-to-twelve foot waves preceding the storm, we had taken down the jib. Now, we were flying a big staysail and a double-reefed main. Exhilarating, but when the storm broke over us, it was going to be a whole lot more exciting. Both the wind and the waves would be much higher. We were ready to change down to the storm staysail.

Several minutes passed before Rick saw the light again. The right combination of swell height with a big wave on top and timing of the light only happened occasionally. When Rick saw it, I saw it, too. A single blink. After seven-and-a half-days, and 1,200 miles at sea, it felt good to see the first sign of New Zealand. Visibility when it started raining might be a problem, and finding the entrance and navigating down the entrance to Opua in heavy winds might be difficult, but we wouldn't have far to go in unprotected water. And it would be dawn soon. Our mood was lighter than before and carried down below.

"What's going on up there?" Sandy's head and shoulders popped up out of the main hatch. "Did you say you saw land?"

"Well, not land, but the light from a light house."

"Which one?"

"Cape Brett."

Several light houses dotted the northern coast of New Zealand. "Maybe we ought to check that." I'd heard too many stories of boats making landfall and not being where they thought they were.

Every light identified itself with a different timing. We needed at least two flashes in a row to time the frequency of the light.

We watched over the port bow as the boat surged along over the swells in the heavy wind. Occasionally, we saw the light, but not two flashes in a row. Nearly half-an-hour later, we were close enough to time sequential flashes. When we did, the two-and-a-half second interval confirmed the light was Cape Brett.

The Cape Brett light wasn't at the entrance to the Bay of Islands. The entrance lay several miles to the west. There was no light at the entrance. We would have to find the entrance visually.

The gathering storm clouds overhead delayed the arrival of dawn. Daylight first began to come as a sense of the black not being quite as black as it had been. When the gray light of dawn finally gave us some visibility, we could make out the roiling underside of the storm arriving from the Tasman Sea.

Below, I had to turn on the light over the chart table. Dawn had not arrived inside the boat. I sat down to do with accuracy what I tried to do in my head when Rick first saw the light.

The last fix on the Sat Nav was over two hours old. I plotted the latitude and longitude noted in the log, and then updated it with our course and distance run.

While I worked at the nav station, Rick took the bearing to Cape Brett Light with the handheld compass. The bearing to Cape Brett on the chart and the bearing to Cape Brett on the handheld compass were roughly the same. I assumed the dead reckoning was correct and plotted a course to the entrance into the Bay of Islands, well to the right of Cape Brett.

I shouted the new course up the hatch to Rick and Sandy, and they adjusted the autopilot a few degrees. We believed we were headed directly at an entrance we couldn't see yet.

Our early morning arrival was good fortune. We saw Cape Brett Light before the light of day obscured it. And, by the time we got to shore, visibility would be as good as daylight could provide on a stormy day. In my experience, this happened more often in textbooks than in real life.

I joined Rick and Sandy on deck as the light of morning increased the size of our world. We all had cabin fever and watched ahead for signs of land. Our lack of patience was heightened when we spotted the first small black bump rising from beyond the horizon. Landfall! New Zealand itself was in sight!

Excited, we brought the chart on deck. We all looked to see what the bump was.

Several high spots were shown by the contour lines on the chart. Some were near the shore, some were inland, some a little to the right, and some to the left. With a storm coming in, it could already be raining in places, obscuring the hills in the rain. We had no way to tell which high spot on the chart was the bump we saw over the horizon.

The thrill of landfall, the closeness of our destination, and the excitement of almost being there kept us all on deck, staring forward at the tiny, but growing, bump on the horizon. No one could sleep. The watch system was broken. We were victims of landfall fever.

Slowly, our progress toward land enabled us to see more and more of New Zealand. The first bump grew and was joined by a second bump to the left. Eventually, more bumps to the right and left showed over the horizon.

Each time we saw more definition, we tried to identify the bumps on the chart. But, each time we failed.

Slowly, the distant bumps on the horizon grew. Dark lines began to develop between some of the bumps. At eight miles an hour, our vision of New Zealand grew slowly as the dark lines on the horizon grew in length and thickness. The whole formation slowly gained a little contour.

With more detail to match with the contour lines on the chart, everyone had an opinion. But, no one was sure.

The Bay of Islands on the north end of New Zealand was just that—a bay full of rocks and islands. These were roughly scattered between Cape Brett on the left and Cape Wiwiki on the right. The entrance we needed to find was two-thirds of the way from Cape Brett to Cape Wiwiki—two-thirds of the way across those rocks and islands.

Cape Wiwiki didn't have a light. We had to identify it by land contour.

Looking at the chart, we thought we should see land to the right of Cape Wiwiki, but no land to the left of Cape Brett. Looking ahead, we weren't certain of anything, other than the Cape Brett Light, which was still visible in the dreary light of the cloudy morning.

Every mile the boat sailed toward land brought more detail to the formation ahead. Every ten minutes the detail increased, giving us more to talk about and more to support our differing theories.

We tried to identify Cape Wiwiki, just to the right of the entrance. We even imagined we could see it. Then, more detail appeared and we became uncertain again.

The land ahead grew and gained definition. The areas closest to us began to show color. Distant areas receded into gray.

Cape Wiwiki continued to elude identification. The chart showed the coast line just to the north of it was fairly perpendicular to our line of sight from this position. No wonder we couldn't see much color change along that coast. If we found the entrance and sailed into it, though, the shore to the right of Wiwiki would no longer be perpendicular to us; it would recede off to the right. Then, we would see a color difference, but not until we got there.

With the field glasses, we began to make out the smaller contours of the islands. We also saw many tiny black spots that looked like rocks sticking out of the water.

Many of the names on the chart were created before white men came to "The Land of the Long White Cloud." This complicated our communications as we bounced ideas back and forth.

The chart showed clear water between Tikitiki Island and Te Nunuhe Rock, the entrance to the Bay of Islands. Both seemed too small to see now, but when we found the entrance, Cape Wiwiki would lie just behind Tikitiki Island.

We knew we must be absolutely certain of our position and which islands we would sail between before we sailed in. We needed to know we had clear water in front of us, not rocks and shoals.

We knew where Cape Brett was. The key was to find Cape Wiwiki. Then, the rest would fall into place. We went back to waiting for more detail to immerge from the indiscernible.

Slowly, the coast line began to have heights, and near and far distances. Other places began to look like islands. The largest rocks began to show to our naked eyes.

Headed toward what we thought must surely be the midpoint of the entrance, we watched the time and advanced the dead reckoning as we went. As our dead reckoning slowly approached the spot we'd marked on the chart as the entrance's midpoint, the land to the right of Cape Wiwiki began to recede into the distance. The distinct color variation caused by the recession of the coast under a gray morning gave away the position of Cape Wiwiki. We finally had visual confirmation of our location.

As we arrived at the entrance, we could clearly see the big, tall rock, Tikitiki Island, on the starboard bow. And, nearly abeam on our port, we could see Okahu Island. Just to our side of Okahu Island, some rocks, which must have been Te Nunuhe, were awash in the water.

Again, we updated our dead reckoning, this time with the notation of "Fix." Everything fell into place and it felt good to be certain. Opua lay seven miles ahead, shortly after the entrance turned into a tidal river.

The pressure of determining where we were was over. We knew. The land formation suddenly turned into the wonderful island paradise of New Zealand, and we became tourists.

As we relaxed, someone remembered hearing about a VHF radio station in Kiri Kiri that was supposed to be "a friend of the cruising boats." We gave Kiri Kiri Radio a call on the VHF, just for fun. With a distinct Kiwi accent, our VHF announced, "Welcome to New Zealand! I'm John."

John assumed we were still making our approach and wanted to know our location. When we told him, he wanted to know if we'd seen Ninepin Rock yet. When we said no, John got a little concerned.

He told us if we were where we thought we were, we should be able to see it right now. After a short discussion, we discovered Tikitiki Island, which we'd been navigating on, and Ninepin Rock were the same rock, just named by different peoples. We relaxed again.

It turned out John, who ran Kiri Kiri Radio, operated on both VHF and short wave. My ham radio also worked on short wave, which would have let us talk to John long before we could have on VHF, if only we'd known to try.

Kiri Kiri Radio was the primary communications link for the fishing boats working around northern New Zealand. John would make phone calls for the fishing boats, take calls from land lines, and relay messages via either VHF or short wave. Occasionally, John would get a request from a fishing boat for a spare part or piece of equipment, pick it up on his next trip to Auckland, and then rendezvous with the boat at the Opua dock.

John also enjoyed the cruising yachts and offered to help in any way he could. He offered to be our phone contact if we wanted to give out his number to our friends back in the States. And John was the one who gave us the details on the Thanksgiving dinner the "Yanks" held each year at the Opua Cruising Club. John called Customs, too, and had them on the dock about the time we tied up on that stormy morning. "And the next time you enter the Bay of Islands, please call me earlier," John instructed. "I like to help you Yanks find the entrance."

After we put Denouement on a mooring, Rick and Sandy flew back to California. I rested and did maintenance on the boat, and signed up with Kiri Kiri Radio. Each morning, I listened to John's weather report and tidbits of news over breakfast.

Several days after our arrival, the storm had passed through, but a thick morning fog was hanging over the moorage in Opua. I was scrambling eggs when I heard a call on the VHF: "Kiri Kiri Radio. Kiri Kiri Radio. This is the sailboat Horizon. Come in, please."

Almost immediately I heard John's voice, "Yes, Horizon. This is Kiri Kiri Radio. Over."

"We're coming in from Tonga, bound for Opua," the first voice said. "We're just approaching the Bay of Islands and it's pretty foggy out here. Can you tell us what Ninepin Island looks like? Over."

"Yes, it's foggy here, too. What's your location? Over," asked John.

"Well, about 20 minutes ago, we were at 35 and 7 south, and 174 and 13 east. You know, we had cloud cover all day yesterday, so we didn't get a Sun shot. We are working on a two-day-old DR. Over," came the reply.

"I take it you don't have electronic navigation? Over." queried John.

"No. But we seem to be on track OK. We just want to verify Ninepin. Over."

"Well, it's a big rock. Rather tall. Stands quite upright. Over."

207

"OK, I guess that could be it. I can just barely make it out in the fog. We'll come in a little farther. Horizon standing by. Over."

"Do be careful! Kiri Kiri Radio standing by."

Wow. That's pretty gutsy, I thought. *I'm glad I'm not trying to find the entrance in this fog.*

About halfway through breakfast, I heard the second call, "Kiri Kiri Radio, this is Horizon again. Over."

"Yes, Horizon. This is Kiri Kiri Radio. Over," John answered immediately.

"We're closer now, and I can see Ninepin. Tell me again what Ninepin looks like. Over."

"It's quite big. More tall than wide. Over."

"What I'm looking at is just in front of an island. Does that sound right? Over."

"Yes, as you approach, land would be just behind Ninepin. Over."

"OK." Silence on the VHF for a moment. "You know, we're not quite sure yet. The fog is a real problem. It's not helping anything. Over."

"Yes, the fog seems to cover the whole area. I was talking to some of the fishing boats this morning and everyone is reporting quite sticky conditions. The weather report says it might lift in the heat of the afternoon. Have you seen Cape Brett Light yet? Over."

"No. In this fog, I doubt we would see anything unless we were right on top of it. Over."

"Quite right. Over."

"Well, we'll go on in a little farther. I wish we were more certain. Horizon standing by."

"Horizon, what's your course and speed? Over."

"We're headed about 195 magnetic, at about 5. Although I think we should slow down some. Horizon standing by."

"Thank you. Kiri Kiri Radio standing by."

Several more minutes passed with silence on the VHF. I wondered how many boats in the Opua moorage were listening this morning. Probably a lot, it was almost time for the Kiri Kiri weather report and news. The silence on the VHF made me think everybody listening was trying to keep the channel clear for Horizon.

As I was washing the dishes, John's voice broke the silence. "Horizon. Horizon. This is Kiri Kiri Radio. Over."

"Yeah, we're here," Horizon replied.

"Kiri Kiri Radio serves as the communications link for all the boats in northern New Zealand. This morning, we have several at sea in the area. Since my last conversation with you, I did a general call to them and asked them each to check their radar for any blip headed 195 magnetic at about 5 or less. I got no response, so I asked them to check again. These boats are fairly scattered about the north end of the North Island, which means we don't have complete coverage by any means. Horizon, none of them had you on their radar. I asked them to continue watching and to call me if they got a blip that might be you. Over."

"Sounds like they don't know where I am either." The voice on Horizon was quieter now. "Well, we took the jib down. We are doing more like 3 now. Thanks for trying." Then, in a moment, "We've got a lookout on the bow. So far, nothing. Horizon standing by."

"Kiri Kiri Radio standing by."

When the dishes were done, I sat down by my VHF to listen. When Rick, Sandy, and I made our approach, I was glad to be ahead of the storm. Now, I was thankful we didn't have any fog.

It seemed like an eternity while I relived our entrance into The Bay of Islands and thought of Horizon out there in the fog trying to find her way in.

"Kiri Kiri Radio. Horizon here." The voice sounded farther away this time and was hard to understand.

"Horizon. Horizon. Horizon. I can hear your call, but you're breaking up." John was obviously quite alarmed. "You cannot be where you think you are. You cannot be in the entrance to the Bay of Islands. I have clear reception in that area. Your transmission is breaking up. You have to be somewhere else. There must be a rocky hill between us now. You cannot be in the entrance!" John was nearly shouting now, hoping his transmission could be heard on Horizon.

"Turn around and go back out to sea! You are not where you think you are. Do not come in! Go out to sea! Over."

"I think you said go out to sea. Is that right?" came the distorted voice.

"Yes, go out to sea! Turn around and retrace your path back out to sea. I'm not sure where you are, but you are not in the entrance. If you're in the Albert Channel, it becomes shallow and has rocks strewn about. It's not recommended without local knowledge and a clear day. Retrace your path back out to sea."

"I can't do that. We'll turn around now and go back out to sea, but I can't retrace our path back out. We've been going downwind and I'll have to beat going back out. That'll take me off to one side or the other." Then, a moment later, "We're heading up now. Over."

"Right. Over."

And, then, as if there were nothing else to say, "Horizon standing by."

"Kiri Kiri Radio standing by."

I was sure everyone in the harbor listening to the VHF held their breath at the same time.

And we waited.

And waited.

It felt like half an hour later when Kiri Kiri Radio finally called again. "Horizon. Horizon. Horizon. This is Kiri Kiri Radio. Over."

"Horizon here. We haven't hit anything yet. Still can't see anything. But as best as we can tell, we must be getting into clear water. Over."

"Yes, Horizon, you are. One of our fishing boats just picked up a blip headed out from shore on a course of about 080 true. There's no harbor there. Just a small bay with rocks along the shore. Stay on your present course and he'll rendezvous with you. Over."

There was more, but I lost my concentration at that point. I was back sailing Denouement the morning we made our approach into the Bay of Islands.

Chapter 33

Thanksgiving in Opua

In the hot summer months, The South Pacific islands lie in an area occasionally swept by hurricanes. Each spring, October and November in the Southern Hemisphere, the sailboats in the southern tropics all head to safer waters. Those on their way north sail to Hawaii. A very few wait out the hurricane season anchored in an island lagoon near the equator. Most of the boats, however, head to New Zealand for the summer.

The most northerly harbor in New Zealand, and the closest to the tropics, is Opua, which becomes the summer home for many cruising boats. The annual migration of boats brings an economic need that the local Kiwis seem to enjoy satisfying. Moorage, boat yard, repairs, supplies, and even showers are available to the new arrivals.

The people of New Zealand have a close relationship with the ocean and genuinely enjoy welcoming the sailors. For those living a nomadic life on a boat, the gathering in New Zealand is an opportunity for social events.

"Yes, Counterpoint is anchored a good ways down the lagoon," came the reply on my ham radio. I was still anchored in Tonga, planning to leave for New Zealand in another week. I'd been looking for John and Mary since leaving San Francisco. They were friends from my Cal 2–27 days, who had departed San Francisco for the South Pacific shortly after I did.

I knew they were somewhere behind me in the islands, but I had no idea where. They didn't have a ham license, so making contact with them was almost impossible. As my trip progressed down

211

through French Polynesia to Niue and Tonga, I had occasionally tried to contact them, but without success. Now summer was approaching, and we all needed to leave the tropics.

I was already planning my passage to New Zealand. I knew John would be driven by the same weather patterns, so he should be making the same plans.

"Stand by a minute and I'll try to raise them by VHF." This afternoon, during the warm-up session of the Pacific Maritime Net, I put out a call for anyone knowing the whereabouts of a boat named Counterpoint. Water Lace responded.

"Denouement, I have the VHF mike in one hand and the ham mike in the other. John sends his best to you and wants to know where you are."

What a thrill to finally make contact with an old friend in a new place, even if it was only by radio!

With Water Lace acting as relay, John and I went through the basics. They had been delayed in San Francisco and hadn't left until nearly six weeks after I did. They were still in French Polynesia, hoping to leave in a couple of days. Yes, they were much later than they expected. Yes, they certainly felt the pressure of the approaching hurricane season and were moving along as fast as they could. No, they couldn't possibly catch up with me. In fact, they wouldn't arrive in New Zealand until late November, but they would be in New Zealand for the hurricane season. We would see each other then and compare adventures.

With thanks to Water Lace, John and I signed off. I was disappointed we couldn't get together before leaving for New Zealand. But thirteen hundred miles at six miles an hour was a hard reality. John couldn't possibly catch up in the time left. We would just have to see each other in Opua.

The middle of October came and went. Rick and Sandy arrived, and we sailed Denouement to New Zealand before the tropics got warm enough to support hurricane activity.

In Opua, I rented a mooring for the six-month hurricane season and began working on the many boat projects that had been accumulating on my list at sea. I bought a rusty old Datsun for transportation to the hardware store and for sightseeing in New Zealand.

I wasn't the first boat to arrive in Opua, but I must have been near the front of the migration. Every day, a few more boats came in, tied to the dock, went through Customs, and found a mooring. Many of the boat names were familiar to me. Most had been on the Pacific Maritime Net roll call and several I had talked to directly for more information about something.

On land, I began to meet the people behind the voices on the radio. On the dock, people would say hello, and introduce themselves by the most likely thing to ring a bell—the name of their boat. It didn't take long before I had a whole new set of friends.

Every day, more and more boats came in. I began listening to Kiri Kiri Radio each morning for the weather and news. John loved to welcome the boats coming in from the tropics, and he always told the rest of us who had arrived since yesterday's news.

Whenever a boat I knew came in, I would drive my dinghy around the moorage looking for them, so I could personally welcome them.

Some of the boats had summered here before, and a few "permanent cruisers" had been here several times. Those with knowledge offered advice and directions to those who needed it. I gave rides to people until they got their own transportation.

The boats were mostly American and it was the middle of November. Everyone who had been here before talked about Thanksgiving dinner at the Opua Cruising Club. Truly, we all had so much to be thankful for. It would be a lot like going to Grandmother's house to renew relationships with the relatives and to catch up on the gossip.

Still the crowd grew, although more slowly now. John and Mary on Counterpoint were still out on the ocean somewhere, headed toward Opua.

Then one morning, it happened. Kiri Kiri Radio announced they had just heard from Counterpoint. They were expecting to be in this morning.

I was so excited I couldn't sit still. John and Mary were finally here. I grabbed my foul weather gear and jumped into the dinghy. With the outboard at full throttle, I headed down the river toward Ninepin Rock and the ocean. I wanted to greet them and escort them in. I wanted to share all my experiences with them and to hear about theirs. I wanted to share my happiness with them and be a part of their joy.

As I powered down the river, the wind blew against me, raising a goodly chop for a little dinghy. Every wave splashed water over the rail. I didn't care. I bailed and hunkered down in my foul weather gear and kept the dinghy headed toward Counterpoint.

When I found John and Mary, I drove along beside Counterpoint back to the Customs dock. We chatted about our experiences and the options ahead of us in New Zealand and beyond. It felt warm and good to welcome old friends.

After clearing in, John and Mary found a mooring, and settled in for some sleep. They barely had time to rest up for turkey dinner, but they made it.

Thirty-four boats attended Thanksgiving dinner at the Opua Cruising Club. We carved 15 small turkeys to feed nearly 80 people. We stuffed ourselves, just like Thanksgiving at home. Unlike home, no one fell asleep after dinner. We spent the rest of the day sharing our experiences and meeting old friends for the first time.

Chapter 34

Stitches in Tonga

No one sleeps well on a beat in the ocean. On a beat, the boat moves upwind as the waves roll downwind. On the passage from New Zealand to Tonga, 1,200 miles to weather, the boat has to cross a lot of waves.

With the boat lurching from wave to wave, everything you do inside the boat takes more effort. Putting on your pants, brushing your teeth, fixing breakfast, navigating, trimming the sails . . . everything. After several days on the wind, things don't get put away as well, or cleaned as well, or repaired as well.

We arrived in Tonga with the decks and our foul weather gear wet and salty. Below, we'd created an eight-day clutter.

After going through Customs in Vava'u, we anchored in front of the Paradise Hotel, and began picking up and reorganizing the boat. We attacked everything at once. Two of the crew flaked the jib we'd been using and zipped it into its deck bag. Another person was sorting out the mess below, stowing things rightly, and getting what was dirty ready to go ashore for washing. Someone opened the deck hatches to let them air out and dry.

One of the crew was washing the breakfast dishes that, somehow, got dumped in the sink when we first sighted land. I was making the final entry in the log when we all heard a loud thud and a muffled scream topside.

Darrel, who had been carrying a big armload of wet foul weather gear from the cockpit up to the mast to hang over the boom to dry, stepped into an open deck hatch. The first point of contact on the way down was his shin on the edge of the open hatch.

If we'd still been out on the ocean, Darrel would have been wearing pants and foul weather gear. In shorts, the side of his shin was cut rather badly by the edge of the hatch. He needed stitches.

Darrel had taken vacation from his job at a hospital in Marin County north of San Francisco to make the passage from New Zealand to Tonga. His idea of medical treatment—and mine, too, for that matter—was that of a modern facility in the States with doctors in white coats and framed degrees on walls.

In Vava'u, the situation was a little different. I had a medical kit on board that was significant by any mobile standard, except that of a paramedic. In the kit were all the needles, sutures, and locking forceps needed to sew up Darrel's leg. It also had antibacterial medicines to control infection. In the three-ring medical binder were drawings showing the method of holding the needle and making the knots. What was missing was experience. And, to make up for that, I was reading as fast as I could.

The other option was to go to the local island infirmary on Vava'u. None of us could speculate what level of medical help might be available there. This certainly wasn't the USA. The Kingdom of Tonga was a group of small tropical islands in the middle of the Pacific.

Our patient probably had more medical knowledge than all the rest of us put together. After much discussion, Darrel made the decision for himself. He chose to go to the infirmary for local help. If an infection should develop, then Darrel would rely on the onboard medicines.

Two of the crew quickly put the dinghy in the water and, with Darrel in the middle, they motored off to shore. The Paradise Hotel made arrangements to drive them to the infirmary.

In Tonga, an old story is told about a group of men who went out fishing in the ocean in a sailing long boat. A bad storm came up and they were driven away from the island. The men turned the boat on its side—swamping it—and jumped into the water beside the boat. The boat was washed by crashing wave after crashing wave. For the men to swim in the violent water, they stripped off their clothes and swam naked, hanging onto the gunnel of the boat.

When the storm was over, they righted the boat, bailed it out, and sailed back to the island. The Queen of Tonga was worried about the men being on the ocean in the terrible storm. When their sail was sighted approaching the island, the Queen went down to the shore to welcome the men home.

The men, ashamed of their nakedness before the Queen, cut down the pandanas woven sail, and cut it into small pieces. They used the pieces as skirts to cover themselves in front of the Queen.

To this day, the well-to-do men in Tonga wear small, formal, pandanas skirts as an outer garment in honor of the Queen. They often wear black slacks, with a pandanas skirt tied over their slacks, a black shirt, and sandals.

When Darrel arrived at the infirmary, he looked around, trying to gauge the level of medical help he was about to receive. The room was clean and bright, but some of the equipment was rather old. In fact, he saw rust spots here and there on some of the sterilization pans. Swallowing hard, Darrel reminded himself this was the tropics and he tried to accept the rust. Then, the doctor came in, asking how he could help.

What Darrel saw was a barefoot Tongan native, dressed in a grass skirt, ready to perform witchcraft on his leg.

As it turned out, the doctor had considerable experience stitching up patients and he did an excellent job on Darrel's shin. He gave Darrel a few antibiotic pills, which worked fine. Darrel returned to the boat and, a few days later, flew home to Marin County.

When Darrel returned to work at the hospital in Marin County, I suspect every white-coated doctor reminded him of a big, barefoot fellow in a grass skirt.

Chapter 35

Swallows' Cave

"Palangi" in Tongan literally means "from the sky."
Long ago, the men in square riggers who explored the South
Pacific came to Tonga from the horizon. To the Tongans, it
seemed as if they came from the sky.
In a similar manner, I, too, had arrived in Tonga by
coming from the sky. I, too, was called a Palangi.
Swallows' Cave is, in a way, a tribute to Palangies.

I turned off the dinghy motor at the mouth of Swallows' Cave and unshipped the oars. The entrance was wide enough to extend the oars, but not big enough to pass two dinghies side-by-side. Rowing inside the small cave, the sound of water dripping from the oars echoed loudly off the close, damp walls.

Swallows' Cave had two caverns. The front cavern was narrow, tall, and half-full of water. The only way to enter was by dinghy. The only place to get out of the dinghy was the entrance to the second cavern at the back of the water in the front cavern. The floor of the second cavern was a few feet above the water level and completely dry.

In the old days, the secluded second cavern was used as a meeting place by the Tongan Chiefs. Sometimes, their meetings would last several days. The local Tongans would lower food down with a vine rope through a small hole in the overhead, from the surface of the island above.

For the Tongans, Swallows' Cave was a sacred historical place. If the meeting room of the Tongan Chiefs was sacred to the Tongans, the front cavern in Swallows' Cave was overwhelming to me.

The front cavern had been visited by white men ever since they had first come to Tonga. Well before rubber dinghies were ever invented, men had slipped inside in long boats and painted their names on the walls at high tide.

The earliest names and dates I could read were: J. C. Christensen, 1897; Fletcher Emery, 1874; Peter Hansen—"Norwar," 1863; and J. Milton, 1828.

In the dim light and damp echoes of Swallows' Cave, I was overpowered by the presence of those who had crossed the same ocean I had to arrive at this place.

Chapter 36

Just a Beautiful Sail

The passage from Apia to Hawaii was really the end of my South Pacific adventure. I still had one more passage to go before arriving in San Francisco, but it would be in the cold waters of the North Pacific. This was the final passage of tropical sailing for me.

The sail back across the date line and the equator was the stuff dreams are made of.

Clearing out of Apia was simple and quick in comparison to most tropical countries. Bill and Nick had flown in for the passage and were duly noted on the crew list stamped by Western Samoa Customs, a document US Customs would never bother to look at.

The direct course to Hawaii was mostly north and a bit east. We studied the prevailing winds on The World Climatic Chart[6] and the typical currents on The World General Surface Current Distribution Chart[7] looking for the best sailing route from Apia to Honolulu. The northern trades typically blew out of the northeast, and the currents close to the equator would set us west. The typical southern trades would allow us to sail northeast before entering the Doldrums. If we could get far enough east before we entered the Doldrums, we should be able to lay Honolulu in one tack.

Our plan was to sail northeast out of Apia, and then stay as far east as we could going across the Doldrums. We could only hope we

---

[6] World Climatic Chart—July in *Ocean Passages for the World*. 3rd ed. Crown, The Hydrographer of the Navy, Copyright 1973.

[7] World General Surface Current Distribution chart in *Ocean Passages for the World*. 3rd ed. Crown, The Hydrographer of the Navy, Copyright 1973.

would be far enough east to lay Honolulu from where ever we entered the northern trades.

We loaded what last-minute provisions we could find and pulled the dinghy up on board. We stowed it in its locker below decks and secured the motor on the transom. We did a little meal planning and stowed the provisions we would need for the trip in cabinets where we could easily retrieve them while on a beat. Everything that had crept out of its place during our sight-seeing in Apia was stuffed into a safe at-sea storage place.

We checked the navigation charts for hard spots in the water between Apia and Hawaii, and then preprogrammed the Sat Nav with all the way points we might possible need for the passage.

The boat was ready. With a good night's sleep, we'd be ready too.

This was my final departure in the South Pacific. After nearly a year-and-a-half, I was on my way back home.

Dawn pressed the sleep from my eyes, ending my last full night's sleep before Hawaii. Nick and Bill began to stir. I knew we'd be off soon.

We opted to raise the anchor first and have breakfast underway. Excitement was quiet, but strong.

Nick and Bill were both accomplished sailors and easy to live with. I was delighted to have them on board for the passage. As a teenager, Bill had sailed from New Orleans to San Diego via the Panama Canal. Bill had also raced and cruised on Lake Michigan and the San Francisco Bay. Now, he wanted to return to the sea and do a long passage again.

This was Nick's first long passage, but he had done a lot of coastal racing around San Francisco. He was eager for a longer ocean experience.

I had sailed ten thousand miles on this trip already and I loved sailing. But it felt good to be going home again.

All three of us were looking forward to being at sea. We all loved the ocean.

Going out the entrance to Apia, we looked back at the harbor and the brightly painted Victorian buildings with red and green roofs.

Then, we looked ahead to the horizon, where blue met blue. Time to start sailing.

Once we were out on the ocean, the wind didn't conform to the prediction in "Ocean Passages for the World." The wind was blowing gently out of the northeast, not the southeast as predicted. We had to decide between going north toward Hawaii and going east just because we might need the easting. Throwing our plan for early easting into the ocean, we decided to sail north toward our destination. The easting would have to take care of itself.

We chose the Swedish system, but modified it for three watches, instead of two. We would each stand one four-hour watch and have eight hours off during the day. And at night, we would stand two watches of two hours and have two periods of four hours off watch. During my year-and-a-half at sea, I had tried many different watch systems and this was the one I like the most.

This departure from Apia solved another problem. Typically, I was always exhausted for the first two days while my sleep pattern adjusted from eight hours at night to whatever was available during the off watch hours.

By leaving the day *after* getting the boat ready, we all had a good night's sleep and departed rested. Then, by setting watches early in the day, everyone was able to get a good nap during the day before the first night of interrupted sleep. The sleep transition turned out to be easy. I was getting smarter about cruising.

The first evening out, I got on the roll call with the Pacific Maritime Net. When I called in, I was welcomed by several familiar voices, people I'd been talking to for over a year, people who had become good friends.

Being familiar with the drill made roll call easy. I now had a special page where I copied the weather conditions the other boats reported. I had changed the sequence of the columns in my own log to the order I was supposed to use when reporting my weather information. Roll call was no longer a new adventure, but a familiar routine with friends.

Crossing the date line turned out to be a nonevent. I was experienced with the change of day at the date line.

The best thing was the weather and the sailing. Leaving Apia, the wind was further north than we expected and lighter. We never had too little to sail by, but the direction changed a lot.

Bill had the first wind shift and did a normal racing tactic. When the wind backed far enough, he tacked. Nick and I were below at the time. We looked at each other, but not at a compass, and knew something was wrong. Both of us scrambled to get on deck to help in any way we could.

Bill was just finishing cranking in the jib top—an easy job in the light air. He pointed at the compass and explained the shift. With a twinkle in his eye, Bill suggested we relax and go back to whatever we were doing before. He had it under control.

The winds continued to oscillate for all three of us. For three old racers, deciding when to tack was automatic. In the middle of the ocean—with no race course in thousands of miles—one by one, on our own watches, we each tacked on every wind shift.

The starboard tacks were a lot longer than the port tacks. Maybe the port tacks weren't entirely necessary. Maybe we were each showing the others we could do it, too. Or, maybe we'd just had too much sleep.

Slowly, the wind shifted east and filled in a little. We stopped tacking and let the boat sail itself. All day the wind held steady. Then all night. And the next day. And night. And on, until we each drifted into that timeless place between sunshine and sparkling water.

The light wind out of the northeast made for steady sailing. Enough wind to power up the boat, but not enough to create big waves for us to beat against. Denouement's big jib top and staysail were well matched to the breeze, so we sailed hour after hour on a good beat. With a split rig, the boat wouldn't point as high as with a single big genny, but the slant of the wind was still giving us some easting.

With three of us on board, we each stood watch alone. Alone at night under the stars, with no city lights and few requirements other than sailing, we each felt the power and beauty of the ocean. Nowhere have I ever found this feeling so strong as at sea in the dark, in warm and gentle conditions. Life there is truly good.

On the net one evening, a boat described a problem they had. No one was hurt, but they had turned a battery over. The acid had run out of the battery into the bilge. Did anyone have any recommendations?

One of the land-based ham operators in Hawaii took on the problem. He reasoned Hawaii was still as early in the day as anywhere, perhaps he could get a recommendation by evening.

I had a very large box of baking soda on board. The boat with the problem and I were roughly headed toward each other. I would have to divert west by a hundred miles when I really wanted to gain all the easting I could. It would be a couple of days before our paths crossed. Then, we would have to find each other in this big ocean. After having said all that, would the baking soda be any help? I was told to stand by while the ham in Hawaii worked on the problem. I held course for the time being and roll call continued.

Just before the end of roll call, the ham in Hawaii called the boat with the problem and me, and then took us both off frequency. When we connected, the ham had a recommendation from the head of the chemistry department at a university there in Hawaii. The recommendation was to open a seacock and let ocean water into the bilge until it was fairly full. Let it slosh for a few minutes, and then pump it all out. This process should be repeated at least three times, raising the water level each time. After three or four times, the acid would be diluted to the point where it wouldn't be a problem anymore.

The boat with the problem thanked the ham operator in Hawaii and set about flushing out the bilge. I also thanked the ham operator, because I now could hold course for Hawaii.

The steady sailing conditions made for good sleeping. Well rested, we all had the energy to take on projects. Books got read. Meals got more elaborate. Reflections got written in personal logs.

In secret, I made a mask on three or four successive night watches. I found a three-foot piece of laid Dacron line and unwound the three strands. Then, I cut lots of three-inch lengths of white curls. I made a headband from a sail tie with bands going down the sides of my face to my chin and across my upper lip. I sewed the white curls onto the forehead and face bands making a mask of white curls.

King Neptune was at my command and the equator lay only a few miles ahead. This time I was the shellback!

With only one shellback and two polliwogs, I judiciously decided the proceedings should be more presentation of awards than hazing. So, at the absence of both north and south latitudes, I dressed in a sheet, put on my curly white face mask, and carried a trident made from a boat hook and aluminum foil. King Neptune formally awarded Bill and Nick the official Denouement Document of Equatorial Crossing Under Sail.

Crossing the ITCZ (Intertropical Convergence Zone), or the Doldrums, for short, turned out to be a great sail. The wind held strong all the way across. We were on a beat and crossed the Doldrums at six knots. We even worked a little farther east.

The breeze held as we sailed into the northern trades. When the northern trades filled in, we found we were making better boat speed than in the Doldrums, and we were laying Honolulu. We had made our easting. We wouldn't have to tack again.

We caught a Dorado and feasted on fresh fish. Two days later, I was in the galley looking at the leftover fish as Nick offered cooking advice. I wrote it all down on a blank page in the onboard cookbook I'd been developing. Years later, I would come across "Nick's Fish Stew, between W. Samoa and Hawaii" and remember this wonderful passage.

With only four days to go, it became obvious we were coming in high of Honolulu. We cracked off ten degrees and felt the boat ease its motion a bit. Then, the full force of the northern trades settled in. The wind indicator showed a steady 30 knots with gusts to 40. A little overpowered and rounding high of our desired course, we eased off another ten degrees to a close reach. With the stronger wind, we were roaring into Hawaii!

Our course to Oahu took us a hundred miles to the west of the Big Island. As we began to pass downwind of it, the trade winds began to die. Slowly, they died completely, and Denouement came to its first stop since leaving Apia. The explanation came from the Pacific Maritime Net. We were in the wind shadow of Kilauea, the volcano on the island of Hawaii. Furthermore, the wind shadow had been observed by other boats as far west as two hundred miles. Never mind it was only two-and-a-half-miles high.

We turned on the engine. Because we had sailed across the Doldrums, we still had plenty of diesel left, so we pushed the throttle up high.

Once we sailed out of the wind shadow, the wind returned, and we resumed our mad rush to Oahu. It was an exhilarating finish to a wonderful 21-day passage.

Apia to Honolulu is 2,252 miles on the great circle, but we had sailed 3,158 miles through the water to get there. We had tacked some and done a small curve to the east, but most of the miles were on the starboard tack. One big factor causing the extra miles was current. Both the ocean current and the surface water driven by the wind drifted in the same direction—against us. The Sat Nav had nearly always registered a 1-knot current against us. For a few days, it never got below 2 knots.

Arriving back in the US, and being in a major American city again, was a shock. For the previous year-and-a-half, I had crossed a good part of the Pacific Ocean, visited with the people of six foreign countries, anchored in about 50 coves surrounded by beautiful sand beaches, and watched hundreds of tropical sunsets.

If the experience of travel broadens one, then the experience with the time to reflect on it resonates at a deeper place. For the last year-and-a-half, I had traveled the waters and lands of simpler people. Slowly, I had left behind the pressures of a modern city and a high-tech job. I had adjusted to simpler pleasures, finding them just as satisfying and, somehow, more real. I had begun to measure dangers with a less drama and more pragmatism.

As the press of civilization in Honolulu brought back the visceral memories of my former life, I realized just how much I'd changed by growing accustomed to the cruising life.

Part IV

Singlehanding

Chapter 37

Rules of Thumb

The rules of thumb for sailing have mostly come from the fully crewed environment. The procedures for everything from backing out of a slip to jibing a spinnaker have been worked out over a long period of time for multiple people working as a team.

I learned to sail as a part of the crew on other people's boats and I learned the rules well. When I started racing singlehandedly, I found the rules of thumb from a crewed environment led to disaster. No one was around to do the rest of the jobs.

Racing singlehandedly in a fleet of a hundred boats in the winds and tides of San Francisco Bay presents an opportunity for rapid learning. Beating upwind in the thick of the fleet, I quickly learned to bring the main sheet back to the cockpit. Before I learned to do that, the main sheet was led to a winch on the cabin top, totally unreachable from the helm.

On a normal summer afternoon in San Francisco Bay, Giggles, my Baltic 38, would not steer down in the heavy winds without first releasing the main. In a crossing situation where I had to give way, I had to choose between not steering and not releasing the main. Sometimes, new rules-of-thumb need to develop quickly.

The first time I took down Giggles' spinnaker in the ocean, I almost joined the boat in being dragged through the water by the sail. I immediately added a spinnaker sock to control the 3-percent-of-an-acre of sail cloth.

The Singlehanded Farallon Race is one of the best-attended singlehanded races in San Francisco. Each boat, between 25 and 50 feet long, is sailed by one person, 30 miles out into the ocean and back. Some call the race "The Rites of Spring for Testosterone."

The return to the San Francisco Bay from the Southeast Farallon Island is normally a broad reach. After rounding the Southeast Farallon Island, the winds out in the ocean are usually lighter, perfect for singlehanded spinnaker practice. The 30-mile reach back to the Golden Gate is a wonderful sail, and the course home is full of colored spinnakers.

On one of my early Farallon races, I stayed too high on the way back in. As I neared shore, the wind backed and I steered up to keep from going by the lee. My new course was bringing me in to shore, just north of the entrance to the Golden Gate. I had to either jibe or douse the spinnaker.

Being green at the time, I chose to take down the spinnaker. So, I pulled in the spinnaker sheet and cleated it, eased the guy forward until the pole rested on the headstay, eased the guy another six or eight feet through the jaw of the pole collapsing the spinnaker, went forward, opened the forward hatch, pulled the sock down over the spinnaker, went to the mast, uncleated the spinnaker halyard, grabbed the foot of the spinnaker now in the sock, eased the halyard with one hand while guiding the spinnaker down the forward hatch with the other, released the halyard from the top of the sock and clipped the halyard onto the base of the mast, cleated off the spinnaker halyard, closed the forward hatch, uncleated the pole-topping lift, went to the headstay, grabbed the outboard end of the pole while easing the topping lift, set the forward end of the pole in the pulpit to weather of the jib, went back to the mast unclipping the topping lift from the pole as I went, clipped the topping lift onto the base of the mast, cleated off the topping lift, went to the bow pulpit and made sure the jib halyard was clear, went back to the mast, uncleated the jib halyard, raised the jib, went back to the cockpit, and trimmed the jib. When I looked ahead, I was almost on the rocks.

New Rule of Thumb: allow more time.

The entrance to the Golden Gate is like a funnel, causing the light wind at the mouth to gain speed as it flows down the funnel. In the entrance to the Golden Gate, the wind normally backs. When it backs enough, the boats are forced to sail dead downwind in a strengthening blow. Eventually, the course to the finish forces boats to jibe their spinnakers in the heaviest part of the wind. What had been a wonderful sail turns into a serious learning experience.

Many singlehanded boats take down their spinnakers and sail the last few miles under jib and main. Those who are bitten by the racing bug hold their spinnakers as long as they dare. The last spinnakers to come down are the best known.

The first few times I carried the spinnaker into the funnel, I took it down early. Then I watched the best-known spinnakers sail away from me.

As I got more experienced—or more foolish—I held the spinnaker longer and longer, deeper and deeper into the funnel. My takedowns occurred in heavier and heavier winds.

Once I came into the entrance, but too far north. As the wind backed into the west, I found myself sailing a little by the lee in strengthening conditions. I eased the pole forward, somewhat narrowing the chute, and sailed on. Eventually, the boat started doing death rolls, causing me to wonder if singlehanding was a reasonable sport.

Another time, my approach was perfect. I carried the chute under the bridge and all the way into the Bay. Now, the wind instrument was occasionally showing 30, and the boat speed read a solid 8-plus. What was I doing carrying a spinnaker singlehandedly in 38 miles of wind? Well, let's see, it was light back at the entrance to the Golden Gate. I never crashed, so here I was reciting the list of things I needed to do to get the spinnaker down.

Reciting the list turned out to be much easier than accomplishing it. When I tried to pull the sock down over the spinnaker, it wouldn't come down. The wind was so strong, the spinnaker had more force in flagging than I had in pulling the sock down around it. In serious problem-solving mode, I ran back to the helm and set the autopilot to steer the boat a little by the lee, risking a jibe. I cranked in the sheet until the leach of the spinnaker was tight behind the main. While I ran forward again, I wondered, if all else

233

failed, could I sail this mess into the lee of Angel Island? If so, I hoped I could get the sock down there.

When I got to the foredeck, I grabbed the sock haul down and nearly lifted myself off the deck by pulling so hard. It worked! The spinnaker was now in the lee of the main, and the sock did come down. I never set the jib. I finished under the main alone.

During the takedown, I never got frightened. That happened the next morning. I woke up in a cold sweat. My stomach was so upset, I couldn't eat breakfast. My jangled nerves didn't calm at all until around mid day. Then whenever I happened to think back over the previous day, my nerves clenched into a panic all over again.

Another new rule: allow more time.

Only once did I carry the spinnaker all the way to the finish line on the city front. I finished the Long Pac Race in mid morning. That early in the day, the wind hadn't built to full strength yet. I crossed the finish line with the spinnaker full and drawing.

Yet another time, I finished a race under spinnaker in the Richmond estuary at the Richmond Yacht Club. After getting the finish whistle, I set the autopilot, eased the pole forward, and ran out enough guy to collapse the spinnaker. I ran forward, grabbed the sock-haul-down line, and started pulling the sock down. When I set the autopilot, I must have hit the wrong button, because it never started to steer. The wind was light and boat slowly started rounding up, driven by the main way out on the low side of the boat. *No problem,* I thought, *I'll just get the sock down around the spinnaker and run back to the helm.* As I pulled the sock down, a tug coming out of the estuary beeped its horn.

The beep wasn't the standard authoritative five blasts saying Get Out Of My Way! It was more like I'm over here, real close, and coming pretty fast. Please do something!

I glanced in the direction of the horn, only to see how close the tug really was. Now I was headed directly across his path. I ran back to the helm, pulling on the down haul as I ran. At the helm, I violently turned the boat back down to its original course and passed the tug starboard-to-starboard with only a few boat lengths between us.

As we passed, I looked up into the face of the well-seasoned tug captain. Remembering the way he gently hit the horn when I started across his path, I said, "Thank you."

He smiled back at me. In a voice more steady than mine, he pointedly replied, "Thank *you*."

Another new rule: well, I guess this one isn't so new.

Maybe the new rule should be: *stay* out of trouble. Once you're in trouble, you won't have time to get out.

I started trying to do everything I could to *stay* out of trouble. I tried to do everything earlier. I made my sandwich before the race instead of during. I started rigging the boat the night before the race, instead of the morning of the race. I tried to start spinnaker jibes and takedowns well before they needed to be done. And, I tried to have lots of room at the marks.

Often singlehanders shared marks with doublehanders and, occasionally, with fully crewed boats. In one race, I was beam-reaching toward a jibe mark in heavy weather. At the mark, we would all jibe and head into the Golden Gate to the finish line on the city front.

With lots of wind, all the boats were sailing at hull speed. I began to overtake a smaller boat with a full crew. Being competitive, I did the tactically smart thing. I overtook him on the side that would be inside at the jibe mark when we got there. As we approached the mark I pulled up even with him.

Then I realized being the inside boat at the jibe mark meant I would have to singlehandedly pull off a perfect jibe in heavy weather at hull speed. The boat outside of me would be expecting me to jibe in a timely manner. Sure, the rules gave me the right to take a normal amount of room. That meant a normal amount of room for a fully crewed boat.

If I turned slowly and he turned fast, his whole boat might end up in my cockpit.

When we got to the mark, I was barely clear in front of him. I hollered, "Go inside. Cross my stern!" and steered up a little. Unfortunately, the helmsman couldn't hear me or maybe he was timing his jibe.

I took another look at the distance to the approaching mark. It was NOW!

Just as I headed down, I heard one of his crew behind me shout at his helmsman, "Cut across this guy's transom. You're clear!"

We both turned at the same time. They made their jibe fine, but mine took a lot longer. I was frantically hauling in main sheet, steering, and easing the jib sheet when I heard their bow wake cross right behind me. It must have been close. I never saw it.

The biggest singlehanded race is the Singlehanded Transpac. Two thousand miles across the open ocean from San Francisco to Hawaii. When I bought Giggles, I dreamed of making the race.

Preparing for the race was a major effort. All the normal things for a race that long, plus all the extra things related to singlehanding, needed to be addressed.

The Singlehanded Sailing Society was a great help in getting us ready. Whether it was setting up the boat or learning what to do, the old hands regularly helped and advised those of us who were rookies.

One of the things they helped us understand was the danger of sleeping on watch. They had calculated a minimum of 15 minutes for an ocean freighter and a sailboat, both traveling at full speed directly toward each other, to go from behind the horizon to colliding with each other. For complete safety, I should check the horizon every 15 minutes—meaning I never could sleep more than 15 minutes at a time.

The Singlehanded Sailing Society meetings were given over to a series of lectures by experts on the problems we might face on the Hawaii race. One of the speakers was a doctor specializing in sleep and sleep deprivation. He explained the deep-sleep cycle was about an hour-and-a-half for most people. Between deep-sleep cycles, the need for sleep would slowly accumulate. To gain any recovery, we would need at least two deep-sleep cycles in a row or three hours of uninterrupted sleep.

I tried to determine how I could maintain a watch every 15 minutes and still get enough sleep to survive the two-week race. Again, the old hands tried to help. They suggested maintaining the 15-minute watch for the first 200 miles leaving the coast, because most of the freighter traffic was there. Then, I might switch to an hour-and-a-half of sleep at a time.

I thought, *If I do it that way, I'm guaranteed to be in sleep deprivation after the first two days.* After that, sleeping only an-hour-and-a-half at a time would never get me back out of sleep deprivation.

Sometimes, I guess, there just isn't any rule of thumb. You make the tradeoff as you go between what you have to do and what you can do.

Sometimes, you prepare the best you can, but there's no good way to find out whether your plan will work. Recovering a man overboard was one of those things where the normal rules of thumb for a fully crewed boat simply don't work in singlehanding.

Recovering a man overboard is normally an all-hands effort. Getting the boat back to the man overboard and lifting him back on board requires lots of people. But, I would be alone on the boat.

My plan was never to go overboard. Well . . . that's everybody's plan. If I did leave the boat, I must stay attached to the boat. It wouldn't come back for me. I resolved to use a harness and tether whenever I left the cockpit.

Then I created a ladder made out of webbing, attached it to the front of my harness, and carried it in a small cloth bag all the time. My idea was, if I did go over the side, I would remain attached to the boat by the tether, and I'd have a ladder to climb to get back on board. Then, I could lift my body weight and wet clothes with my legs, instead of my arms.

I never did go out to sea, set a spinnaker, and jump overboard to test it.

Sometimes rules of thumb need to develop slowly.

Chapter 38

The Crusty Old Tug Captain

The Singlehanded Transpac, which is held in even years, requires an applicant to show significant singlehanded experience in the ocean, specifically a nonstop 400-mile passage that went at least 50 miles offshore. In the off years from the Singlehanded Transpac, the Singlehanded Sailing Society holds the Long Pac Race as a means for applicants to meet this requirement. Starting in San Francisco Bay, the Long Pac Race requires contestants to cross a north-south line passing through a point 200 miles due west of San Francisco and to finish back in the Bay.

This course requires the single-hander to cross the north-south freighter lanes twice and to deal with the worst of the weather expected on the Singlehanded Transpac. The length of the race almost guarantees each contestant will be in sleep deprivation when approaching and reentering the Golden Gate.

Day three of the Long Pac Race. Two in the morning. I was just past the Southeast Farallon Island on my way to the Golden Gate.

The wind was directly astern and too light to do any good. The spinnaker wouldn't fill, no matter how I trimmed it. The bubbles in the water showed I was moving forward, but the knot clock was undecided about any movement at all.

During the race, I had kept a freighter watch every 15 minutes, just as the more experienced singlehanders talked about. Every 15 minutes for almost three days I had scanned the horizon for any sign of traffic. That was the only way to make certain I wouldn't be run down by a freighter in the ocean.

I was seriously motivated. I had kept the watch. Now, I was exhausted.

Giggles, my Baltic 38, and I were in the lead. With any luck, we would be the first to finish. My closest rival was a few miles back and a little to the north. I could see his strobe light blinking in the night from the top of his mast. I tried to judge which of us was gaining. My eyes burned too much to trust them.

The VHF radio was tuned to the Vessel Traffic Control channel run by the Coast Guard. It had been mostly quiet. A little while ago, a freighter south of Point Reyes, 40 miles to the north, called the Coast Guard and reported he would be passing through the traffic control zone outside the Gate. Other than that, nothing.

I scanned the horizon for lights, but the only lights I could see were the city lights of San Francisco, far ahead. Time for my 15 minutes of sleep. I started toward the main hatch and my bunk below. I hadn't had my foul weather gear off in three days . . . I'd been sleeping in it. I'd just set a couple of egg timers, clip them to the neck of my foul weather jacket, and then lie down, fully dressed.

"Vessel Traffic Control, Vessel Traffic Control," the VHF blared with a crusty old voice. "This is the tug and tow Mud Runner, haulin' a barge out to the dump site." This guy sounded like he was born at low tide. "There any traffic out here in the western sector with me?"

"Sir, there is no reported traffic in the western sector," replied the high-pitched voice of a young Coast Guard recruit in the middle of the night.

"Well, what am I looking at then?" demanded the voice of the tug captain. This question, unanswerable by the young coastie who'd been assigned the night shift, was followed by silence on the VHF.

A tug and tow, I thought. *Where are they?* I hadn't seen him on my last visual sweep of the horizon. I got up and looked again. I couldn't see any running lights. He must be out there. I looked all around again. No tug. No tow. I scanned the lights of San Francisco far ahead. Were his lights mixed in with the city lights? I knew he must be coming out of the Golden Gate, exactly where I was headed. If he were coming straight at me, then his lights wouldn't move against the background. I was too tired. The lights seemed too far away to make out anything clearly.

I was concerned. I didn't want to get run down by a tug in the middle of the night. The worst danger was the barge. A tug in the ocean tows a barge with a very long, heavy, wire cable between the tug and the tow. If I should happen to sail just behind the tug, I wouldn't be able to cross the cable. My keel would catch on it. The tug would continue on its way, pulling the cable past me. Eventually, in the dark, the cable would pull the barge up and over Giggles.

I was wide awake now! I scanned the horizon one more time. I didn't dare go down to sleep until I knew where he was. I needed to know I would pass both the tug and the tow safely.

"Vessel Traffic Control, Vessel Traffic Control. This is the tug and tow Mud Runner," the same crusty, life-on-the-ocean voice called again. "There any traffic out here with me?"

"Sir, there is no reported traffic in the western sector," replied the coastie in exactly the same voice as before. He must have recognized the raspy voice and remembered which sector Mud Runner was in. He had probably already assigned the name "Mud Runner" to the two blips on his radar screen traveling outbound at the same speed, one behind the other.

"Well, I don't understand what I'm looking at." The tug captain sounded confused and crusty at the same time.

I knew I had the strobe light on the top of my mast turned on. I could see the strobe on the sailboat just behind me. More than five miles offshore, this was a legal way of attracting attention. Most of the singlehanded sailors turned on their strobe lights when they slept. Often, they left them on all night outside the five-mile line. I wondered if the tug captain was seeing our strobes. Fully crewed sailboats racing at night usually don't turn on their strobe lights. The tug captain, in fact, may have never seen scattered strobe lights in the ocean.

Maybe I ought to ask the tug captain if he was looking at strobe lights. Maybe it might answer his question and also tell him not to approach us. Maybe I could find out where he was and if we were on a collision course.

I grabbed the VFH and, just as I lifted the mike to my mouth, I realized how this was going to sound to the tug captain. The first part was easy: "Mud Runner. Mud Runner. Mud Runner." The next part just didn't want to come out. "This is . . . ahhhh . . . the sailboat . . . er . . . . Giggles." VHF protocol says I had to wait for him to recognize me, and I wasn't sure he ever would.

A minute passed before he found his VHF mike. "Yeah. Whadda ya want?"

Too late now! I forged on. "Well, some of my friends and I are having a sailboat race out here. We went 200 miles offshore and now we're on our way back in. There's not much wind, so none of us is moving very fast." I wasn't sure what to say next.

Oh yes, the strobe lights. "I have my strobe light turned on. And the next boat behind me has his turned on. Are you looking at a couple of strobe lights?"

"Well. That could explain it." *Explain what?* I thought, but I never got an answer. The VHF remained silent.

The next time I swept the horizon, I thought I could see a white light ahead and a little to port. I stared at it, trying not to lose it. The harder I stared, the more the light danced in my vision. I tried looking a little to one side. Slowly, the light got strong enough to see and slowly became three white lights.

Were they moving to one side or the other? I sure hoped so. After a while, I saw they were moving to the left against the background, but ever so slowly. At least I knew he would pass to port.

Now, where was the tow? I strained to see its lights. I knew the tug was passing to port, but at what angle? Which way was straight back from the tug? Where was that darn tow? Would I cross behind the tug and in front of the tow?

Minutes passed. Then a few more. An eternity seemed to pass. I was exhausted.

Then, I caught the first glimpse of the running lights on the tow. They were much dimmer than the white mast lights on the tug. I wondered if the electricity was supplied by a generator or simply a half-dead battery.

After a few more minutes, I could see the tow would pass to port also. I would pass safely behind both the tug and the tow. I was relieved to be safe, but overrun with fatigue. Now I could go below for my nap.

Below, I set the egg timers, and stretched out. Instantly, the egg timers went off. I knew I had been asleep, but with no sense of how long. I only knew it was time for my next sweep of the horizon. I wondered where the tug and tow were. Would I still be able to see them?

I stood up beside the bunk, and started toward the main hatch. As I put both hands on the edges of the hatch to pull myself up and out, I looked out and noticed lights behind Giggles and a little to the right. Wow, there was a boat there! As I came out through the hatch, I saw another set of lights behind and to the left. Gosh, another boat there, too, with a dark space in between.

My exhausted mind tried to deal with two boats passing close astern. Then, it hit me. The two sets of lights were on the front and back of the same freighter. The blank area in between was the steel side of the freighter just behind Giggles' transom.

I stood in the hatch and wondered if the freighter was going to hit me. Then, I realized it was already halfway past me. I watched it continue to slide on to the left, until it was totally past me. As the freighter steamed off into the night, it became dark again.

Now I was awake . . . rattled, but wide awake. I tried to put the freighter out of my mind. It wouldn't go away. Where did it come from? How did it get so close without my seeing it on a horizon sweep?

I was hours from the finish line, but I didn't sleep again. I continued to puzzle about the freighter until my exhausted mind began to fit the pieces together.

Before the tug and tow entered my life, a southbound freighter had called Vessel Traffic Control from Point Reyes. That must be the same freighter. Intently watching for the tug and tow, I must not have noticed any other lights on the horizon in a different direction. The time I spent looking for the tug and tow, and the time I spent napping would have been about the right amount of time for the freighter to travel from Point Reyes at 20 knots.

The freighter had probably heard the tug captain call Vessel Traffic Control about his confusion. And, he had probably heard my comments about strobe lights on sailboats headed for the Golden Gate. So, he probably had his forward lookout watch for strobe lights and set a course to pass just astern of me.

To this day, I am immensely grateful to a crusty old tug captain who stubbornly tried to understand what he was looking at.

Chapter 39

The Singlehanded Transpac

Downwind racing has drawn sailing enthusiasts for years. Sailing to Hawaii has the added attraction of sailing from cold and stormy weather into warm, tropical trade winds. The last few days going into Hawaii are such idyllic sailing that four races are run regularly from the mainland to Hawaii.

Three of these races, departing from Los Angeles, San Francisco, and Victoria, are for sailboats racing with full crews. Surfing for several days down big waves driven by the constant trade winds is high adventure and deepens most friendships.

The fourth race, departing from San Francisco, is for singlehanders. Surfing down big waves for several days in the trades is still the same high adventure. But, with only one person on the boat, the task of sailing the boat is far more difficult, and the accomplishment is far more electrifying.

Racing alone on a sailboat for 2,120 miles across an open ocean is not an activity for beginners. In the 20-year history of the race, no one had died and no boats had been lost. But, the prospect of a storm on the ocean with no harbor of refuge tends to keep all but the most certain at home. Singlehanders at this level of racing are some of the most independent and self-sufficient people in the world.

With great insight, the Race Committee required us to spend the last week prior to the Singlehanded Transpac gathered together at the Oakland Yacht Club for some nice male bonding.

The list of contestants ran the gamut from internationally known names to normal people. Well, they seemed normal to me.

John Guzzwell, one of the better-known names, was sailing Endangered Species, a custom 30-footer that looked like a miniature BOC boat from the Open 60 class. Thirty years earlier, John had written *Trekka Round the World,* which told of his remarkable four-year circumnavigation. Trekka was 21-feet long. Together, they set a record for the smallest boat to sail around the world. Endangered Species was shorter than Giggles, but she was designed and built for downwind speed. Her rating said she was 33 seconds a mile faster than Giggles. After sailing the 2,120 miles to Hawaii, John would owe me a little less than a day of time.

Steve Fossett was sailing a 60-foot trimaran—Lakota. Steve already held several world records in sailing and hot-air ballooning. He had swum the English Channel, run in the Iditarod Dogsled Race, driven in the Lemans auto race, and run the Ironman Triathlon. Steve's objective in the Singlehanded Transpac was to set a new world record for the fastest singlehanded sailing passage from San Francisco to Hawaii. Lakota, the only multihull in the race, could probably hit speeds three or four times faster than the rest of us in monohulls. This wasn't a race for Steve. This was a record-setting attempt, and the Singlehanded Sailing Society was the authenticating body.

Another "normal" contestant was Ken Roper, affectionately known around the docks as "The General." This was Ken's sixth Singlehanded Transpac. His boat, Harrier, a Finn Flyer 31, rated a minute a mile slower than Giggles. At the finish line, I would owe him about a day-and-a-half.

I would also be racing against Bruce on Razzberries, his Olson 34. Bruce and his wife had sailed with me several years before when we drug our circle of water from San Francisco to French Polynesia. That passage had been Bruce's first ocean crossing. More recently, while I was learning to race single-handedly in and around San Francisco Bay, Bruce had been both a friend and competitor. Eventually, we seemed quite equally matched, trading wins over each other as often as the wind shifts. For the Singlehanded Transpac, his Olson 34 was rated one-second-a-mile slower than Giggles. After two weeks of racing, I would owe him about 35 minutes. We were essentially racing boat-for-boat.

The boats were divided into two classes. Harrier and six more boats made up Class II, the smaller boats. Endangered Species, Giggles, Razzberries, and two more boats made up Class I. Lakota was all alone in the Multihull Class.

The competition certainly wasn't lacking in skill and knowledge. But, then, racing two weeks alone across an ocean wasn't for the unskilled.

By comparison, I was an unknown. I had spent the last two years learning to race single-handedly. I normally finished near the top, but I was far from a consistent winner. I certainly wasn't as well known as some of the big names.

When I submitted my application to the Race Committee, I was somewhat in awe of the magnitude of what lay ahead. I'd attached all the required documentation to my application for the race: my sailing résumé, the last boat survey, a list of the work I'd done to correct all the problems noted, my qualifying log from the Long Pac, proof of my celestial navigation ability, as well as photos of the boat and myself. When I gave the package to the Race Committee, I was a bit timid that I was going. Half-joking, I commented I was turning in my application, but I wasn't committing to going on the race. The application was just in case I did decide to go.

I also gave them a check for the entry fee. So I don't think they paid much attention to my lack of commitment.

Of the 14 boats that originally applied, one dropped out prior to the start. Preparation for the race was too big of a job. In the end, the Race Committee inspected and passed 13 boats.

The start was just off the Corinthian Yacht Club, where they made slip space available for us the last night before the race. On the way from Oakland to Corinthian, I stopped at my own slip at the Richmond Yacht Club. I had a last-minute appointment with my regular bottom cleaner. On that last cleaning, I think he polished the bottom with a burlap bag before he let me go.

After I put Giggles in the slip at Corinthian, it wasn't long before the Race Committee came around and asked if I were ready to have my prop shaft sealed. This time, I was certain my total lack of commitment showed in my face. Without concern, they put the seals on and told me they would take them off in Hawaii. That way, everyone would know for certain the boat had not been propelled by the engine during the race. *Thanks,* I thought, *I sure hope I don't have any emergencies along the way.*

Later, I walked down the dock and wished the other contestants good luck. In particular, I wished Bruce good luck with Razzberries. His Olson 34 was a good downwind boat and I felt Bruce had as good a chance as anyone at winning. I sincerely wished him the very best.

Trying to sleep the last night before heading into sleep deprivation was a Catch-22. I concentrated hard on not worrying about getting too little sleep and the length of the trip. What should have been my last full night of sleep turned out to be a mixture of anticipation and fear.

In the morning, a friend from San José was already on the dock as I dragged my tired body up the main hatch. He was making a last-minute delivery of the frozen beef stews, and chicken and rice dishes I had made and frozen at home. Frozen solid, they went into the coldest part of my cooler, next to the cold plate. Now I was completely ready.

I watched the wind and tried to decide which headsail to use — the 120 or the 90. I changed my mind more times than was reasonable. Finally, I ended up with the 120 on the forestay, ready to go up. I dressed in my best polypro underwear and foul weather gear, and I waited.

Friends and strangers alike wished me good luck as they walked by on the dock. Finally, the Race Committee came by to take my drink order for the finish line and to wish me good luck.

Then, they untied my dock lines and pushed Giggles backwards out of the slip. Without an engine, I was totally helpless. I retied one of the dock lines to the bow cleat. In a moment, the Race Committee tender was beneath the bow and took the line. They towed Giggles out to the starting area, and then slowly upwind while I raised the main. Then, they cast me off with a quick "See you in Hawaii!"

I started sailing.

Under the main alone, I sailed away from the starting area and the other contestants. In Raccoon Straight, I found enough room to raise the jib and set the halyard tension. By the time I finished, the flood tide had swept me half the length of Raccoon Straight. Noting the strength of the tide, I sailed back to the starting area for the prestart free-for-all. After saying hello to Bruce on Razzberries, I remembered I was required to check in with the Race Committee via VHF. When I turned on my radio, check-in was well in progress.

At a lull in the check-in, I called in. When they recognized me, I explained, "I'm checking in, just in case I decide to go on the race. Uh . . . I'm still not certain if I'm serious about this race or not, or how far I'll go if I do race. But, just in case I do start, this is my check-in."

In every race, the decision to continue racing is always the decision of the skipper, so they could say little except, "We have you checked in, Giggles." Their tone of voice on the radio told another story. They still didn't believe me. I'd have to keep trying.

The start was in the cove in front of the Corinthian Yacht Club. A strong flood tide was running in the Golden Gate and through the Bay. With the strength of the flood, I guessed the best course to the Golden Gate Bridge was to cross the Bay from Corinthian straight to the City Front, short-tack up the city front, if necessary, and then try to go out the Golden Gate from Crissy Field.

Day One:

The start of the race was fairly normal. Bruce and I were both on the line, within talking distance. In the heat of competition, we didn't say much. It was silly to be so competitive when we had 2,000 miles to go.

After the start, I found I wasn't alone in my reasoning about the best course to the Golden Gate. Leaving the cove in front of Corinthian, we all headed across the Bay in front of Angel Island, in the teeth of the tide. I was glad Giggles was fast enough and windward enough to work upwind against the strong adverse tide.

The smaller boats in Class II found gaining distance to weather over the bottom difficult. The current robbed their upwind progress.

Lakota, the big tri designed for downwind reaching, undoubtedly had the worst of it.

The wind picked up as I left the cove in front of the Corinthian Yacht Club. By the time I arrived at Harding Rock, the wind was blowing hard. When a gust hit the boat, I looked up at the mast, and remembered I'd never finished tuning it. I'd never had this much wind when I had time to work on the tuning. Hoping the mast was OK, I decided to look.

I reached down and pushed the button to turn on the autopilot. Instead of it steering the boat, the autopilot gave me an error message: Main Current Error. I tried it again. Same result. Now what? I was a quarter of a mile into a 2,000 mile race and the autopilot wouldn't work.

Main Current Error. That sounded like an electrical problem. I'd have to check the wiring to see if I kicked something loose while I was crawling around in the bottom of the boat working on other projects. If it were a loose wire, I should be able to fix it under way.

Right now, I wanted to look at the mast. Oops . . . the autopilot wouldn't work; I couldn't get off the helm.

OK. I could use the wind vane to steer the boat.

Uh, oh. The wind paddle was down below. I hadn't planned on using the wind vane until I was in the open ocean. So, the wind paddle, the most delicate part, was still stowed safely below, well out of reach.

The race instructions defined the course: "From the start, leave the south tower of the Golden Gate Bridge to port, and then by any course to the finish."[8] It didn't say anything about hand steering 24 hours a day for two weeks.

I wondered if I tied off the helm, could I make a dash below for the wind paddle?

I grabbed the tail of the lazy jib sheet and tied off the helm. With a little experimenting, the boat balanced quite nicely. I started to

---

[8] Singlehanded Sailing Society, 1998 Singlehanded Transpacific Yacht Race, Supplemental Sailing Instructions — Additions to the Rules & Conditions.

go below and remembered the mast. So, instead of going below, I scrambled up to the high side for a look at the mast.

No good! The top of the mast was leaning off to leeward—not badly, but I didn't dare go across an ocean like that. The starboard upper shroud needed tightening.

Well, I wouldn't be able to do anything about it until I tacked and that would be at the city front. Tacking then should give me plenty of time on the other tack to adjust the turnbuckle. I hoped the mast would be OK all the way to the city front. No more wind! Please!

Nature didn't care what I wanted. The central Bay was where it blew the hardest.

I noticed Bruce had worked out in front of me a little way, but he wasn't holding as high. No time to speculate why, I dove below for a pliers, a knife, and some rigging tape. As I started back up the ladder, I remembered to grab the wind paddle for the wind vane.

Back on deck, the wind was blowing a little harder. The boat was balanced, but a little higher than when I went below. I shortened the lazy sheet length to put a little more helm in, and looked for traffic. The bubble came out of the main and the boat felt as though it was being driven a little harder. Bruce was lower now and not much farther ahead. I was surprised at how well Giggles was doing with the helm tied.

When I approached the shore in front of the Marina Green, I untied the helm, waited as long as possible, and tacked in 15 feet of water. As soon as I got the boat trimmed and balanced on the new tack and the helm tied, I headed for the starboard shroud, now slack on the low side. As I crossed the cabin top, I stopped and sighted up the mast. The tuning on this side was OK. I dropped down to the low side and attacked the upper shroud. I cut the tape and pulled the cotter pins. As I reached for the turnbuckle, I wondered how much to tighten it. I decided on a turn-and-a-half, and then arbitrarily changed that to two turns.

I replaced the cotter pins and wrapped tape over them. I wondered if two turns would be enough. Then, I wondered if it would be too much. Unsure, I looked for traffic, grabbed the tools and tape, and headed back to the helm.

Approaching the Golden Gate Bridge while fighting a heavy flood and a big chop was slow going. I looked around for my competition. Bruce was short tacking up the city front, probably headed for the south tower. If he went under the bridge near the south tower, he would undoubtedly go for the tide relief along Baker Beach. That was probably the best way to go out against the tide. With no autopilot, I thought I might be better off to tack fewer times and go for the relief along the north side. I wondered which of us would go under the bridge first.

The tidal current was setting us all back into the Bay fast enough that everyone was having a hard time getting to the bridge. Eventually, I sailed into the shadow of the bridge. I thought I was first one there, but Bruce went into the shadow at almost the same time.

On the other side of the bridge, a power boat was loafing around just below my course. As I passed by, they hailed me. It was the staff of *Latitude 38* magazine getting a close-up view of the race. What a sloppy place for a power boat! They were bouncing around worse than I was.

I waved at their hail and tried to tell them I had an autopilot problem, but we were far enough away from each other that shouting didn't work well. I would tell the Race Committee tonight at check-in.

The bash out through the entrance to the Golden Gate settled down as I sailed away from the narrow part where the bridge was. As the entrance widened, there was less wind and current. Sailing got better. I set the wind paddle in the wind vane and it took over the steering job I'd given to the lazy sheet.

By Point Bonita, the wind was lighter. Then, the lighter wind slowly turned into too little wind and I went back to hand steering. When I cleared Point Bonita, the wave structure became confused. The combination of too little wind and confused waves was decidedly unkind to sailboats.

The going was slow, with an irregular boat motion and occasionally slatting sails. Bruce drifted by close enough to wave. Neither of us was happy with the lumpy water and fickle wind. This would be the last time I saw any of the other boats until I was at anchor in Hawaii.

About 8 P.M., the jib slid down the forestay for no reason at all. The port jib halyard had broken or worn through, I didn't know which. I had a personal dislike for jib furlers and I fussed at my decision to put mine back on for the race. I was sure it was the furler's fault. While the jib was down, I took the upper swivel of the furler out of service and re-tacked the sail on the stem fitting. Then, I raised the jib back up on the starboard jib halyard without the furler. I wouldn't use the furler again until the return home.

At the 9 P.M. radio check-in with the Race Committee I reported my position and my problem with the autopilot. I told them I was on the wind vane now and had switched from race mode to cruise mode. I wasn't sure how long I would keep going.

I didn't realize it at the time, but the sloppy conditions had sapped a lot of my energy.

Day Two:

Sailing out past the Farallones and away from shore, I slept 15 minutes at a time, keeping a watch for freighters. I had two egg timers clipped to the neck of my foul weather jacket, both set for 15 minutes. When I slept, I lay down in a bunk in my foul weather gear and gloves, and closed my eyes. When the egg timers went off, I got up, looked around the horizon, and lay down again.

During the night, the wind came back, and I threw in a reef. At 5 A.M., it was blowing 35, and I threw in the second reef. Then, I changed the first reef line to the third reef point, in case I would need to go to the third reef.

The wind eased a bit, and then came back and held. The waves built all day long. By late afternoon, I began to feel as if I were sailing the rinse cycle in a washing machine. I still wasn't far enough offshore to get more than 15 minutes of sleep at a time. Early in the afternoon, I managed to change to the Number 4 jib, but the exertion and overheating started my inner ear rolling in a bad way.

Now the boat seemed to have too much main and wouldn't sail as low as I wanted. I fretted about being unable to sail my desired course. If I sailed too high now, I'd have to make it up later. Once I crossed the trough tailing off southeast from the North Pacific High, the wind would come around behind me. Then, it would be much harder to sail lower. I had to sail low now. But, I just couldn't get the boat to sail down.

I didn't realize it at the time, but I was already exhausted and in sleep deprivation. All I needed to do was let the main out. I couldn't figure it out.

In another hour, I felt the onrush of seasickness. I wasn't normally prone to mal de mer, but there was no denying it. I looked at the low side of the boat and rejected it as too dangerous. Hanging out over the side of a rolling boat seemed unsafe. I was uncertain of myself. I ran down the ladder to the head just inside the main hatch.

I made it. Just.

When I'd spent the last of my energy into the head, still staring down into the bottom of the bowl, I reflected on my situation. The autopilot didn't work. The tuning of the mast was suspect. One of the two jib halyards broke at the top of the mast after only one day of use. I couldn't get the boat to sail the course I wanted to Hawaii. The sea conditions were awful. And I was seasick.

With my arms still around the head, I thought, *This is not a good beginning.*

I crawled into a bunk and crashed, totally exhausted. The effort of getting the boat ready, starting the race single-handedly in heavy weather, and worrying about everything had worn through all my normally excessive stamina.

I slept without awareness of any ships at sea or my need to keep a watch every 15 minutes. I slept for two whole hours.

At 4:30 P.M., the wind was still blowing 30. I checked the sail trim, eased the main, and corrected the wind vane. The boat was now sailing only ten degrees above my desired course. I felt better and had some dinner on a totally empty stomach. In the log, I wrote, "My first meal . . . I chewed well . . . just in case . . . for the head's sake."

Slowly, the wind came down to manageable. With better weather, I settled down to sailing the boat. I tried to get some sleep— 15 minutes at a time.

254

At radio check-in, I heard the highest wind reported by the other boats was 42 miles an hour. Giggles wasn't the only boat having a rough time of it. Two boats had dropped out, damaged by bad weather and heavy conditions. Magic Carpet Ride had suffered a broken goose neck and a torn main, and decided to retire. Leilani Too had broken open the hull-to-deck join near the bow and was taking on water. Both boats were returning to California.

The rest of us smiled and tried to convince ourselves we were having the time of our lives.

Day Three:

In the middle of the night, the wind eased to a nice 25 nearly on the beam. I put the # 3 back up and could finally adjust the boat down to my desired course. The cloud cover was still 100 percent, but the waves were slowly coming down from awesome to just serious.

I knew I was pretty beat. I tried to keep the boat going and somewhat on course. I couldn't do much more.

Finally, I decided I was far enough offshore to begin sleeping an hour-and-a-half at a time. Each time I woke, I felt better. This seemed like getting well after being sick. Each time I realized I felt better, I knew it was a cumulative improvement. And, each time the accumulation increased, I realize how bad I must have felt when I was in the worst part of it.

Radio check-in had been pretty much just facts up until now. Tonight, more chit chat came through and even a few stories. Most of the stories seemed to result from sleep deprivation. Steve on Solitaire reported, "I got whacked in the head and bled on the deck a little. I decided to leave the blood there to remind me I wasn't invincible. I need to be more careful in the future." Gregg, sailing Color Blind, said, "Something hit me in the back of the head, so I turned around to see what it was, and the boom hit me in the face."

Day Four:

Overnight, I continued the 90-minute sleep periods. By mid morning, I began to think a little, but physically, I was still struggling. The wind was now mostly on the beam. I knew if it went any further aft, I'd need to switch from the wind vane to the autopilot, and that probably wouldn't be too long.

I dragged together what energy I could muster and resolved to crawl down into the after-cockpit area and look for the broken electrical wire. I needed to fix the Main Current Error soon or I really would be in cruise mode for the rest of the race.

With a lot of reservation, I forced myself to squeeze down into the space aft of the cockpit, just forward of the transom. The space was so tight, the rolling of the boat made little difference. I was tightly wedged securely in place.

Below deck, I could see on the bulkhead in front of me the wires from the switch panel and the autopilot were still attached to a terminal strip. I searched for a break anywhere in the electrical line, but didn't find one. I couldn't find the cause of the Main Current Error.

I mumbled something seaman-like, reaching for a handhold to pull myself back up and out of the below-deck hole. As I pulled up, I turned my face to miss the bulkhead and glanced at the quadrant. Oh! There's a problem! The autopilot ram wasn't attached to the quadrant. The end of the autopilot ram was hanging in mid air. How could a disconnected ram cause a Main Current Error? That didn't make any sense.

At least I'd discovered a problem that would certainly make the autopilot inoperable. I lowered myself back down and lifted the end of the ram back onto the stud attached to the quadrant. The end of the stud was threaded, and I remembered putting the washer and nut on when I installed the autopilot. Now, they had come off, allowing the ram arm to drop off the stud.

I twisted around hoping to find the nut and washer beneath me in the bottom of the boat. Of course, the rolling of the boat didn't help. I kept getting rolled onto one shoulder. In the cramped space, I couldn't get the leverage to lift my body off the bottom of the boat and out of the way. Finally, I managed to roll enough to see the low spot in the bottom. Lying there next to a stringer was the nut, just out of reach. Eventually, I contorted my left arm enough to grasp the nut.

I relaxed a few overused muscles and breathed deeply. For a moment, I wondered where the washer was. Then, I realized the obvious. It wasn't with the nut and I wasn't going to find it.

I wondered if I really needed it. I hoped I didn't because I had no spare washer that size on the boat. I realized just how thankful I was I'd found the nut.

After a moment of resting, I realized if the nut came off once, I'd better put it back on better than I had the last time. The stud had no hole for a cotter pin, but at least I could fill the threads with Loctite®.

I climbed up out of the after-cockpit area, rising into the cockpit. In the main cabin, I found the Loctite® in the toolkit and a wrench that fit the nut. I returned to the tiny, below-deck compartment by the quadrant. Putting the nut back on with Loctite® was easy. The quadrant was where I could reach it. I wondered how long it would take for the Loctite® to harden and climbed back out of the below-deck confinement.

The sky had a low cloud cover, with occasional mist. I was glad to be back on deck, even in the mist. And, I was thankful I didn't get sick again from being confined below.

That evening during radio check-in, Steve reported blowing out his ¾-ounce chute. Etosha reported a close encounter with a freighter and I reported getting the autopilot fixed.

Day Five:

Later, while tinkering with the sails and the wind vane, I wondered how far south I should be going. Before the race, I talked to other skippers who made this race before and planned "my best route." I wanted to sail a little north of the great circle route to get offshore, and then a little south across the great circle route and into the trades as soon as was reasonable. Then, I would sail a straight line to the finish. This all seemed so easy before leaving the dock.

Well, I certainly had sailed north of the great circle route leaving San Francisco. While I was sick in the heavy weather, I didn't try too hard to maintain course. I just kept going . . . pretty much wherever the boat wanted to go. Yesterday, I started trying to work more south. I didn't have a good feel for how I was doing.

A review of the chart showed I was on the great circle route, but my preferred track had already swung well south of the great circle route.

The next question was where was the high? If it was far north, my wind might hold. If it was getting closer to me, then I should try to sail farther south, to stay away from the high.

The 2 A.M. weather-map broadcast showed the high was closer than I liked. North of my position, the isobars were already well spaced. If the high came any closer, I'd probably lose some wind speed. The 48-hour projection showed the high moving a little closer to where I'd be in two days, but not much. I decided to try harder for more southing. Fiddling with the sails and the wind vane, I got the boat to sail another five degrees south without giving up much boat speed.

At 7 A.M., I passed the one-quarter mark. Three-quarters of the race was still in front of me. I tried not to think about my exhaustion level.

The Loctite® under the nut holding the autopilot ram had been drying for almost a day, so it should be set up now. I hoped. I turned the autopilot on and it worked. No more Main Current Error message! I prayed the Loctite® would hold because there was no lock nut.

I celebrated with a big nap. Both the functioning autopilot and the nap made me feel better.

Up on deck, I let out the jib and main a bit, and I tried to get the boat to steer down even more. The wind was a little aft of beam, and the boat felt sluggish when it went a little low. Knowing the spinnaker would create more boat speed than a jib and main, I adjusted the course down some more and set the spinnaker with the pole well forward.

Most of the time, the autopilot steered well under the spinnaker. But the boat wanted to head up on every big wave, and the autopilot response was too slow. On the biggest waves, the spinnaker and waves combined forces to round the boat up more than the autopilot could control. Each time the boat headed up more than was wise I shut off the autopilot and steered back down by hand.

All afternoon, it was back and forth between the autopilot and me. I had good boat speed, but I couldn't get too far away from the helm. I missed my afternoon nap.

I realized I couldn't go on this way.

Time for Plan B. I took down the spinnaker. Under the main alone, the boat seemed to bob up and down, rather than charge forward. I set the good 120 jib on the starboard groove in the twin stay with the starboard jib halyard and poled it out to weather. Then, I set a cut-down 120 jib in the port groove. Because the port jib halyard was broken, I used the port spinnaker halyard.

The boat responded to the power of the twin headsails and built up good boat speed. I wondered how good my speed was compared to the other boats flying spinnakers. I cared, but after missing my afternoon nap, I didn't have any other options. I was exhausted.

I adjusted the pole position on the high side and the sheet lead on the low side. When I finished the sail change and tuning, it was so close to check-in that I missed my nap again.

At check-in, Magic Carpet Ride and Leilani Too were reported in port. We all felt a little better for that. Then, I realized I'd been getting position data on the other boats and I hadn't paid any attention to it. Bruce on Razzberries was now 21 miles north of me and 19 miles ahead, and I owed him a bit of time. The rest of the boats in my class didn't seem to be a threat after allowing for handicaps. Etosha was well ahead of me, but she was a 60-foot boat and owed me more time than she was saving.

With meager energy, I went back on deck and tuned the double-head rig. I wondered again just how much I was giving up by not flying a spinnaker.

I looked up and saw the first stars of the trip. Finally, the overcast was beginning to clear a little. Maybe now the weather would ease up a bit.

Day Six:

I crashed until the 2 A.M. weather fax transmission. Again, it looked like I ought to work farther south, but not drastically so.

Occasional mist wet my face and the clouds filled in again. The wind was holding and the boat was moving nicely under main and double-head sails. The autopilot was steering well. Best of all, the double headsails didn't round the boat up like the spinnaker had.

All day, I wondered how I was doing against Bruce. I knew he'd be flying a spinnaker. Somehow, I just didn't have the energy to take down the double headsails and put up the spinnaker.

I tuned the sails, napped and caught up a bit, tuned the sails, and tuned them again.

About 4:30 in the afternoon, a sailboat crossed behind me. I hadn't seen anything except water and sky for five days. A sailboat! I ran to the VHF to see if they'd seen me. Yes, the boat was Dry Martini sailing on the Victoria to Maui Race. I told them I was sailing in the singlehanded race from San Francisco to Hawaii.

When they realized I was single-handling, they regaled me with a great description of the gourmet dinner they were about to have. Roast tri-tip, mashed potatoes, fresh vegetables, salad, and rare old wine. I was drooling by the time they finished.

I was probably more in awe of having someone to sit down to dinner with than the dinner itself, but I didn't tell them that part. I told them about the week-old cold stew I was about to heat up and take up on deck.

In a half hour, they were out of sight. I was back to water and sky, trimming the sails, trying to maximize boat speed, and driving further south.

At check-in, I was amazed at Bruce's report. In the last 24 hours, I held even with Razzberries and, at the same time, I managed to work farther south than Bruce. More than anything, I was mystified. How could double headsails be as fast as a spinnaker?

Day Seven:

At 2 A.M., waiting for the weather map, I was still pondering Bruce's position report. I didn't understand. I didn't think it could be right. Tomorrow, I expected to lose ground.

On the weather map, the high had hardly moved.

All morning and throughout the day, I alternated between tuning the sails and napping. I tried to maintain a balance between keeping the boat speed up and sailing as low as I could.

The day passed quietly, as we all ground off more miles toward Hawaii.

At check-in that evening, I said hello just before the appointed hour. Someone asked me what sails I was flying. Somehow, I didn't want to answer. I didn't want to tell them I wasn't flying a spinnaker. Mumbling something evasive, I asked someone else a question. Etosha talked about having an accidental jibe and wrapping the chute. Solitaire reported a spinnaker wrap so bad, it had to be cut off the forestay.

During the position reports, I found I'd gained three miles on Razzberries. Bruce was now just 16 miles ahead. I gave my report, but I couldn't get Bruce's position out of my head. I was gaining on him? I gained three miles?

Day Eight:

Finally, the Sun came out. It was beautiful. Today was the first pretty day since the race began.

Last night's weather map showed I'd just crossed the trough on the southeast side of the high. Sure enough, today's wind was more aft.

From here on, it would be harder to work south. The penalty for not being south now would be to sail nearly dead downwind. I was glad I'd worked so hard to get as far south as I had. I was particularly glad Bruce was north of me. I hoped I would hang on to him for the rest of the race.

Again, I spent the day making as much boat speed as I could, and I tried to rest as much as possible. I finally felt I was recovering because I didn't feel as physically fatigued as a few days ago. But, then, I couldn't remember when a few days ago was. I never did realize today was the Fourth of July!

About 1:40 P.M., Giggles was at the halfway point. I had the same number of miles behind me as ahead of me. I made an entry in the log, tuned the sails, and laid down for a nap to celebrate.

Three hours later, I was on deck trying to make the boat go faster when the starboard jib started sliding down the headstay. I rushed to the foredeck to find the problem. When the sail was about a third of the way down, it stopped descending. At the top of the mast, I could see the end of the starboard jib halyard. Only the snap shackle was sticking out of the mast and it looked like it was open. I wondered if the pin was gone or if, somehow, it had just opened.

The pole had both a foreguy and an afterguy, so it stayed in place when I eased the starboard jib sheet. From the cockpit, I jibed the half-down starboard jib to the port side of the boat. It lay on the port jib, making the rest of the takedown fairly easy. I attached the starboard spinnaker halyard, and then raised it again still on the port side. When it was fully up, I jibed it back to the starboard pole. Again, I was at full power.

With the binoculars, I looked carefully at the snap shackle. It was open and looked like the pin was still there. If I wanted, I guess I could go up the mast to the very top and retrieve the halyard. I remembered going up the mast on the way to French Polynesia. I knew I didn't want to do that again, especially not alone. I'd wait until the situation was critical.

At check-in that evening, I talked to Bruce about the shackle. "Yes," Bruce said, "I've had them open before, so I always tape the pins now." Then, Bruce told me about the terrible spinnaker wrap he had today. It took him four hours to get it untangled.

Later, when Bruce gave his position report, I was dumbfounded to find he was now 50 miles north of me and three miles behind me. I owed him a little time. I thought three miles would just about do it. Bruce and I were now dead even!

The General, sailing Harrier in Class II, reported a bad spinnaker wrap had caused him to go back to his twin jib headsail. Harrier was 80 miles behind me.

When I gave my report, I told the Race Committee, "I passed the halfway point today. Now that I'm closer to Hawaii than San Francisco, I think I'll go on to Hawaii, rather than turn back. I'm not certain yet if I'll cross the finish line. I'll keep you posted."

Too tired to think about the position reports, I lay down for a nap before the weather-map transmission. Having crossed the ridge to the southeast of the high, the strategy for the race was mostly over. I'd gotten as much southing as I could before passing through the trough. Now, the race was nothing but boat speed to the finish.

Day Nine:

The weather map was interesting, but I couldn't take much action based on it.

Reflecting on last night's position reports, it finally sank in that I was now tied for first in class. Razzberries was 50 miles north of me. We were exactly even after I gave him time for the difference in our handicaps.

Mulling it over, I decided to change my mental picture of the situation. Instead of thinking about this being another day in the middle of a 2000 mile race, I pretended it was the first day of a 1,000-mile race to Hawaii. Instead of letting myself be lulled, I decide to take the mental attitude of the first day of a race.

Well, if this were the first day of a race, I'd be all over the boat—trimming sails, checking leads, and adjusting course—trying to maximize any tactical advantage. So, let's get busy, Dale!

OK, let's see. If I were racing from here to the finish line, was any course better than just a straight line? Well, I knew more wind ought to be south of me. I started thinking about the tradeoff of more wind to the south versus sailing more miles in a curved course. How deep of an arc should I sail? I went on deck, and started adjusting my course and sails, looking for the optimum. I didn't know what was best; no one ever does. At least I was back to looking for the best! I was no longer just trying to finish the race.

This became the first day of the second race. I pushed harder than I did yesterday and it felt good.

I also tried to take better care of myself. I was more careful about getting enough sleep during the day.

In the evening, the wind picked up. The autopilot began to wander back and forth across a wider course. I wondered if I should reef the main, and I pondered the tradeoff between slower and straighter. At 8:30 P.M., the seas were becoming sizable. I threw in the second reef and rushed below for check-in.

Someone asked me if I were having any trouble with my spinnaker. I dodged the question by talking about downwind racing. Then, someone else mentioned Lakota had crossed the finish line in Hanalei Bay at 10:28:26. Steve Fossett had set a new record for the fastest sailing passage from San Francisco to Hawaii, taking almost a day off the old record. In the position reports, Razzberries was now 25 miles behind me.

On deck, the wind was higher. A storm was building astern. The autopilot was steering with greater course swings, so I rushed back to the helm to help. I needed to sleep again, but I was uncertain about the autopilot and the double-head rig in the approaching storm. I decided to play it safe and reduce sail area. Maybe I was just tired.

I jibed the starboard jib across to the port side; it rode nicely on the port jib. Then, I turned up 20 degrees, enough to get the two jibs on port to fill and fly as one. Net result, the boat was going just about as fast, but 20 degrees above the course I wanted. Then, I reminded myself—the course I wanted in this *new* race.

At least now I could sleep without worrying about the boat.

Day Ten:

At midnight, the wind was about the same. I decided to stay on the "single" jib for now. At 2 A.M., when I got up for the weather map, the wind was still blowing too hard for the double headsail.

At 4:30 A.M., the wind had eased off some and I jibed the starboard jib back to the double-headsail configuration. When I got the boat back down to my desired course, I wondered how much I'd given away by sailing 20 degrees above course for six hours.

This was the second day of the new race. I tried to think and act as if it were only one day after the start. Mostly, this was freshness and attitude. I tried to pretend I was fresh: I adjusted course and tuned the sails again. Maybe freshness wasn't being satisfied, always searching for something better. I tried to think about better tactics or a better course.

I tried to worry more about my competition. Last night, Razzberries was 25 miles behind me and seemed to be falling back, ever so slowly. The only problem was, today, I'd sailed 20 degrees high of course for six hours. I wondered where Razzberries would be tonight?

I got on the radio a little before 9 P.M., the official hour for check-in. As normal, chitchat about the race prevailed, plus everyone had a spinnaker story to tell. Someone noticed I hadn't mentioned a spinnaker and asked me directly, "What color sails are you flying, Dale?" Everyone else got curious and waited for my answer. Finally, I was trapped into admitting I was sailing an all-white double headsail.

The General came to my rescue and told me about a special sail he'd had made for his boat. His double jib was really two half-weight jibs sewn together onto a single luff tape. The General normally flies his spinnaker 24 hours a day, but, when it's simply unwise to fly a spinnaker, he switches to his double jib. The last few days, the wind was so strong, the General had been flying the spinnaker during the day and the double jib at night, even though changing back and forth slowed the boat.

When we went through the position reports, I was delighted to hear Razzberries had fallen back another nine miles. Bruce was now 34 miles behind me.

Up on deck under the stars, I realized I'd gained on Razzberries every day. I shouldn't have been able to do that, but I had. Staring off across the dark ocean, I tried to figure out why. Perhaps it was just too hard to fly a spinnaker well shorthanded, at least in the trade winds when you're tired. Maybe the cost I was paying by not flying a spinnaker was less than the cost everyone else was paying by flying one. Certainly everyone had told many gripping stories about spinnaker wraps.

Whatever the reason, I now believed I would beat Razzberries. I was going to win Class I. Well . . . assuming I didn't break something between here and the finish.

So where would I place overall? I had no idea. I hadn't been watching Class II much. I went below and looked at my notes from the daily check-ins.

After comparing "miles to go to Hawaii" for the boats in Class II and their handicaps, it looked like Harrier was the leading boat in Class II. At the last check-in, she was 124 miles behind me.

At the finish line, I would owe the General over 35 hours. In the last 24 hours, he had sailed 165 miles, for an average boat speed of 6.875. At that speed, when I finished, I'd have to be more than 243 miles ahead of Harrier to win.

I'd have to put another 119 miles between us, and I only had another 688 miles to the finish line. Was that possible?

I looked back over my notes from the last few check-ins. Three days ago, Harrier was 51 miles behind me. So, in those three days, I'd gained an average of 17 miles a day. And, yesterday, I gained 30 miles on him. I had no way to know what I would gain on the General in the next few days: I'd just have to race as hard as I could.

Race fever drove me and I drove the boat. Together, we plowed a wake of white water across the ocean. It didn't take long until I was exhausted again and I had to rest.

Day Eleven:

At 2 A.M., waiting for the weather fax, I reminded myself this was the third day of the new race. It helped me hold my focus on racing. I set aside all thoughts related to anything prior to three days ago and concentrated on right now.

Instead of waiting for the weather map transmission, I went up on deck and checked the sails and my course. The wind had gone aft again. I trimmed the weather jib aft to square up the pole, and then eased the leeward jib out. Looking at the apparent wind, I wondered if the leeward jib might be more effective if I rigged the second pole on port and poled out the leeward jib.

Trying to maintain my new race mindset, I focused on getting the port pole up and the jib poled out. I tried to stay focused on what needed to be done, rather than relaxing and enjoying the ride or drifting off into a haze of fatigue.

Back below, I was too late for the weather map, but it wouldn't make much difference in the race. Changing the sail trim and putting up the second pole, however, might have. I realized I made the right choice to go on deck and adjust the sails rather than wait for the weather fax. I was actually acting as if this really were Day Three of the race. I was worn out all the way through, but I was pleased.

After my nap, I made two signs on the back of a log sheet and stuck them up on the bulkhead above the nav station. One sign said, "Mid-Race Mind Games," and the other, "Go Fast!"

Late in the afternoon, the wind went dead astern. As I decided to jibe, I remembered my first race to Hawaii 18 years before when we jibed on every wind shift. Back then, we were in about this same area when we did our first jibe. We called the whole crew on deck and efficiently jibed to the port tack.

Well, here I was again with the whole crew on deck. All alone, I jibed the main to the port tack, came up 20 degrees on the new tack, and adjusted both poles. Just as I'd done 18 years ago, I congratulated myself on not collapsing the forward sails and told the entire crew how good they were!

An hour later, I jibed back, wondering why man ever invented spinnakers. In this wind, the double headsails drew just about as well. In addition, the lower center of effort allowed the autopilot to steer the boat better.

OK. OK. I know. If the wind weren't so strong, a spinnaker would probably be more effective than the double headsails. *Spinnakers are beautiful,* I thought, *and they're a lot more dramatic.*

Stop daydreaming and get back to racing! I don't need drama.

This was the third day of the race. What else could I do?

Nothing? Well, then, go get some rest.

At check-in, Razzberries had fallen back some more. Now, she was 50 miles behind me.

Harrier, in Class II, was 164 miles behind me. I was pulling away from her, but was it fast enough? Last night, I'd figured I needed to be 243 miles ahead of her when I finished. In the past 24 hours, I'd gained 40 miles on the General, so I'd have to gain another 79 miles before I finished. I'd finish in another two or two-and-a-half days. And, if I could gain just 40 miles a day, I'd make it. Wow!

Before I could spend much time thinking about that, it was time to go up on deck. The autopilot was having trouble steering again. Whenever a squall came over me, I ended up steering instead of using the autopilot. Even with a heavy displacement IOR boat and double headsails, when the wind was heavy enough, I could steer better than the autopilot. I could even get the boat to surf a little. Every time the boat surfed, it gained on where it would have been.

Wiped out from hand steering, I hit the sack.

Day Twelve:

Before dawn, I was back on deck, checking everything. I jibed to port and, four hours later, I jibed back. *Every wind shift. Just like the big guys,* I thought, and then laughed.

Make the boat go fast. Mid-Race Mind Games. Drive. Drive. Drive.

Be careful. Don't break anything. Just keep everything going smoothly.

Drive. Drive. Drive.

Late in the afternoon, I began to hear a tic in the steering. I couldn't have anything go wrong now. Frantically, I checked the whole system. I couldn't see any broken links in the chain or any broken strands in the cable; the shives all turned and were well greased. The cable lay smoothly on the quadrant. I couldn't find anything wrong. I could only worry.

At check-in, Razzberries was 61 miles back and Harrier was 188 miles back. I only gained 24 miles on Harrier in the last 24 hours. I would have to gain another 55 by the finish line. With only a day-and-a-half to go, gaining 24 miles a day wouldn't get me there. Feeling my exhaustion, I went back up on deck, looking in vain for a way to make the boat go faster.

I adjusted everything anyway, more from habit than making any improvements.

I lay down to rest again.

Day Thirteen:

I slept through the weather map transmission, which was no longer significant. Whatever would come to me, would come to me. I couldn't get out of the way, or in the way, for that matter. I'd just have to sail with whatever came.

I continued to adjust things whether or not they needed it. Harrier and Giggles were both going as fast as possible. This was the General's sixth Singlehanded Transpac. What did he know that I didn't?

I couldn't think of any different strategy. I'd done all I knew to do. Now, I could only surf on the big ones.

In the current wind, the autopilot steered as well as I could. At least as well as I could this tired. I let it steer.

I looked back at the horizon. I knew Harrier was back there, out-of-sight, coming as fast as she could. I looked forward and wished, but I knew wishing didn't make any difference.

I rested and tuned sails. That was all I could do.

At check-in that night, Harrier was 219 miles behind me. I only gained 31 miles on her. *I need to gain another 24 miles by the time I finish tomorrow,* I thought, *and that's less than 24 hours away.* This was much too close to call.

At the end of check-in, the General called me on the radio. When I responded, he congratulated me on winning. He figured he couldn't catch me now.

I tried to respond the race wasn't certain yet, but the General congratulated me again.

After I got off the radio, I thought about how nice the General was to do that. I always thought generals were supposed to be hard-bitten, tough, old codgers. This guy was anything but. Was he really a general?

Up on deck, I knew I still had another 24 miles to gain. I cleared my head and tried to go back to work. The warmth of the General's congratulation was still with me as I tinkered in the cockpit.

Day Fourteen:

Shortly after midnight, I marveled at the brilliance of the Moon. It made working on deck a lot easier. The twinkling reflection of the Moon's light on the surface of the waves was beautiful.

A bright-red dawn unfolded, as only seems to happen at sea in the tropics.

The tic, tic, tic continued in the steering, but was no worse.

About mid morning, a tropical storm built up behind me. When the autopilot could no longer steer, I took the helm.

With the wind increasing this was the best of sailing. At full power, I turned down on every wave and Giggles responded by surfing. I watched the speedometer climb to exciting new highs.

Over and over again we surfed down the big ones. I screamed and laughed at the thrill. The fatigue of racing was gone now—the roar of water as it passed the hull and the rush of adrenalin in my ears filled my world.

A half hour later, the wind was even stronger. Still grinning, I began to look for a way out of this violent charging. Now, the knot clock rarely returned back to hull speed. On the face of the biggest waves, it registered two knots greater than anything I'd ever seen before on Giggles.

The bow wake was spraying sheets of water out sideways, as it did from a dinghy on a plane. Only this was a 16,000-pound displacement hull.

After the first hour, I wanted to end this high-risk madness. I didn't want to lose the mast this close to the finish. I definitely didn't want to break anything.

I looked for a way to steer and jibe the weather jib at the same time. I'd had too much excitement and adrenalin, and far too little sleep. But, I couldn't see a safe way to reduce sail while steering. And, I didn't dare let the autopilot steer. I was caught. The safest thing to do was continue being unsafe.

As long as I didn't make a mistake, I thought everything would be OK.

At least with the double-head rig, the boat was easy to steer. Easy, but I knew I had to be very quick or the boat would spin out. If I lost my concentration and spun out, the boat would stop, and the apparent wind would shoot up another ten miles an hour.

An hour-and-a-half into the storm, I was totally spent. The wind was beginning to ease a bit, and the knot clock was no longer climbing as it had. I wanted off the helm. I wanted to rest. But I couldn't get off. Not yet.

More and more, the wind eased as I became less and less able to keep going.

Finally, I decided the autopilot could steer better than I could in this condition.

On my way to the closest bunk, I realized I might be within VHF range of the Race Committee in Hanalei Bay. I tried to call them, but I didn't make contact.

I barely made it into a bunk before I was asleep.

I hurt when I woke up . . . more all over than in any one place.

I tried to call the Race Committee again on the VHF. This time, they responded, loud and clear. They said they'd heard me last time and had called back, but I hadn't responded. Now, they were glad I could hear them.

I gave them my position, course, and speed. They calculated my ETA and told me they would be on station.

Still sleepy, I tried joking with them. "I've sailed all this way and now I'm in the vicinity of the finish line, but I'm not sure if I'll actually go across it." They responded, saying, "If you aren't committed to finishing, then we aren't committed to bringing your smoothie out to the finish line."

Well! Now we were talking Real Motivation! Immediately, I committed to the race, finishing, and anything else necessary. Right now, my smoothie was the most important thing in the world!

However, finding the finish line turned out to be more difficult than I expected. Before the race, the Race Committee handed out materials to help each of us. One page was an 8 ½ by 11 picture of the finish line from our approach direction. The photo showed the mountains behind the finish area bathed in sunlight. And, an overhead arrow pointed to where we would find the finish line.

With the picture in one hand and the helm in the other, I tried and tried to match the photo with the horizon ahead of me. Nothing looked the same. The picture showed the skyline, but the island in front of me was half-covered with low clouds. I could see the base of the mountains, but not the peaks. I couldn't match any part of the photo with my view of the island.

271

I waited until I got closer, thinking everything would fall in place. The random contour of the shoreline ahead either seemed to match any number of places in the picture or none at all. The closer I got, the more worried I became.

Finally, I threw the photo below and returned to navigating as I had in all the landfalls on the New Zealand trip. During my years of sailing, the miracles of modern electronics had improved continuously. On my first ocean passage, we were dependent on a sextant and sight-reduction tables. We could determine our location only twice a day: at twilight and dawn. On the New Zealand trip, the Sat Nav was dependent on a satellite being in the right position, which happened every hour or three. Now, my GPS updated itself continuously. Every second, the GPS told me which way to steer to the finish line and how far I had to go.

The finish line was an imaginary line at 290 degrees magnetic from the Race Committee Headquarters, located at 22 degrees 13 minutes and 20 seconds north, and 159 degrees 29 minutes and 50 seconds west. I'd heard the Race Committee Headquarters was someone's condo overlooking Hanalei Bay, and the actual finish line was a line sighted from the balcony door jamb across a pencil stuck in a flower pot on the railing: a definition never found in print. The race instructions only said, "The Race Committee will advise the skippers via VHF when they finish."

I raced toward a finish line I couldn't identify, while the Race Committee calmly said things like, "Yes, Giggles, we have you in sight. Yes, you're approaching the line. Yes, we'll tell you when you finish. Yes, you're getting closer. Yes, you're almost there."

And, finally . . . "Giggles, you have finished!"

The time was 16:39:28 P.M. PDT. 13 days, 5 hours, 50 minutes, and 32 seconds after starting.

Having finished, the next task, and one of the most difficult tasks of the race, had to be completed as quickly as possible. Giggles could only sail one more mile in this direction before running up on the rocky shore of Makahoa Point. The boat was still going at racing speed and I was the only crew. I had to take down both jibs and turn Giggles away from the shore before I drove her up on the rocks.

And I had to do it without the engine. The Race Committee needed to come on board and remove the seals before I was cleared to go under power.

It wasn't pretty, but being high from the finish helped. I did get both jibs down and tied to the lifelines. When I turned the boat away from shore, I was so tired, I forgot to release the preventer. I tacked and back-winded the main, which was now being held out on the wrong side of the boat by the preventer. Giggles was quickly losing steerage way. I judged the distance to the rocks.

I felt as if I'd been in a fire drill for the entire race and this was only one more in the continuing list of events. No problem. I'd just go on around. When I jibed, the wind returned to the right side of the main and the boat started sailing again—toward the rocks.

This time, I removed the preventer before tacking, and then sailed away from shore while the Race Committee ignored my low-skill maneuver. At their instruction, I sailed into the bay. In calmer water, the Race Committee tender came along side and, for the first time in two weeks, I was no longer alone on the boat.

A smoothie never tasted so good!

The Race Committee removed the seals, kindly lowered the main, and helped me get the anchor set securely. Then, as Race Committees do, they departed without saying a word about how well I'd done. Actually, they probably didn't know yet either.

Physically, I felt pretty good. I ate dinner and slept for eight hours. I marveled at how well I felt after driving myself so hard for so long.

Then for the next month, I marveled at my inability to get anything done. My mind and body had a big case of the "I don't wanna's."

What happened to the competition? Where was Harrier? I listened at check-in, but had no way to tell where Harrier was when I finished in the afternoon. I'd have to wait and see.

So, I waited. I waited on the boat. I waited on shore under the big tree. I waited as I tried to exercise my legs. I waited as I carried my laundry to town.

273

Razzberries finished about half-a-day behind Giggles and corrected out to 11 hours behind. My old friend, Bruce, placed Second in Class I, and fourth overall.

Harrier finished a day-and-a-half later, about five in the morning. When the handicaps were applied, Harrier corrected out to an hour and eight minutes behind Giggles. I had put the necessary 243 miles and probably another 7 miles between us. After two weeks of racing around the clock for 2,120 miles, 7 miles was so close anything could have tipped the scales either way. As it turned out, the General won his class and got second overall.

When the last boat was about to finish, I tied a fender to the end of my anchor line and slipped the whole anchor line overboard. The Race Committee brought the wife and daughter of the last skipper to finish out to Giggles on a tender. I motored around to the other boats and picked up anyone who wanted to go, and ended up with more people on Giggles than ever before. Certainly, there were more fog horns than ever before.

About a mile before the finish, we waited as his sail grew bigger, and then passed a few yards away. His wife was in tears and his daughter was in awe as we all sounded our fog horns and welcomed the last of the 11 boats to make it to Hawaii. I must admit, Bob looked better than I felt when I finished.

Two days later at the Awards Ceremony, Giggles was declared First in Class I, and First Overall. In the history book, Giggles had the tenth fastest corrected time in the history of the race.

The trophies were impressive. But the most important of all the trophies was the diamond engagement ring the Race Committee gave me for my commitment to the race.

Singlehanded

Eight tons of sailboat, food, water, and gear.
Across the start, out the Golden Gate, into the deep ocean.
San Francisco to Hawaii, a race for experienced sailors.
Alone on the boat.

Day ends, night begins.
Visions of freighters turn sleep into naps.
Cook . . . navigate . . . adjust course . . . trim sails . . . check weather.
Spinnaker up. Faster! Unstable. I dare not sleep.
Night . . . Day . . . Night. The first week is logged.
Alone on the boat.

Wind and rain blast out of passing squalls. Smaller sails, bigger sails.
Beautiful weather most of the time. Wonderful sailing!
Another squall. Braver now, I leave the big sails up, steering by hand.
The storm builds. Need to reduce sail.
I can no longer leave the helm.
Alone on the boat.

Landfall!
Double-check the navigation. Must not sleep approaching shore.
Find the finish. Thirteen days and four hours.
Exhausted.
Alone on the boat.

The Awards Dinner:
First in Division. First Overall.
Tenth fastest time in the history of the race.
Inside my head, a feeling I'll carry forever.
I did it. I did it all myself.
Alone on the boat.

Chapter 40

Three Close Calls

After the Singlehanded race to Hawaii, Bill and John joined me in Kauai, and helped sail Giggles back to San Francisco. With three of us on the boat, we divided the 24 hours into three watches. We each sailed singlehandedly a total of eight hours a day.

Together, we kept a lookout for ships during the whole passage. I'm glad we did.

When I first saw the light, it was just aft of the starboard beam, way out on the dark horizon. *Wow,* I thought, *we've got company!* In the middle of the night, the light was tiny, but unmistakable.

Rarely have I ever seen a ship in the middle of the ocean. The ocean is just too big and the number of ships too small.

Fascinated, I watched the speck of a light. It blinked out. The blackness of the horizon was monotonous.

The ship was well over the horizon. Maybe we both had been up on swells at the same time.

I watched where the light disappeared. Eventually, I tired of staring at a black space on a black horizon. After a few minutes, the yaw of the boat and the absence of any visual reference points made identifying the original location impossible. I was no longer certain where I had seen the light. I just knew I'd seen it for a moment.

Giggles continued to beat north. With the helm under the control of the wind vane, Giggles stayed at the same relative angle to the wind. In the steady trade winds, our course would stay constant as long as we had wind enough to drive the boat and move the wind vane.

Scanning the rest of the empty, dark horizon, I verified we were alone. That felt good. I liked being alone better. We were five days north of Hawaii, bound for San Francisco, and I would be just as happy not to see any ships at sea.

Ever since we left Nawiliwili Harbor, we had been sailing pretty much north, scanning the horizon for ships every few minutes—bumps on the horizon in the day or lights at night. This was our first sighting.

Now I scanned more frequently. Curiosity about the light I'd seen kept drawing my gaze back to the starboard quarter. In time the light was there again. It blinked, and disappeared.

The next time it reappeared, it had not been gone as long as before. When it came back, I was ready. I sighted over the pedestal compass and got a bearing on the light. Then, I sighted once more before the light blinked out. The light was at 115 to 120 degrees on the compass.

Now I had to let some time pass for our relative positions to change.

When I saw it again, I checked the compass. Still the same 115 degrees. The light went out again. *Patience,* I thought. It was still mostly over the horizon.

A few more minutes and the light began to show more frequently. I resisted taking another bearing because I knew it was too soon. This far apart, our relative positions would change slowly.

I sat back in Giggles' cockpit and tried to think about something else. But my gaze kept going back to the light on the quarter.

Slowly it stopped blinking out. In the daylight, the ship would have been hull down behind the horizon.

I roused myself and scanned the rest of the horizon. The starboard quarter held the only interesting thing in sight. I watched some more.

Now the light turned into two lights, one slightly higher than the other. Looking at the lights again, I could see the lower light was slightly to the left of the higher light, which made it look as if the ship would pass on the starboard side of Giggles. But, Giggles was headed towards the ship's track. If we were both going at exactly the right directions and speeds, we could arrive at the intersection at the same time. The only way to tell was to see if the relative bearing changed.

After waiting as long as I could stand it, I took another bearing. This time I got 120 degrees, maybe even 125. Looking first over the binnacle compass at the light on the horizon, and then looking down at the compass to get the reading made being accurate difficult. Frustrated, I went below and dug the hand-bearing compass out of the nav station.

Now I could read the bearing with some accuracy. This time, I read 113 degrees. The previous readings were from the ship's compass—less accurate and a different compass. I didn't have two comparable bearings, so I'd have to wait to get a second reading from the hand-bearing compass. I needed to see the *change* in relative position.

The rest of the horizon remained dark. I took another bearing at 113 degrees. *Too soon. I'm too anxious,* I thought.

Giggles continued to sail on unattended, balanced between the sail trim and the wind vane. I couldn't do anything, except wait here in the cockpit in the dark and be ready.

A red port light now showed below the range lights. It was a big ship of some kind. The relative position of the lights said it was headed to my starboard. The increasing brightness said it was coming this way.

I fidgeted with the hand-bearing compass and took another bearing: 111 degrees. Maybe it was going to pass ahead of me.

Then, I realized I'd made that decision on a two-degree change. Was I really that good?

I'd better check again. I did and I couldn't tell if it was 111, 112, or 113. *I'll have to wait some more,* I thought.

The range lights began to get brighter and a little farther apart. Now I could see small lights, maybe on deck or in the superstructure. The ship clearly was coming closer.

Still, the hand-bearing compass read somewhere between 111 and 114. I wasn't as sure of my readings any more. I certainly couldn't tell if the bearing was changing. The only thing for sure was the lights were getting brighter and farther apart. And, the ship was still on my quarter.

The longer I watched the ship come in on me, the more I realized it was going to be close. I thought back over all the stories I'd ever heard about collisions at sea and, while many well-told and scary stories came to mind, only one involved actual contact. That was a story about a man who liked to sleep on his boat in the ocean.

The man would sail far enough offshore from San Francisco to be in the ocean wave structure, and then he'd go to sleep for the night. Eventually, he got bumped by a freighter. Considerable rigging damage occurred, as well as some damage to the hull, but nothing really serious. Just a glancing blow – a glancing blow from a metal structure the size of a freighter.

That was the only incident I knew of where contact had happened.

Then, I realized if the man had been hit head-on by the freighter, he wouldn't have returned to tell the story. I wondered if the reason I'd never heard any stories about collisions was because a collision normally resulted in no one being able to talk about it.

I looked up at the lights bearing in on the quarter. I wanted to be able to tell this story after it was all over.

I watched the ship's lights continue to get brighter and more spread out, and wondered if I should steer off course to avoid a collision. Which way should I turn?

I took another bearing with the hand-bearing compass. Still about the same. Still no clear change in bearing.

Clearly, the ship had to pass on one side or the other of Giggles. I just couldn't tell which side. And, I certainly didn't want to change course to sail back in front of it.

I got behind the wheel and disconnected the wind vane. I steered with one hand and took another bearing with the other. Still the same.

Now I saw the first dim outline of the hull in the fading moonlight. It was hard to see, though I thought it was pointed a tiny bit to the starboard of Giggles. I wanted to steer left, but I wasn't sure.

I stared intently at the ship, now taking shape in the moonlight. Indecision about which way to turn to avoid collision had kept me on a constant course. Our two constant courses had maintained a relative bearing since we were over the horizon from each other.

Now the ship was closing with Giggles and moving much faster. I tried to make out the gray image of the hull emerging from the dark. It sure looked like it would pass to starboard. Yes, that was clear now.

In the dark, I had nearly waited too long. The ship was almost on top of me.

I grabbed the port jib sheet from the self-tailing winch and eased out a big bunch. At the same time, I spun the boat down to port, away from the ship overtaking me. Giggles turned to a beam reach and began picking up a little speed.

I looked back at the ship, now passing just a little to the right of where Giggles would have been.

An old freighter, I thought. *I wonder if anyone is on watch?* All ships are supposed to keep a watch. I didn't want to think about the Singlehanded Race and that none of us had anyone on watch much of the time.

Bill's head and shoulders popped up out of the main hatch. He asked, "What's going on?"

My easing sheets and spinning the boat had brought him out of his bunk to see if I needed help. I just pointed astern at the old freighter. Bill looked, nodded, and said, "Oh."

With the freighter passing astern, there was nothing to do. No danger. Bill's head disappeared.

The rest of my watch, I wondered how close it would have been if one of us hadn't been on watch.

The second close call occurred about a week later on this same passage. We had just come out of the North Pacific High and we were sailing again, although the wind was fairly light.

Again, in the middle of the night, a light appeared on the horizon. This time, it was very bright, brighter than what a range light should look like that far away.

And, again, the bearing remained constant as the light got closer and became a ship. I could see the ship, it was bathed in its own light. Its lights were turned down on itself. But why would a ship do that?

As it came close enough to make out detail, I could see it was a commercial fishing boat headed straight downwind. Thinking it over, I realized the minimum roll provided by its course would provide the best sleeping.

This crossing, too, was too close for comfort, so I altered course to avoid collision. Again, I wondered if anyone was on watch, or if they were all sound asleep below.

A few days later, we were approaching the coast of California and a fog had settled in over the whole area. Being unable to see very far made standing watch much more nerve-racking. Normally, it took more than 15 minutes for a ship to come over the horizon and collide with a sailboat. In the fog, the ship would be much closer when it became visible.

I was off watch and sound asleep when the third close call occurred. I barely remember the boat rolling to the other side, and then rolling back. I didn't wake completely until I heard the pounding of a winch handle on the cockpit seat just above my head and Bill shouting, "Dale! Get up here!" Now I was wide awake!

With a call like that, I didn't even put on my pants. I just ran for the main hatch and stuck out my head. I opened my mouth to say something, but Bill was pointing out to port. "What do you see?" he demanded.

It was early morning, but the fog limited the circle of vision to about half a mile. Over to port, I saw a freighter well inside the fog line, but on a course to pass astern of us. A second glance told me the freighter was also turning to pass farther astern. "He'll go behind us," I said. It was close, but there was no danger of being hit. I wondered why Bill was so hyped.

"Yeah, that's what I see, too. I just wanted some conformation." Bill replied. I must have looked at Bill like he needed some sleep.

"When he popped out of the fog, it looked like we were on a collision course, so I jibed to turn away from his track," Bill explained, a chill in his voice. "As I completed the jibe, I realized he was leaning to port. The only reason I could think of for him to be leaning to port was he had the rudder hard over and he was already turning to his starboard when he came out of the fog. So, when I jibed, my new course kept us moving back into his track as he turned.

"He didn't have time to turn the other way and miss us, so I jibed back. That meant I had to pass in front of him." Bill's voice was clearing a little, "Trying to cross in front of a freighter going full speed is one thing I really don't want to do in a sailboat. The odds just aren't all that good."

Bill was a little calmer now. "That's when I wanted someone else to look at him."

"Go back and get some sleep . . . and thanks for your help," Bill wound down.

Suddenly, I was shivering, and not just from standing in the north Pacific night air in my skivvies.

I did climb back into my sleeping bag, but I couldn't sleep. On one passage, we'd had three close calls—close enough that, each time, prudent seamanship caused us to change course to avoid collision. And, in two of those situations, I doubted anyone was on watch on the other ship to notice our presence.

On the Singlehanded Race, I'd just sailed the same passage going the other direction, sleeping an hour-and-a-half at a time. I wondered how many ships had passed close to Giggles that I'd never known about. Had any of them altered course to avoid me?

In the Long Pac Race, a year before the Singlehanded Race, I'd had a close call with a down bound freighter, just after looking for an outbound tug and tow. I had put it out of my mind and entered the Singlehanded Race to Hawaii.

Now, I felt as if I were in the middle of a huge wake-up call.

Part V

Two Last Memories

Chapter 41

Singlehanded Cruising

Several years had passed since I won the Singlehanded Race to Hawaii and several more since cruising to New Zealand. All in all, I made five return passages from Hawaii to the mainland, but they, too, had all turned into memories.

I longed for the next grand adventure, although perhaps something a bit less-strenuous than before.

The guest speakers at the local yacht club included two who had been cruising singlehandedly. At the receptions for the speakers, they both assured me they hadn't been lonely. Sure, they did the passages alone, but other boats were always around in the anchorages. As singlehanders, they reported the opposite problem: too many social invitations. The people on the other boats would normally feel a little sorry for the singlehanders and make doubly sure they were invited to everything going on.

My plan was to leave today. I had my Visa application, my Mexican ham license, charts, medical kit, diesel, water, and provisions for two months. Somehow, cruisers never leave on time.

Giggles and everything on board was ready by mid morning, but with a rain storm coming, I decided not to make the 12-hour sail to Ensenada right now. The low 300 miles west of San Diego was supposed to go through between noon tomorrow and noon the next day. I decided to start after that. No point in going out looking for bad weather.

I went home, looking forward to a hot shower and a big nap. After pushing hard for the last few days, it felt good to relax.

Getting my boat insurance extended from the San Diego area to the Mexican coast while I was singlehanding was a real challenge. In the end, I documented my experience and my broker went to bat for me. Finally, the underwriters agreed, provided I sail only in daylight hours.

The Mexican charts showed anchorages all down the coast. My plan was to sail a series of short passages from one anchorage to the next and see how far I could get. I thought I might be able to get all the way to Magdalena Bay without having to enter an anchorage after dark.

A few of the day sails were a little too long to complete in only daylight hours. On those days, I planned to leave before dawn to provide reasonable time for the distance. Leaving in the dark from an anchorage I'd seen the night before would be safer than entering after dark into an anchorage I'd never seen.

In any event, I resolved not to enter an unknown anchorage after dark. I'd stand off, if I had to, until dawn. Or, if I simply had no way to go on, I'd have to turn back. My plan was a series of short sails, however far down the coast I could go.

I wondered if Lance might want to make the first hop with me. As appealing as it was, I remembered my trip was an experiment to find out if I wanted to go cruising alone for an extended period. No, I wouldn't call Lance. I held to my plan to make this trip alone.

I wished the storm would move through. I was tired of waiting. I wanted to go sailing. Eventually, the storm, more light rain than wind, dampened San Diego and began to clear. I went down to the boat and turned in well before dark, planning to leave before dawn against a light flood in the morning.

The alarm got me started at 4 A.M. and I backed out of the slip 40 minutes later. In the dark and dead calm, I raised the main as I quietly powered out of the marina at just over an idle.

The dew on the decks and the cockpit seats slowly painted my jeans a darker blue. The damp haze in the air fuzzed the harbor lights along the shore. I knew this harbor and its lights. It was home and it felt good.

Being off on an adventure again also felt good. At Zuniga Light, I set a course south toward Mexico and unknown anchorages.

Shortly after sunup, I raised the Mexican courtesy flag and the Q flag on the starboard flag halyard. I wondered how long it would be before I sailed back across the border into the US and took down the Mexican courtesy flag again.

The chill of the night air was gone now and my jeans were returning to their original color. About ten, the wind began to fill in from the shore. As soon as the jib would stay filled, I rolled it out and let it help the motor. In another hour, the wind was strong enough for me to turn off the motor and sail in silence. Only the sound of the bow wake and an occasional gull overhead disturbed the bright blue morning.

The rest of the day, the wind slowly strengthened and shifted into the northwest. By afternoon, the wind was blowing 18 knots, raising small waves and frequent whitecaps. I sailed most of the day under wing and wing. My boat speed increased with the wind, climbing from 5 to 8 while surfing a little on the biggest waves. Wonderful sailing!

Even the dolphins came to play, first a pair, and then six or eight. They led Giggles down the coast to Ensenada, swimming just in front of the boat to get the push from the high-pressure area ahead of the bow. All the time, they entertained me with their grace and power, quick turns, and spouting beside the bow pulpit. We raced down the coast, Giggles driven effortlessly by the wind, and the dolphins swimming easily and yet faster.

I arrived at the hotel marina at 3:30 P.M., just 11 hours after leaving my slip. I was in Mexico. My new adventure had begun.

I flaked the main, put on the sail cover, and made up all the lines. I was tired from the 60-mile dash down the coast, but it felt good to be on the way.

The check-in process in Ensenada had changed since my last visit. The new process was easier for yachts entering from the US, and it gave the Harbor Master, who watched the boats coming and going, more authority. Customs, now handled by the hotel Harbor Master, went smoothly. Immigration was still done downtown, by the Immigration Office. It was OK to take down my Q flag, but my check-in wasn't complete. I had to go to Immigration on Monday.

I ate cold chicken and potato salad, and then hit the sack. Because tomorrow was Sunday, I decided to take it easy.

By Monday, I was well rested and went to Immigration to present my papers. They stamped and scribbled on my visa application, and then sent me to Banjercito Bank, about three blocks away, to make a $20 payment for the tourist card fee. Then, I went back to Immigration, where they noted my payment and gave me my official Tourist Card. This turned out to be my stamped and scribbled visa application.

On my way back to the hotel Harbor Master, I picked up fresh bananas and milk from the Gigante Grocery Store. This would probably be my last provisioning until Turtle Bay. At the Harbor Master's office, I surrendered a copy of my Tourist Card. Now, I was officially a tourist in Mexico.

Frozen homemade beef stew, black bread, pistachios, and chocolate cake for dinner tonight. The easy cooking on a boat lasts as long as the precooked foods.

The next morning, I climbed out of my bunk and my feet landed on a cold cabin sole. Up on deck, it was even colder. It reminded me all too much of mornings in San Francisco Bay. After I retired from work, I moved from San José to San Diego to get away from the cold. I still didn't like it.

After breakfast, I entered way points for several anchorages into the boat's GPS and checked distances. It looked as though I were a little optimistic about my sailing plan. The last hop, to Magdalena Bay, was 90 to 95 miles. Too much for a day sail, even a long one starting a little before dawn.

It was clear I wouldn't be able to go all the way to Magdalena Bay. So, I decided to go as far as Turtle Bay, where I could get fuel and probably supplies. Then, I'd decide if I wanted to go any further.

Mexico had just changed its regulations for cruising boats. Each cruising boat had to check in and out with every Port Captain as she traveled along. Ensenada was my port of entry into the country of

Mexico. Now, I needed to check out of Ensenada under the new cruising rules to sail down the coast.

I took my paperwork to the hotel Harbor Master, who checked boats in and out for the Port Captain. I needed to carry a despacho naming the people onboard with me from the time I checked out with one Port Captain until I checked in with the next Port Captain. The Harbor Master asked me where I was going next and to which Port Captain I would give my despacho?

I didn't know. Each day I'd sail a little farther south. At some point, I'd turn around and sail back north.

Was I going to stop at Magdalena Bay? I could check in with the Port Captain there.

No. Probably not. I didn't expect to get that far south. Maybe Turtle Bay, but no further south. I named the anchorages I could remember on the route to Turtle Bay.

The hotel Harbor Master picked Cedros Island out of my list and stared at me for a while without smiling. Cedros Island?

Yes. It looked like about the right distance between the other anchorages along the coast. I expected to anchor there for a night or two, and then go on.

Cedros Island? Again the long face, while he pondered something. Then, he seemed to decide. "Is bad place. Bad men there. You alone on boat. Maybe robbed. Not go to Cedros Island."

Realizing what he'd just told me and his desire to help me stay safe, I thanked him as sincerely as I knew how.

Where was I going? My paperwork was still lying on the desk between us. What was I going to do?

I just want to cruise around a while, and then head back—kind of like a vacation—a vacation on a boat.

"A boat can't go both south and north on the same despacho," explained the hotel Harbor Master. It needed to be reissued by the southern Port Captain before the boat turned around and headed north. Turtle Bay had no Port Captain and, now, I definitely wasn't going to go to Cedros Island. The hotel Harbor Master called the Port

Captain downtown to find out what to do. They couldn't decide. I had to come back in two hours.

They decided the same form could be used for a round trip. But because this was the first time they'd ever issued a round trip on one despacho, the hotel Harbor Master couldn't sign the form. He had taken my form to the Port Captain's office to get the Port Captain's signature. Could I come back in another hour?

Success! I had a despacho showing a crew of one to Turtle Bay with a return to Ensenada. This was a first for the Ensenada Port Captain. Never before had an American sailboat with a crew of one gone sailing for a vacation.

Then, the hotel Harbor Master made four copies and gave them all to me . . . in case I needed them. Maybe the navy would want one.

I took the forms and headed back to the boat with visions of the Mexican Navy boarding Giggles and finding a despacho for a trip they'd never heard of and didn't understand.

Months later, after I returned to San Diego, I was sitting at the yacht club bar telling this story. A friend offered an explanation that absolutely chilled me. He suggested the Port Captain thought I was going to sail around until I made a drug connection, and then return to the US. They'd probably alerted the Mexican Navy to both my sailing plan and the description of my boat!

Innocent and unaware, I got up at 6 A.M. and looked south over the breakwater. Now, I would see no more harbors, slips, fuel docks, running water, restaurants, grocery stores, or telephones. I'd be sailing where I'd never been before and anchoring in coves I'd never seen—singlehandedly.

Civilization would be replaced by a Sun shower. The real adventure was beginning.

I sailed southwest across Bahia Todos Santos, around Punta Banda, and then headed southeast to Punta Santo Thomas. It was overcast and chilly again, almost foggy. I took a few pictures of Punta Banda, hoping they would show the dreariness.

I checked into the Baja Net on the ham radio and talked for a few minutes with a ham operator in La Bufadora. He asked if I were power or sail, and he offered to wave as I went by.

My experience from the New Zealand trip was that most of the ham operators were maritime mobiles on boats, so I made the natural mistake. I thought this ham was on a boat at anchor in La Bufadora and changed course a little to pass by there.

I followed the coast down to La Bufadora and looked for the ham operator in the cove, but there were no boats in the cove at all! He must have lived on the hill or had a vacation house overlooking the cove. Oh, well. I waved at the hillside and took up a course to Punta Santo Thomas.

The jib still had the social-sailing sheets attached, which were a little shorter than the racing sheets. They were just a little short for easy pole handling. In the process of setting the pole, I got whacked in the head. I decided I was rusty. I had to do more full-on racing when I returned to San Diego.

The day turned beautiful and the sail became exhilarating. The point of Santo Thomas grew larger and, eventually, I turned in under its lee. The anchorage was the area most protected from the NW winds. The best part of the area was filled with mooring balls and open fishing boats. The rest of the area had a lot of kelp. I saw some clear places, too, but not so big that finding a spot was easy. I dropped the hook shortly after noon in the best spot I could find.

The anchorage was full of williwaws and was somewhat rolling. As the afternoon wore on, the wind picked up and shifted to the right, coming in more over the hills. The williwaws slowly developed in strength and character, and they pressed their intent on the boat. At dusk, a small cabin fishing boat motored into the anchorage and anchored somewhat close aboard. It was fine for the direction of the wind at the time, but if the wind shifted back to where it had been earlier in the day, his short, all-chain scope might not work well with my longer rope rode.

I slept in the main cabin with my clothes on, wondering which way the wind would shift as it died in the night. I got up every once in a while and checked the relative position of the boats. The wind did die down some, but it stayed stronger than I expected all night. This surprised and delighted me, as the boats stayed well apart. When the

293

morning broke, they pulled up their anchor and got underway quite early. But my all night concerns had left me a little short of sleep.

At breakfast, I watched two whales pass by the edge of the anchorage. The beauty of a momma and her calf in their natural element made me forget my lack of sleep.

Getting the boat ready to sail in the early morning Sun, I realized today would be another beautiful day. The weather felt as if it were going to get warm and, if it did, I'd need suntan lotion today. This would be my first time to worry about a sunburn since leaving San Diego. Finally, some warmth was on the way.

Encouraged by the prospect of warmer weather, I pulled up the anchor and got under way. The wind along the coast was light and from the shore. I set the main, but the wind was too light for the jib.

Two or three hours later, the normal sea breeze filled in from the northwest. Going back home, it would be dead on the nose. Now, it was dead astern on my way to Colnett, my next anchorage. I jibed, headed out to sea a little, and set the pole.

All afternoon, the wind increased. When I jibed to come back in, it was blowing 22 knots. This felt like San Francisco!

A few hours later, about five miles before Point Colnett, the axel of the steering wheel began to slip out of the binnacle. I could see the ends of the roller bearings around the axel peeking out of the binnacle housing. I pushed the whole thing back in as far as it would go, but it only went back in about halfway. I held the wheel with one hand to keep the wheel from working out again. With the other hand, I took the compass off the binnacle to see if I could fix the wheel axel under way. No such luck. I couldn't steer or let the autopilot steer, and make repairs at the same time. The chain was still attached and functioning, but the end of the axel was riding on the housing. The roller bearings were no longer supporting the axel.

The autopilot steered the boat with a hydraulic ram directly attached to the quadrant. As long as I used the autopilot to steer the boat, the chain and wheel bearings wouldn't have any load. I wondered if I could maneuver the boat in an anchorage with the autopilot. That would certainly be a new experience. But, then, that's what adventure is all about, isn't it?

I also had visions of the wheel slipping out far enough to lose the roller bearings or other small parts. I could see them rolling around in the cockpit floor until they dropped down the scuppers and into the ocean. Just in case, I blocked off the scuppers in the cockpit with paper towels.

With a strong autopilot and a nervous stomach, I sailed in under the lee of Point Colnett. When I got the boat anchored, and stopped steering, I was able to repair the assembly. My dinner of homemade stew was a little late, but all the better for it.

The anchorage at Colnett was open to the south and west. At sunset, I sat in the cockpit and watched the sky turn red and the land turn into a dark silhouette. Looking seaward from where the boat was anchored, the sea was red from the bow of the boat to the setting Sun on the horizon.

No other boat was anywhere to be seen.

Back on shore, not a single light came on at dusk. The darkening red turned to black as I sat in the cockpit wondering about singlehanded cruising. I truly was alone. The two speakers never said I wouldn't be alone. They said I wouldn't be lonely.

A month before leaving San Diego on this trip, I had an atrial fibrillation. My heart eventually reset itself and my doctor said, "Resume your normal life." I told him about my plans for this trip and said I'd be unable to obtain medical help if anything went wrong. He simply repeated his suggestion.

So, here I was, alone, 150 miles down the coast into Mexico, anchored in a place where I probably couldn't take a dinghy through the surf and land it on shore. Even if I could land it on shore, I had no way to get from the lonely beach to a hospital. I wondered if the doctor completely understood what my normal life was like.

The anchorage itself was a challenge. After last night in Santo Thomas, I thought the rest of the anchorages would have to be better.

Wrong. The south side of Point Colnett was a bluff, which ran along the north side of the anchorage. It provided pretty good protection from the prevailing northwest wind. But the anchorage was open to the ocean from the west to the southeast, probably 160 degrees. The prevailing swells in the ocean also came from the NW and refracted somewhat around the point. The diminishing remains of the refracted waves rolled straight east across the anchorage to spend themselves on the beach behind the boat.

The refracted swells didn't have the punch of full-sized waves. The anchorage was tolerable and the holding was good, so I stayed the night and rolled. When the wind blew, I listened to the whistle in the rigging. In the lulls, I listened to the surf between the boat and the shore.

Overnight, the wind changed from the nice sea breeze I had all afternoon to a weak offshore flow. As the wind shifted, the boat turned with the wind. During the night, the boat was first bow to the refracted waves from the ocean, then broadside to the waves, and then, finally, stern to the waves.

Two bad nights of sleep in a row. In the morning, I wondered how much I liked this. Tomorrow night, the anchorage simply had to be better.

Earlier than I planned, I ate breakfast and pulled up the anchor. Again, I had a light offshore breeze, so I powered most of the morning. Eventually, the wind came up from the NW again. I wondered if this was normal or if the low was having some effect.

Wind makes a sailboat go and I had another great afternoon of downwind sailing.

Once inside the anchorage at San Quintín, the area was open to the wind, but protected from the ocean waves and swells. Actually, the anchorage only provided protection from the wind and swells coming from the north and northwest. This anchorage was also open to the south and southwest. I motored north inside the anchorage, looking for a spot in the lee.

Two boats were already in the anchorage: Hoptoad and Margarita. Their transoms said they were both from San Francisco. Finally, I'd have company in an anchorage! As I passed close aboard Margarita, someone stuck his head out of the main hatch and welcomed me to San Quintín. They found out where I was from and I learned they were headed north, waiting here for better weather.

Better weather would certainly be nice. In fact, the wind was so strong we didn't talk long. Giggles couldn't stand still in this much wind. So, I slowly moved off, found a spot close up under the weather shore, and anchored.

With the hook down, I flaked the main, made up lines, and put the pole back in its chocks. But, my heart wasn't in it. The cold and blustery weather in the anchorage made being neighborly difficult.

The next day, the wind continued, raising waves in the anchorage. I decided not to blow up the dinghy. It was much too choppy to go anywhere in a dinghy. I wondered what the ocean was like. The lumps were probably a lot bigger out there. Maybe I'd just relax here for a day or so. On the radio, I heard it was raining in San Diego. I tried to feel better.

I took the next day off. I read, played my banjo, did nothing, and waited for the weather to lift. I got bored and unsuccessfully tried to talk to the other boats on the VHF. Then, I did nothing again.

When I charged the batteries, I tied the engine-room doors open to let the engine heat into the cabin. It helped, but it was still too cold for me.

I thought back over my trip so far. At each anchorage, in the cold of the morning after a night of marginal sleep, I knew it hadn't been what I'd expected. I wondered if I wanted to go all the way to Turtle Bay. I dug out Charlie's Charts and began reading with more clarity and less daydreaming than I'd had in San Diego.

Charlie's Charts[9] said the next anchorage, Punta Baja, had many kelp patches and was "one of the rolliest anchorages in Baja." Punta Baja was a popular area with surfers. The anchorage after that, San Carlos, was less rolly. The last two days of sailing had been 40 miles each. To pass by Punta Baja and go straight to San Carlos was 56 miles. I could make it south in a long day. However, coming back

---

[9] *Charlie's Charts of the Western Coast of Mexico*, by Charles E. Wood. Surry, BC, Canada: Charlie's Charts, 2001.

upwind, I'd have to put in at Punta Baja or sail outside the hours defined in my insurance endorsement.

I checked the weather on the ham radio and found the low over southern California had moved eastward. Maybe in a day or two, the weather would be better again. Then, I'd have to decide which way to go.

A fourth boat came in to the anchorage, but it was too cold and rough to be social. I hadn't talked to anyone since I left Ensenada.

I did more reading in Charlie's Charts and found I was now in one of the best anchorages between Ensenada and Turtle Bay. I made a list of what lay ahead from Charlie's Charts:

Miles:	Anchorage:	Charlie's Charts comments:
27	Punta Baja (Rosario)	Full of kelp and the rolliest anchorage along Baja
29	San Carlos	Windy, but offers less swells than Rosario
7	Punta Bluff (Escarpa)	Not recommended
12	Punta Canoas	Not as satisfactory as Punta Bluff
34	Bahia Blanca	Refracted waves cause most boats to anchor in a more exposed area.

From there to Morro Santo Domingo, the anchorages didn't provide much shelter, except in settled summer weather with light northwesterlies.

Morro Santo Domingo was useful only as an emergency or fair-weather anchorage.

I remembered the Harbor Master at the hotel suggested I not go to Cedros Island. Charlie's Charts said a good anchorage could be found in the north anchorage on Cedros, but the loss of sand on the bottom may require the use of more scope or a killick. I'd never heard of a killick and I certainly didn't have one on board! Later, I read on the Internet[10] that a killick was originally a rock tied to the end of a rope, used as an anchor by the early sailors.

At anchor, 200 miles from San Diego, in the cold of the cabin, I slowly began to grasp the reality. My idea of sailing from one anchorage to another down the coast in a series of day sails was broken. I couldn't go on; I'd have to go back. The only decision left was when.

The weather forecast on the Baha Net was for NW winds 10 to 15 today, lighter or uncertain tomorrow, and rain the next day. Rain in my mind meant storm conditions and some probability of wind from the south. Every anchorage I'd been in was completely open to the south.

If I left right now, I thought, I could be in Colnett tonight, Santo Thomas tomorrow night, and Ensenada the following night when the wind turns south, assuming the forecast holds true.

If the wind turned south earlier than forecasted, I wouldn't have any protection at anchor until I got back to Ensenada. Lying at anchor, the boat would be exposed to the waves rolling in from the south.

OK. My decision was clear, I must go—and right now! I had to get to Colnett by dusk tonight to stay ahead of the storm, presuming the forecast was correct.

If I made it to Ensenada, I wondered if Lance would like to sail the last leg home with me. At this point, I had no way to find out. I'd have to start sailing right now or I wouldn't be in by dusk.

My computer told me the time changed today, so I reset my wristwatch before going on deck. Other than my computer, my watch was the only clock on board. I'd been using it as the ship's clock.

On deck, I rushed to get the sail cover off and the anchor up. Then, I hoisted the main and headed straight for the entrance.

Outside, in the ocean, the waves weren't as bad as I expected. Giggles sails well in a medium-to-heavy beat against a good wave structure. I started with a number three and a full main. In mid

---

[10] http://www.Google.com, then enter "killick definition"

afternoon, I put a reef in the main. Even though the deck was a little wet, I had a great sail all the way to Colnett.

In the late afternoon, I measured the height of the Sun in hand-widths to the horizon and realized I only had two hours to sunset. With Colnett still 18 miles ahead, I would not make it in daylight. How could this be? I'd been thinking all day that I'd be at the anchorage right at dusk. Now, I was going to be an hour late. What happened?

Thinking the situation over slowly, I realized my mistake. When I reset my watch this morning, I'd been a little groggy and in a big hurry. I'd set my watch backward instead of forward. I'd sailed all day thinking it was two hours earlier than it really was.

The Sun didn't change with daylight saving time. It was still on yesterday's timetable, so my thinking was only an hour off the Sun's schedule.

No matter what I'd been thinking all day, I had no way to be in the anchorage by sundown. Should I enter and anchor in the dark or sail on to San Thomas, or even to Ensenada?

A week ago, I'd been anchored in Colnett. I departed to the south and remembered it was completely open. I didn't remember any kelp. Being wide open to the south was now to my advantage, I'd have a wide, straight path from the ocean into the anchorage. All I had to do was stop before I ran up on shore and drop the anchor. In the dark. In a good spot.

If I decided to sail on, I'd have to sail all night. And, I'd undoubtedly have to sleep a good part of the time. Not maintaining a lookout at all times was against international maritime law. Worse, it was unwise this close to shore where traffic is common.

Both options were in violation of my insurance endorsement.

Watching the Sun slowly slide toward the horizon, I decided the risk of going into the anchorage after dark was preferable to sailing the Mexican coastal waters at night without a lookout. I simply wouldn't tell my insurance company.

I checked the chart and marked a spot with good depth, swinging room, and protection from the prevailing northwest wind. I picked off the latitude and longitude, and then entered them into the GPS. Then, remembering how easily I had screwed up changing my watch in the morning, I checked the latitude and longitude three times before I stopped sweating.

By the time the depth sounder showed I was approaching the coast, the Sun was down, and dusk had faded away to pitch black. There were no lights on shore to give me a sense of distance. The Moon wouldn't rise until much later. Where shore should have been in front of the boat, I couldn't see anything—only blackness. I grabbed the biggest flashlight on board and swung the beam all the way around the boat. The beam went out into the dark and was lost in the dark. No image came back. With the flashlight in my hand pointing at nothing, I slowly followed the GPS through the pitch-black night toward my selected spot. I kept playing the flashlight ahead of the boat, praying no other boat had anchored in my spot or in my path to it. I never saw anything in the dark. As the minutes ticked by, I became more and more uncertain. I kept going slower and slower through the blackness.

When the GPS said I was at my chosen spot and the depth sounder read 30 feet, I put the boat in reverse and pointed my light over the side down at the water. For the first time, I could see something. With the flashlight pointed straight down, I could see the water and a few bubbles on the surface. I couldn't feel the boat moving forward or slowing down. I couldn't see movement in the water itself. The only movement I could see was a few bubbles on the surface of the water.

In the beam of the flashlight, I intently watched the bubbles as they moved aft along the side of the boat. When they slowed, and then stopped moving, I took the boat out of reverse. The bubbles bobbed on the surface in the same place beside the boat. I was over my chosen anchorage.

In the dark, I ran forward and lowered the anchor into the black water, let out scope, and tied it off. Back in the cockpit, I slowly backed down on the anchor until the boat pulled the line tight. With the engine still in reverse, I went forward again and felt the anchor line in the dark. No jerking in the line. The anchor seemed to be holding. Good. I was in for the night.

Back in the cockpit, I turned off the engine and picked up the big flashlight. I slowly swept it across what should be the horizon. The beam went out into the dark. I swept the beam toward shore, but I couldn't see the beach. I couldn't see the bluffs. I hadn't seen anything since sundown but the bubbles on the water close to the boat. I had no visual connection with the rest of the world and no visual concept of my location.

Later, when I turned off the cabin lights and went to bed, the darkness felt better with my eyes closed. It's supposed to be dark with your eyes closed.

Sleep was limited again by the rolling of the boat. The breeze had quit completely before I went below and the boat wandered at anchor. Occasionally, the boat stood broadside to the swells and woke me. Perhaps never having seen where the boat was anchored and what was close aboard kept me from sleeping well.

The alarm woke me early, just in time to get the weather map at 4:58 A.M. with the ham radio and computer. I was still tired and a little slow getting up. By the time I got reception started, I missed the first two minutes of the transmission.

I missed the area well north, but what I did get looked fine. I would do the 42-mile beat to Punta Santo Thomas today.

I must not arrive late because there was kelp was all around the Punta Santo Thomas anchorage. If I were late today, I'd have to go on another eight-to-ten hours overnight to Ensenada. I was up and underway much earlier today and I expected to arrive at Santo Thomas in fine time.

I started the engine, raised the anchor, and began powering at an idle using the autopilot. There was no wind, so the boat's slow forward movement created a slight apparent breeze right on the bow. Just as I started to raise the main, the engine stopped. The boat coasted slowly as I ran from the main halyard to the anchor and put it back down.

Dirty fuel filters—the most common problem with diesel engines on boats—was the culprit. An hour later, I had them changed and the insides of the boat back in order. Finally, I pulled the anchor up and was off under power again.

An hour or so after breakfast, I heard a ringing in the engine room too metallic to be a belt whine. It was a sound I'd never heard on a boat before. Uncertain, I opened the engine room doors and listened again. It seemed to be coming from the bottom of the engine or below it. Listening some more, I decided it was the dripless packing gland. I stopped the engine, and the whine stopped with the engine.

I burped the dripless packing gland but, when I did, it didn't reseat correctly. Water free-flowed into the pan beneath the engine. Panicked, I burped it again. This time, it seemed to seat OK and the inflow of water stopped.

Back on deck, I restarted the engine again and resumed powering. The whine was gone, but I was still shaky from the flow of water into the boat. Nervously, I went back below and looked at the dripless packing gland to see if it was leaking. This time, I couldn't see the gland—it was completely under water! The pan was half-full of water. I had a vision of the whole boat being half-full of water!

Frantically, I shut down the engine and reached into the water to burp the gland again. This time, I held it open for a long time. If eel grass, seaweed, or something similar was in the gland, preventing it from sealing, I wanted to flush it into the boat. I wanted to flush it away from the two surfaces of the gland that mate and provide the seal.

When I released the gland to reseat it, the water was up around the bottom of the engine block. I couldn't see if the gland was still leaking. I bailed out the pan to get the packing gland above water. As I bailed, I was glad to see how quickly I was gaining on the water level in the pan.

The gland seemed to be seated OK. No water was leaking into the boat. Just like last time. Cautiously, I started the engine and ran it at a much lower RPM, watching the dripless packing gland for any flow of water while the prop shaft turned.

Everything seemed OK. With a vision of the boat half-full of water still in my head, I continued to watch. The seal seemed to be working fine.

Eventually, I got tired of watching.

I felt the boat heel a little under the main. The daily wind was beginning to fill in.

I unfurled the jib and set Giggles on a beat. The rhythm of the boat stepping over the small waves as it beat to weather felt good. I enjoyed the motion of the boat moving with the ocean and began my daily sail.

At the lay line to Punta Santo Thomas, I tacked to port and headed back in. Again I wondered if I'd make it by nightfall. Had the time to clean the filter and reseat the packing gland delayed me enough to miss entering before dark? It would be close.

Right now, the only thing to do was to enjoy the sail. Later, I tucked in a reef. Still later, I shook it back out.

As I neared Santo Thomas, it began to look as though I'd make the anchorage just about dusk. I thought I might have enough light to see the kelp as I went in, so I kept going. I had to stop arriving so close to dark!

As the Sun slid below the horizon, the depth sounder showed the bottom was beginning to come up. I realized it was going to be a little dark when I got into the anchorage. To save time on the way in, I turned on the engine and furled the jib. I planned to have the main down and flaked, and be totally on the engine well before I got close enough to pick out an anchorage spot.

I was on the cabin top ready to lower the main when the engine stopped again.

To anchor under sail, I'd have to sail my way through the kelp bed, find a good spot to anchor, head the boat up just to windward of the spot, and coast to a stop where I wanted to drop the anchor. Then, I'd have to run forward, drop the anchor—hoping it would catch on the first try and that the main wouldn't fill and drive me off into the kelp somewhere. If I missed the spot or if the anchor didn't catch, I'd have to raise the anchor and pick my way back out through the kelp.

Anchoring singlehandedly under sail in a kelp bed involves a lot of risk. On the other hand, by the time I could change the filters again, it would be too dark to find my way through the kelp, even with an engine.

Right at the entrance to Santo Thomas, I decided not to enter at all. I tacked off and headed out to sea. It was the safest place.

Just offshore, and north of my position, were the Rocas Soledad, "the lonely rocks." These offshore rocks lay just west of Punta Santo Thomas . . . upwind of the boat and exactly on the straight-line course from my position to Ensenada. The starboard tack would keep me well clear of Rocas Soledad and take me out into deep water. In the dying light of early night, I took a rather poor bearing on Rocas Soledad. Ten minutes later, it was too dark to see them at all. I was glad I knew where they were.

I sailed out into the ocean in the dark and let the boat run a while to make sure I was clear of Rocas Soledad. After an hour on starboard, I plotted my position and course, and discovered that if I tacked now I would be on the lay line through the pass between Isla Todos Santos and Punta Banda. It was time to tack to port and start north, but I didn't care. The ocean was far safer than the coast. I kept going out a little more.

In the dark, headed out into the ocean, I began to reflect on the day: first the dirty diesel, then the clogged dripless packing gland, and now the engine had stopped again. Too many things had gone wrong too fast.

Was it because this boat wasn't as well maintained as the boat I cruised to New Zealand? Was I pushing harder? Was this what it meant to get older? Was I just lonely and the problems seemed worse? Or, was I just tired?

In the dark, I had no answers, just the motion of the boat and the sound of the bow wake. I was glad the night breeze held. I settled down and it felt good to sail. I tacked toward Ensenada and started making progress toward home.

I sailed between Isla Todos Santos and Punta Banda in the dark with a tug and tow on one side, and a working fishing boat on the other. I had no engine. I was thankful the breeze held. In fact, the boat was doing 5 knots on a Number Three and a reefed main. Was this the beginning of the "more wind on Tuesday?"

In the lee of Todos Santos, I hoved to and changed the filters again. I cleaned the Racor® and flushed it. When I flushed it, a lot of gunk came out. Uncertain, I switched to my other fuel tank. That tank had all US fuel in it, so I expected it would be good. In my exhaustion, I could only hope I'd fixed the problem. Then, I forcefully incanted a seaman's verbal ritual over the fuel system and went back up on deck.

At the hotel harbor entrance, I turned the engine on again, uncertain how long it would run. It got me to the fuel dock, where a dock hand met me, and it got me back into my former slip.

The time was 4 A.M., but I was in a slip with a breakwater to the south, not on the ocean with a balky engine. I hit the sack, dead tired. I didn't want to admit I wasn't as young as I used to be.

As I drifted off, the unresolved questions from the day flitted through my head. Did the collar on the dripless packing gland need to be adjusted? I didn't know of any adjustment like that. Was the remaining tank of fuel good or would I have more problems in the future?

Sunshine on my face woke me at eight. I showered and saw the Harbor Master. No problem. He took care of the check-in.

I called Lance. Yes, he would love to make the trip back from Ensenada with me. I went back to bed for a few hours.

When I woke, I flaked the main, put the cover on, made up lines, and cleaned the boat. After all, company was coming tomorrow.

In the late afternoon when I recharged the batteries, the engine started fine and ran like a champ. I ran it a little extra just to make sure. After a handful of cookies, I lay down for a nap, which lasted all night.

In the morning, I felt great and the boat was ready. This was a day to relax and enjoy. I read, played my banjo, and did nothing. Late in the afternoon, Lance banged on the side of the boat. It was wonderful to hear the voice of a friend.

We talked about everything and nothing. I caught up on what had happened to him and his wife Nita since I left San Diego. This was all small stuff, but it seemed vital to me. He asked me about the trip. I told him how good the sailing was. Somehow, I never got around to the rest.

The next morning, the weather report said the storm had slowed its approach and wouldn't arrive for another day. We decided to go now, rather than wait for the storm to come and go.

In the ocean, the delayed low had shut down the wind. We powered all day with the autopilot steering straight up the coast to home. The engine worked fine.

Lance and I had nothing to do but talk—all day long. I loved it.

At dusk, we were tied up at the police dock in San Diego waiting for Customs. For me, my day powering back home with Lance was better than the whole rest of the trip. Deep down inside, I knew the question I started with had been answered. Singlehanded cruising wasn't for me—it was far too lonely and difficult.

The next morning in my bed at home, I woke to rain pattering on the window. Realizing the wind was now blowing hard out of the south gave me shivers. All the anchorages I'd slept in were covered with breaking waves rolling in from the ocean.

I was glad to be safely home.

Chapter 42

Ring in the Water

My wilder days of sailing were slowing down. The more gentle winds in San Diego made for easier singlehanded sailing than in San Francisco Bay. These winds also provided much less thrill and drew fewer boats. With lower interest, only a couple singlehanded races were held each year.

I kept the boat race-ready and started building a crew. We made a few races, but the typical problems of crew turnover kept us at the beginner level.

In a Viennese Waltz class, I met Zaneta and, two years later, we were married on the shore of Puget Sound. Gregg, a long-time sailor and my best man, rang the ship's bell from Giggles. Sixteen strikes: eight for the old watch and eight for the new.

Zaneta and I had put Giggles in the guest slip in front of the Oceanside Harbor Master's office. We had a lovely sail from San Diego, but we departed a little later than expected. We started on a medium beat and sailed in the diminishing winds of the late afternoon. By dusk, we switched to the engine, and arrived at Oceanside around 9 P.M.

As we put the boat in the guest slip at Oceanside, I jumped off to secure the dock lines, while Zaneta shut down the diesel engine. In the damp of the harbor, we hugged each other and congratulated ourselves on making our first passage together, even if it was only a day's sail. We threw our foul weather jackets and gloves in a pile on the cabin top: hers all nice and new—mine old, dirty, and worn. I felt wonderful introducing her to the world I loved.

The Harbor Master assigned us a slip by VHF, but when we tried to move the boat, the engine wouldn't start.

It was a mistake every rookie sailor has made at least once. Here I was, the old hot-shot sailor. I should have caught it right away. But, no! When the engine wouldn't start, I changed the filters and bled the engine, and then stared at it in dumb disbelief when it still refused to run.

The next morning, the problem revealed itself. The T-handle shut off in the cockpit was still in the off position. As soon as it was pushed back in to the run position, the engine started and ran fine.

With everything working again, we sailed on to Avalon. We spent the next day ashore, sight-seeing and shopping. We walked along the seawall in harmony and bliss, toured the casino, and promised ourselves we would return and dance on the wonderful dance floor. We returned to the boat, happy and tired from an all-day meander along shore, and deeply in love.

The passage back to San Diego was a long, easy broad reach, with Giggles moving beautifully on the waves. Sometime in mid morning, Zaneta looked down at my left hand and realized my wedding ring was missing. I had no idea it was gone. We cried like children. We talked and held each other.

My ring was still gone. I searched the boat, my gloves, everywhere I had laid my gloves, and then searched the whole boat again. It wasn't on the boat. My wedding ring was gone.

Sometime later, an insight about the symbolism became clear to Zaneta. I had fallen in love with the ocean on my first passage to Hawaii. After my 2,000-mile singlehanded race to Hawaii, I was given an engagement ring. Now, my wedding ring had slipped off my hand and fallen into the ocean. I loved the ocean. I was engaged to the ocean. And, now, I was married to the ocean.

The ocean had shown me its vastness, its power, and its beauty. My time on the ocean had brought me good friends and wonderful experiences.

Yes, I thought, *I do love the ocean. And, in a way, I am married to it.*

Not long after, the biggest pod of dolphins ever to approach Giggles came and played in front of the bow, leading us home.

Epilogue

Changing of the Watch

Knowledge in mankind is like a spiral. In applying himself, each man improves on what he has learned by adding his personal experiences and insights to the guidance he has received. As in many men, perpetuating the spiral of knowledge is a charge deeply imbedded in my fundamental self. I have a strong desire to help those following me find what is important and to do it well.

To touch others—this is my dream.

They carried me down to the boat today. This will be my last time on Giggles.

As people step onboard, Giggles moves a little under their weight. The movement beneath me reminds me of the good times we've had together. I remember buying Giggles and sailing her singlehandedly. Together, we bashed all around San Francisco Bay and outside in the ocean. Wonderful times—just a memory now.

There is no wind this morning. The water is calm—still, silent, and glassy—not even a single cat's paw. I look down through the flat, silvery surface, well down into the darker water. In reality, I can only see a foot or two, but the depths feel as though they go on forever.

The engine hums a little louder and Giggles backs out of the slip. Around the cockpit, I see the faces of a few old friends here to help me on my last sail. They're talking quietly, mostly about nothing at all. I can't hear much more than a murmur.

I have been blessed with many good friends. Some taught me how to sail. Some taught me about teamwork. A couple of Olympic medalists helped me understand what *good* really means, and how much I could grow. People all along the way helped me learn the skills that brought so much into my life.

Leaving the slip area, Giggles passes the "no wake" sign on the way toward the entrance of San Diego Bay and the ocean beyond.

When I was young, broke, and not even a beginning sailor, a man I never knew lent me a Penguin that had been built for, and sailed in, the USA National Championship. Since then, so many people have helped me, I can't remember them all.

I don't think they ever cared that I didn't remember them. They were simply glad to help.

Giggles motors down the main channel toward the ocean, pulling a silver *V* in the quiet water behind her—lines in the water no one can see beyond; lines created by something that has gone ahead. Lines with their own movement that continue their own life on the surface of something larger.

I remember sailing at night a long time ago, looking out into the dark, questioning what made sense in my life and how I should live it. Since then, many, many people have given me the opportunity to learn and grow. Sometimes, it came as advice from a friend about a broken mast or as two extra months of leave, so I could follow my dream.

The people who mentored me taught me the things I needed to turn the big adventures into great experiences. They also taught me the little things that helped me understand life. Frequently, I have noticed how the same people were always "lucky."

The kindness of people, the wisdom of friends, and the advice from those who have been there before gave me the wisdom that helped me live my life.

I am one of the lucky ones.

Giggles crosses the wake of another boat and rocks a little on the waves. The box in Gregg's hands moves a little in his lap. He holds on tighter to make sure the box is OK.

We motor past Zuniga Light on the end of the breakwater. The first breeze of late morning cools the faces of the people on board. A small, quiet swell lifts the boat a little and sets it back down as the swell slides away to leeward. Ever so quietly, ever so respectfully, we head out into the ocean.

The ocean is where I've been tested, where I've achieved my highest accomplishments, and where I've received the satisfaction of knowing my own abilities.

Sailing in the ocean always filled me with a sense of high adventure. Whether flying a spinnaker all alone, fighting the fatigue that comes after two weeks of no rest, or sailing in a storm—every time I thrilled at exceeding my previous limits.

Each time I sailed in the ocean, I had the sense of being off on a new adventure. I was always going to try to do something, but I didn't know what would happen along the way. I didn't know how the adventure would turn out. I only knew I would find a way to keep going until I finished it.

Today will be a different kind of adventure in the ocean—something I've never done before.

As Giggles passes Point Loma, the breeze begins to fill in over the low, gentle swells. Cat's paws build into ripples and glisten in the sunlight, scattering sparkles across the ocean. Someone somewhere in the cockpit comments today is a perfect day.

The warm sunshine feels good. The quiet waters outside San Diego aren't as wild as those outside San Francisco. Without understanding, I retired from extreme adventure to easier sailing and more companionship. The very real dangers associated with high risk had tempered the exuberant days of my youth and the high-accomplishment days of my mid years.

It wasn't until my singlehanded cruise into Mexico late in life that I began to understand how much I'd changed. Returning after that adventure was over became more satisfying than the adventure itself. The value of good friends became more important than ultrahigh accomplishment.

The feeling of the sea under the boat continues to mesmerize me. The gentle motion of the boat as it steps over the waves has a familiarity that surpasses anything I've ever known as home. The ocean varies greatly over time and place, and the gamut of its essence has become my true home.

I fell in love with the ocean on my first race to Hawaii, I was engaged to the ocean after the Singlehanded Transpac, and I was married to the ocean when my wedding ring found its way from my finger into the water. I am bonded to and I love the ocean. And, now, I will live there.

Not quite an hour later, Giggles slowly passes the last outbound buoy. "SD" marks the beginning of clear water outside the San Diego entrance. Only the ocean lies beyond.

The breeze is stronger now, forming small waves on top of the gentle swells. Giggles' engine becomes quiet, joining the mood of my friends on board. The waves slap against the hull, and the breeze plays through the mast and rigging, waiting for the sails to be raised. Slowly, we coast to a stop.

This is a beautiful place. The glinting of the Sun on the waves outlines the gentle swells passing under the boat. I've seen so many beautiful sights in the ocean, it's hard for me to recount them all. The memories of the sunsets and the stars at night under the North Pacific High, and the sunrise in the tropics, with the four-masted Sea Cloud framed as a black silhouette in the red reflection on the water. They bring tears to my eyes.

I remember the beauty of the small children dressed in their Sunday best at the front of a church in Tonga and the beauty of crossing the equator on the passage from Apia to Hawaii. And, sailing alone in the ocean for two weeks in the same direction has its own kind of beauty and satisfaction.

I know I'm not alone in witnessing this beauty. I can still see the damp walls of a cave half-full of water in Tonga where I read the names of men who sailed the oceans hundreds of years before me. I feel a oneness with them and all who have had the good fortune to witness the beauty of the ocean.

I've had a beautiful life on the ocean. And, soon, I'll be alone in the ocean.

Flowers are being tossed on the water now. Someone is speaking, telling about my life. All I hear are the murmurs again. Gregg brings my ashes to the rail.

My life in sailing has been like a long-distance passage on the ocean. The experiences of all mankind are as big as the ocean, but a single man can only see what comes within his view. My experiences grew from the moving circle of my perceptions.

316

Early on, I kept a sailing diary. I wrote down whatever my mentors taught me. Over the years, my writings became clearer and more comprehensive.

My desire to pass on to others what was so good in my life flourished. My notes became visual aids and my sketches became physical working models to help others learn.

I taught everything I knew at yacht clubs, on my boat, on other people's boats, and at home in my basement. I shared my knowledge with anyone who wanted to learn.

It was immensely gratifying to watch others become capable. My internal warmth was my greatest reward.

I know sailing is more than just an activity. It teaches the important values of life: honest striving, working together, fair competition, and generosity, as well as respect and honor for nature and all others. Sailing passes these values from one person to another.

More flowers join those already on the water. For the second time, Gregg rings Giggles' bell 16 times—eight for the old watch and eight for the new watch.

Gregg opens the box and pours my ashes over the side of the boat. Most of the ashes fall in a mass to the surface of the ocean. Some of them are caught by the wind, swirl up into the air, and float on the breeze. A few of my ashes are blown back across the boat and onto my friends in the cockpit. And, a few continue to float on the wind.

Perhaps the last of my ashes will float on the wind long enough to touch others.

About the Author

Dale Parshall is currently living in central Texas with his two toy sailboats, Bathtub and Hot Water. He moved to Texas from California after waiting too long for an earthquake to give him oceanfront property. Global Warming, Dale feels, is a more certain bet—and Texas is pretty flat.

Dale studied English in high school, and at Illinois Institute of Technology with a bunch of engineers. After 30 years in the computer industry, Dale finally mastered Assembler Language.

Dale's major races include eight Chicago to Mackinac, two Port Huron to Mackinac, one Port Huron to Chicago, one crewed San Francisco to Hawaii, one Singlehanded Transpac, three Newport to Ensenada, five San Diego to Ensenada, as well as a host of weekend club races and Wednesday evening beer-can races.

He has cruised the waters of Lake Michigan and Lake Huron; the Atlantic coast; the northern California Delta; the California coast from Tomales Bay to the Mexican border; Mexican waters from the US border to San Quentin; and the Pacific Ocean from San Francisco to New Zealand, including the waters of French Polynesia, Niue, Tonga, Western Samoa, and New Zealand.

Dale has sailed upwind from Hawaii to San Francisco five times, but only twice downwind to Hawaii. After five times upwind, he is beginning to think downwind is better.

He has been published in the *Latitude 38* magazine, the Pacific Cup "program," and his own newsletter from the South Pacific. Dale has also lectured, taught, coached, and helped many people of all ages.

Dale's sailing experiences have truly ranged from inspiring to amusing. After all is said and done, how many people do you know who have retired to sailing a Bathtub?

319